A Note from Cherie

I must say that I was quite surprised to hear from so many brothers, uncles and husbands that had gone through the *Go in Peace Biblical Discipleship Curriculum* and that God has used it in these men's lives to help set them free. All I can say is: Praise the Lord! As the original flowery cover portrays I never intended to target men as my readers. But obviously God had greater plans!

I so enjoyed hearing the various ways that men were changing the cover to make it manlier. I kept telling one particular men's group, who met weekly at their church, to just tear off the front cover so as not to cause embarrassment.

Since God is doing such a work in men's lives through the *Go in Peace* curriculum I began to pray for a cover that any man would be proud of. As inspiration, the Lord kept bringing a sentence to mind that He had me put in the curriculum. "Why do we choose to stand in the prison cell when the door is wide open?" Soon I was searching high and low for the perfect photo, but could find none.

Then one day my daughter and I visited the Ohio State Reformatory, an old prison that was used to house prisoners from 1896-1990 which is now a tourist attraction. I prayed and asked God if there is a photo in this place that would speak to men's hearts then lead me to it. And since I'm not a professional photographer or have all the lights and whistles can You Lord be the Light and guide my hand.

We were amazed when we looked at the photos on the computer. In fact, it was difficult for our graphic artist to pick the cover shot because so many had turned out great.

Since my original intent was never to write to men, the pages within remain the same, only the cover has been changed. My prayer for you is to follow Christ. He is the One who walked away from an empty tomb. Won't you join Him? Won't you *go in peace!*

God bless,
Cherie Fresonke

What People Are Saying About
Go in Peace! Biblical Discipleship Curriculum

Easy to understand and apply. It kept my attention! Great!
—From an attendee of *Go in Peace!*

This *Go in Peace* seminar is the beginning of a healing process that we sure all are in desperate need of. I will use it for the rest of my life. As a father, I will teach it to my son.
—From a father who attended a "Go in Peace" Leadership Training

After the passing of my 17-year old daughter Gracie, I was experiencing extreme anxiety which was hindering me from grieving properly. After seeing several doctors, they found nothing physically wrong with me. I found myself desperate much like the Sinful Woman in Luke 7. The Holy Spirit used the *Go In Peace Biblical Discipleship Curriculum* to heal my fears, deep heart issues, to help me forgive myself and to receive God's love fully to set me free!

—From a hurting father
Whittier, California

This curriculum puts into words and explains the struggles every person goes through, guiding them through how God teaches His children to deal with these issues.

—From an attendee of *Go in Peace*

I heard that you are developing a *"Go in Peace"* manual cover for men. I am looking forward to its availability. We are planning our second *"Go in Peace"* retreat for men around late March or early April. Our first retreat was very successful.

—A note from a leader using *Go in Peace* for men's groups

Go in Peace! will expose you to yourself. It will help you look to God for healing and to receive gentle love from His arms.

—Stephanie, Baldwin Park

The Peace Restored Ministries are privileged to use Cherie Fresonke's book, *Go in Peace!*, and the corresponding Bible study curriculum with it, for our retreats and biblical mentoring of the wounded. We have seen the Lord heal and restore many through these books in cases of abortion, sexual abuse, rape, divorce recovery, etc. The book, *Go in Peace!*, is very anointed by the Lord. I highly recommend it be used by all those seeking the Lord's healing in their lives.

—Cynthia Wright,
Associate director,
Peace Restored Ministries

This leadership training was very encouraging. I can now see that my past hurts can now be someone else's hope; to see that what Jesus has done for me, He can, and will do for them as well.

—Attendee of the *Go in Peace Leadership Training*

CHERIE FRESONKE

Go in Peace!

A Bible Study for the Brokenhearted

STUDENT WORKBOOK

SUNFLOWER PRESS

Go in Peace! Student Workbook
Copyright © 1999, 2004, 2006, 2012 by Cherie Fresonke
Published by Sunflower Press
P.O. Box 813
Seal Beach, CA 90740
www.sunflowerpress.net

Graphic design by Albena Tzvetkova
Cover photo by Cherie Fresonke
ISBN: 978-0-9831678-5-3

First edition published in 1999.
Second revised and updated edition published in 2004.
Third revised and updated edition published in 2006.
Fourth revised and updated edition published in 2012.

Contents

THE GIFT

DEDICATION

*To him belong glory and dominion
forever and ever. Amen.*
1 PETER 4:11b, ESV

All Glory and Honor

All the glory and honor belongs to God—the one and only who healed my heart and set me free. The one who taught me how to go in peace. The one who then called me to share this wonderful truth with you. May He receive all the glory and honor.

For this reason, I dedicate this work to my Lord and Savior, Jesus Christ. God gave us a gift, the sacrifice of His Son, so that you and I could have eternal life. In view of God's grace and mercy, can I offer Him anything less than my life? Each year I ask the Lord what He would like for Christmas. In 1999, the year I wrote the first edition my gift to Him was this Bible study. Now, twelve years later, I again give Him this gift. My life, my time, my work—is His! Yet, it doesn't compare to the gift He has given to me! Thank You Jesus!

I also dedicate this Bible study to each person around the world who is hurting deep inside over the issue of sin in his or her life. This gift is for you, beloved. May God touch your life as deeply as He did mine. May you too, *go in peace!*

INTRODUCTION

*The LORD is close to the brokenhearted
and saves those who are crushed in spirit.*
PSALM 34:18

Invitation to the Brokenhearted

One evening, there was a news story on television about a young woman who had committed suicide by jumping off a bridge. In her suicide letter, she wrote that she felt responsible for the death of her child through abortion and could no longer live with herself. For her, this was the only way to escape the pain.

Have you ever been is such a deep pit of despair? Did it seem as if nothing or no one could possibly take the pain away?

Although abortion may not be an issue in your life, most of us have been wounded and hurt at some point in life's journey. These hurts may be a result of our own sin (such as bad decisions or wrong choices) or the result of another's sin against us (as in the case of rejection, abuse or rape). In either case, what we do with these hurts greatly affect us and can cause us to dwell in the pit of despair.

In view of this, for those who dwell in the pit of despair, I write this for you, for I have known a pit as deep as yours. When I was ready to admit that my life was out of control, I cried out to God for help, and He met me there. He began to heal my broken heart and teach me how to give my deep heart hurts to Him once and for all. I learned that He never intended for me to carry the hurt by myself. What He taught me set me free. It enabled me to go in peace! Fear was replaced with strength, depression with joy, anxiety with faith, and rage with rest. Best yet, I experienced peace with God deep within my heart. That's what it means to *go in peace!* Likewise, if you have been hurt in life, this Bible study is for you. God truly desires for you to join with me as we go in peace!

> Why should you be beaten anymore? Why do you persist in rebellion? Your whole head is injured, your whole heart afflicted. From the sole of your foot to the top of your head there is no soundness—only wounds and welts and open sores, not cleansed or bandaged or soothed with oil.
> —Isaiah 1:5-6

My prayer for you is this: that you will come to know in a more intimate way the "Wonderful Counselor, Mighty God, Everlasting Father, Prince of Peace" (Isaiah 9:6b).

For this reason, I pray that you will become spiritually, emotionally and physically whole in regard to the wounds and deep hurts in your life. If you are brave enough to turn these pages and apply what you learn to your life, you will find a peace that surpasses all understanding.

You will discover the hurts that are driving the self-destructive behaviors. You will learn how to give these hurts to God in the manner He intended so that you can be set free. You will discover how to apply God's Word to your life in a tangible way so that you too can go in peace. And best yet, you will learn the truth of who you are in Christ so that you can become all that God created you to be.

Now, there is no need to worry, no need to fret; you will not be asked to do anything you are uncomfortable with or told that you must share your deepest secrets. You see, what you will be taught within these pages is not based on human philosophy or human psychology. Instead it is based 100 percent upon the Word of God and you will find among these pages a love so deep for you its immeasurable. No matter what you have been through, or how deeply you have been hurt, know that you are in a safe place.

The Wonderful Counselor is waiting to restore to you a joy, peace and happiness that you may not have even known was missing. It's amazing! It's a miracle! It's exactly what happened within my own life when God taught me what I am about to teach you. It wasn't until the happiness returned that I even *realized* that it had been missing from my own life since I was a young child. The happiness comes with the joy and peace that only God can give. I can honestly say that all three remain as long as I continue to apply the truth found within these pages to my life. The most amazing part of this, I learned what I am about to teach you over twenty years ago.

Are you brave enough to walk away from the side of the bridge and into a brand-new life filled with love, joy, peace, patience, kindness, goodness, faithfulness, gentleness and self-control (Galatians 5:22)? As you walk away from that ledge, you will discover the best that Jesus has in store for you. May the same words that He spoke to the Sinful Woman (and to me) resonate within your entire being:

> Your sins are forgiven. . . . Your faith has saved you; *go in peace.*
>
> —Luke 7:48,50, emphasis added

Hopes and Goals

Before we begin, I want you to make a list of your hopes and goals. Now, these are not goals like what you want to achieve in life, but spiritual goals. I want you to list what you want God to do in your life about your deep heart hurts. Let me give you some examples I hear over and over again when I work with people: *I want to be set free from the hurt. I want to be set free from the anger. I want to be set free from the depression or anxiety. I want the strength to stop the alcohol or drugs. I don't want my deep heart hurt to affect my family and loved ones. I want to forgive the person who hurt me. I want to know that God forgives me for the wrong I have done. I want to draw closer to God. I want my life to have meaning. I want to be used by God and help other people. I want to go in peace.*

You can write down your list of goals below. As you write think about the following:

- What do you want God to do in your life through this Bible study?
- Do you have a deep heart hurt that needs healing?
- Have you done something that you need to know God forgives you for?
- Do you want to be set free from hurt, fear, depression, anxiety, rage, alcohol, drugs, suicidal thoughts or other things associated with your deep heart hurt?
- Do you desire to know why God gave you life?
- Do you want to be used by God to help others?

Write down whatever your hopes and goals are. In the last session of this Bible study we will take a look at these goals once again. It is remarkable how God will help you meet these goals if you are willing to apply His truth to your life. It is absolutely amazing! This is a practical way for you to see how God is working in your life.

HOPES AND GOALS

What do you want God to do in your life through completing this study? Make a list of your spiritual hopes and goals below.

_____

_____

_____

_____

_____

_____

_____

_____

Instructions

Since I don't want to lose your interest as we read this study together you will see within the text blank spaces. As I read, follow along, and listen for the words that go in the blanks, then fill in the spaces with the words that are read. You will discover that the words you must write are key words to get you thinking.

Note to the Leader: Read Luke 7:36-50 out loud from the Bible.

The Sinful Woman

I know many people who have prayed and prayed and asked God to forgive them for their sins. They continually ask, over and over again, for forgiveness for the same offense. Some come to the point that they realize that God has truly forgiven them, but they cannot forgive themselves.

In studying the portrait of the Sinful Woman notice that Jesus did not say to her, "Your sins are forgiven, your faith has saved you, but I want you to beat yourself up for the next 20 years." No! He told her that her sins were _____, that her faith had saved her, and that she was free to go in _____.

Because these verses in Luke are the foundation of what we will be discussing, we will be examining them in depth throughout this Bible study. We will take a look at exactly what these verses mean to _____ and to _____ as we study the portrait of the Sinful Woman.

We will begin by taking a look at where this story falls chronologically in the life of Jesus as we study the background of the portrait. Although the Gospels—Matthew, Mark, Luke and John—record the life of Christ, they are often not presented in chronological order, which means that they are not written in such a way as to follow Jesus' day-by-day life. Yet if we take the time to put the events of His ministry in daily order, it's interesting to note what took place just before He went to the Pharisee's house that evening for dinner. Pastor Warren Wiersbe, in his commentary on the book of Luke titled *Be Compassionate*, claims that just before this event, Jesus had given this gracious invitation:[1]

> Come to me, all you who are _____ and _____,
> and I will give you rest. Take my yoke upon you and learn from me, for I
> am gentle and humble in heart, and you will find _____ for
> your _____. For my yoke is easy and my burden light.
> —Matthew 11:28-30

Are you weary and burdened? Do you desire rest for your soul? Then come and learn like the Sinful Woman did so that you too can find the rest and peace you so deeply crave.

Imagine what she was feeling just before she heard Jesus speak these words. Was she frustrated, overwhelmed, depressed, broken or at her wits' end? She was known as "a woman who had lived a sinful life" (Luke 7:37a). What tragedies and heartbreaks had brought her to the place of making such wrong choices for her life—choices that everyone in her town knew who she was and that her life was out of control? The most important point to make note of when viewing her portrait is that when she heard Jesus say, "Come," she knew that He was her only _____ and she chose to accept His invitation. You too have the _____ to accept so gracious a gift.

There is another important point that we must not overlook in the detail of our portrait—a fact that is obvious. As the woman's name implies, she was a _____. Many Bible commentaries and Bible teachers claim she was a harlot (a prostitute), but God's Word does not tell us what kind of sin in which she was involved. In fact, I believe that God, in His infinite wisdom, left her sin a mystery. The reason? Because each one of us is a sinner. It does not matter what our sin is—whether it is the sin of abortion, adultery, prostitution, pride, anger or whatever. Each of us is just like this sinful woman. Our sins are _____, and we have no right or ability to enter into Jesus' presence in and of ourselves. It is only by His grace and His love that we can accept His invitation to _____ unto Him.

Our only way to be _____, to be _____, to receive joy and peace is to _____ at the feet of Jesus just like the Sinful Woman did. My prayer is for you to understand and receive His gift so that you too may go in _____.

Basic Beliefs and Disclosers

I want to take a moment to discuss some basic beliefs I had when writing this Bible study. First, as I have alluded to earlier, I want you to understand that the principles in this book are _____ based on human philosophy or human psychology. In fact, in many ways, it is just the opposite. Maybe you are at a point in your life (much like I was) where you no longer want to hear what your friends have to say, or even to hear, for that matter, what modern psychology and psychotherapy have to say. Humans, in all of their wisdom, have only caused you pain and confusion. A verse that is repeated twice in Proverbs states this same viewpoint:

> There is a way that seems _____ to a man, but in the end it
> leads to _____.

> —Proverbs 14:12; 16:25

In fact, it wasn't until hundreds of years after the Bible was written that the term "psychology" was even coined. According to Wikipedia, "The first use of the term psychology is often attributed to the German scholastic philosopher Rudolf Gockel . . . in 1590."[2] And it wasn't until the middle of the nineteenth century in England when the term "psychology" overtook "mental philosophy" in common usage.[3]

The point I am trying to make here is that psychology is a relatively new concept when compared to human history. However, all the issues with which we struggle today—fear, anxiety, depression, rage, relationship difficulties and self-destructive behaviors including the *so-called* new issue of the day, cutting—are all found within the Bible. Best of all, because God is the creator of the universe, He is the One who understands human nature better than any human ever could. He chose to preserve His Word and address these issues within it. Therefore, if we are willing to search, we can discover the _____ to all of these issues within the Bible. This is why I wrote this Bible study—to share with you the truth that I saw become a reality in my own life when God and His Word set me free. Listen to what Jesus said:

> The Spirit of the LORD is upon Me, because He has anointed Me to preach the gospel to the poor; He has sent Me to heal the brokenhearted, to proclaim liberty to the captives and recovery of sight to the blind, to set at liberty those who are oppressed.
>
> —Luke 4:18, NKJV

God sent His Son—Jesus Christ—to set the captives free and to heal the brokenhearted. His Word enabled me to go in peace, and He wants to do the _____ for you.

I would also like you to know that I have had no training in the world's way of counseling. In fact, that was one of my biggest arguments with the Lord when He called me to this ministry. I told the Lord that I did not know how to counsel people and that I was only a woman without a degree. But then, my life verses in Jeremiah became real, because it was as if I were saying the same words that Jeremiah had spoken to the Lord when God had called him to his ministry: "Sovereign LORD . . . I do not know how to speak; I am only a child" (Jeremiah 1:6).

What I realized, however, is that God wants us to be dependent on Him in any work we do for Him. He doesn't want us to rely on our own education or our own ideas or our own strength. He wants us to rely 100 percent on Him. He wants us to turn to Him so that He can do His work through us. That is why He answered Jeremiah with these words:

> Do not say, "I am only a child." You must go to everyone I send you to and say whatever I command you. Do not be afraid of them, for I am with you and will rescue you. . . . Now, I have put my words in your mouth. See, today I appoint you over nations and kingdoms to uproot and tear down, to destroy and overthrow, to build and to plant.
>
> —Jeremiah 1:7-10

In view of this, it is God on whom I am relying as I write this Bible study. It is Him whom I am asking for the perfect words to reach your heart as I share the truth of His love—His love, which has the power to _____ even the deepest _____. It is Him whom I am asking to speak through me, because I know without a doubt that just as He called Jeremiah, He has called me to write this Bible study of _____ to you.

So I write this study to simply share with you what God taught me as He healed my broken heart. As the apostle Paul states:

> Praise be to the God and Father of our Lord Jesus Christ, the Father of compassion and the God of all comfort, who comforts us in _____
> our troubles, so that we can comfort those in _____ trouble
> with the comfort we ourselves have received from God.
>
> —2 Corinthians 1:3-4

It is this comfort that I received from God that I am now able to share with you. So, dear beloved, are you at the place where I have been? If so, are you tired of hearing all of the empty answers that human wisdom has to say? Are you ready to go to Someone who really knows the _____ and can really set you _____? Have you come to the place where you recognize that Jesus Christ is the only one who has the answers you seek?

With this in mind, I would like to comfort you with the same comfort I myself received from God—a comfort that does not include any form of psychotherapy but is solely based on the foundation of Jesus Christ.[4] To become victorious over any issue—whether it is the issue of abortion, the issue of abuse, the issue of whatever—will depend strictly on your response to God's truth. As Jesus said in Matthew 22:37, the greatest command of all is to "love the Lord your God with all your heart, with all your soul, and with all your mind." And as God said through the prophet Jeremiah:

> You will seek me and find me when you seek me with all your heart. I will
> be found by you . . . and will bring you back from _____.
>
> —Jeremiah 29:13-14

Perhaps you have been in the captivity of guilt, shame, fear, anxiety, depression, rage, over-protectiveness, relationship difficulties, and/or self-destructive behaviors such as alcohol, drugs, eating disorders, self-harm or even suicidal thoughts. If so, God desires to bring you back. He wants to set you _____.

Are You Right With God?

In view of what God desires to do in your life, let's look again at the Sinful Woman. In reading her story, do you realize that she became a believer? How do I know? Because Jesus said to her, "Your faith has _____ you" (Luke 7:50).

Many believe that they are saved for all kinds of reasons—they attend church, or a family member is saved, or they are a good person, or they do good works. However, according to God's Word, the only true way is by _____.

> For it is by grace you have been saved, through faith—and this not from
> yourselves, it is the gift of God—not by works, so that no one can boast.
>
> —Ephesians 2:8-9

By faith it is simple to accept Jesus Christ as your Lord and Savior. Simply cry out to God as the book of Romans teaches:

> That if you confess with your mouth Jesus as Lord, and believe in your
> heart that God raised Him from the dead, you will be saved; for with the

heart a person believes, resulting in righteousness, and with the mouth
he confesses, resulting in salvation.

—Romans 10:9-10, NASB

If you haven't accepted Jesus Christ as your Lord and Savior and you want to do so, it is as easy as this verse says! Simply _____ with your mouth that Jesus is Lord and _____ in your heart that God raised Him from the dead and you will be _____.

On the other hand, if you have no desire to accept Jesus Christ as your Lord and Savior at this time, I encourage you to complete this Bible study. Do not stop! However, you need to realize that not all of the promises of God, which will be taught in this study, will apply to you. You are loved by God, but the additional promises, such as you are forgiven and you are set free, only apply to those who have accepted Jesus Christ as their Lord and Savior. If at any time you decide to accept Christ into your life, simply do as Romans 10:9-10 teaches. At that moment, all of the promises of God will be yours—every single one of them! (If you would like more information concerning salvation make sure to read chapter four "Are You Right with God?" in the book *Go in Peace!*)

1. Has your faith saved you?

   _____

   _____

   _____

2. If so, when did you accept Jesus Christ as your Lord and Savior? How did it happen?

   _____

   _____

   _____

3. If not, do you want to accept Jesus Christ as your Lord and Savior right now?

   _____

   _____

   _____

Confidentiality (For Group Workshops)

Lastly, confidentiality is of the utmost importance! Many things may be shared which are very personal and private. For this reason, we must respect each other's privacy at all times, especially if you attend the same church or know each other. Do not discuss what was shared here with others unless you have the other person's permission. According to God's Word, we are called to love others as ourselves. For this reason, God would want us to be kind and considerate and respectful of another's privacy.

Assignment

The book *Go in Peace!* is excellent to read on your own to reinforce what was taught in the session. Many times the correlating chapter in the book is closely related to what you learned in the session, but don't skip it. Find a quiet place to sit with God and allow Him to reinforce what you learned. Below you will see the best way to read the book depending upon whether you are going through this Bible study weekly or as a weekend workshop.

Note that I wrote the book *Go in Peace!* specifically for those suffering with the issue of post-abortion. However, I have found over the years that God has impacted the lives of those who read the book in which abortion was not an issue just as powerfully as the post-abortive woman. (This applies to the book only. This Bible study, on the other hand, is for any issue.) Therefore, if abortion is not an issue in your life, whenever you see the word "abortion," simply change it in your mind to the word "sin" and apply what is being taught to your life. God's Word is all-sufficient and has the power to change lives—including yours—if you are willing. Though it grieves me deeply to see the depth of a person's pain, know that it grieves our heavenly Father even more. God has a love so deep for you that it is immeasurable, and His desire is for you to *go in peace!*

FOR WEEKLY BIBLE STUDY:

Read the Preface, Introduction and chapters one through four in the book *Go in Peace!* This will be the only week with so much reading. The following weeks you will only be required to read one chapter per week.

FOR WEEKEND WORKSHOP:

The reading of the book *Go in Peace!* is recommended to be read *after* the workshop is completed to reinforce what was learned over the weekend. The weekend workshop is intense and it is best to read the book slowly and contemplate what is written so that God can complete the deep heart work He began during the weekend. "Being confident of this very thing, that He who has begun a good work in you will complete it until the day of Jesus Christ (Philippians 1:6, NKJV).

DO NOT BE DECEIVED

Do not be deceived, God is not mocked;
for whatever a man sows, that he will also reap.
GALATIANS 6:7, NKJV

The Portrait of the Sinful Woman

*I*n the previous session, when viewing the portrait of the Sinful Woman, did you notice Simon the Pharisee and his placement within the scene? Did you pay attention to his interaction with Jesus? And furthermore, whom do you relate to within this story—the Sinful Woman or Simon?

Since the story of the Sinful Woman is the foundation of what you will be learning in this Bible study, we will examine it once again. As we do, I want to encourage you to look a bit deeper within the scene. Close your eyes, and see with your heart, as you listen to the words read aloud. What is Simon doing? What is he thinking? And more importantly, what point is Jesus trying to encourage Simon to grasp?

Keep in mind; God preserved this passage throughout the ages out of His love for you. And He divinely orchestrated events to bring you to this place to find rest for your soul. But that rest, and the peace we have been discussing, will only be achieved if you are willing to learn what He desires to teach you. So listen with both your heart and your mind, so that you can learn, so that you can become all that God created you to be.

Note to the Leader: Once again read Luke 7:36-50 out loud from the Bible.

Do Not Be Deceived

I have discovered in my many years of discipling that there are typically two types of people who come into my office for help: those who are like Simon and those who are like the Sinful Woman. Those like the Sinful Woman can be helped. Those like Simon, on the other hand, cannot be helped, because they _____ *want to be helped.* They think there is nothing wrong with them and that all their problems are a result of someone else's actions. This is what Simon thought, but, as the story clearly shows, he was _____! He was the one who went away from Jesus unchanged and hopeless.

With this in mind, let's look a little bit deeper at Simon within the portrait. Although the Sinful Woman had a heart ready and willing to learn from Jesus, Simon did _____. In fact, as he watched the Sinful Woman kneel at Jesus' feet broken and filled with humility all Simon saw was a sinful woman at Jesus' feet. In his judgmental attitude, he thought:

> If this man were a prophet, he would know who is touching him and what
> kind of woman she is—that she is a sinner.
>
> —Luke 7:39

I so enjoy Jesus' answer. God _____ knows what we are thinking, and we cannot fool Him! "Simon," Jesus said, "I have something to tell you" (Luke 7:40). Simon was busted! Jesus then went on to tell him the parable of the moneylender. As Pastor Warren Wiersbe notes in his commentary *Be Compassionate*, "Simon's real problem was blindness: he could not see himself, the woman, or the Lord Jesus. It was easy for him to say 'She is a sinner! But impossible for him to say 'I am _____ a sinner!' Jesus proved that He was indeed a prophet by reading Simon's thoughts and revealing his needs."[1]

Let's not make the same _____ that Simon did when he believed he had no sin. There is no one who is without sin. As the apostle Paul wrote:

> For _____ have sinned and fall short of the glory of God.
>
> —Romans 3:23

In view of this, it is my prayer that you will have a heart like the Sinful Woman. If you have such a heart, your life will be miraculously _____. When you take what you read in this Bible study and _____ it to your life you *will* go in peace. As the author of Hebrews states, God's Word has the power to change every person's heart:

> For the word of God is full of living power. It is sharper than the sharp-
> est knife, cutting deep into our innermost thoughts and desires. It
> _____ us for what we really are.
>
> —Hebrews 4:12, NLT

When we get to the point where we are _____ to allow God's Word to _____ the ugliness found in the depths of our beings, we are ready to allow Him to cleanse our hearts and change our lives. That's the place where the Sinful Woman was in her life, and that is why she went away changed.

Are you willing? Are you ready to receive what Jesus offers? Remember His gracious invitation:

> Come to me, all you who are weary and burdened, and I will give you
> rest.
>
> —Matthew 11:28

Well to begin, it is important to realize that there are consequences to the _____ we make in our lives. Listen to what Proverbs 6:27-28 has to say:

> Can a man scoop fire into his lap without his clothes being burned? Can
> a man walk on hot coals without his feet being scorched?

Of course, the answer to these questions is no! There are consequences to sin; there is no getting around that. That's why the apostle Paul tried to warn the people with these words when he wrote Galatians 6:7:

> Do not be deceived, God is not mocked; for whatever a man
> _____, that he will also _____.
>
> —NKJV

Yet, God is a good God. I have seen over many years of discipling with *Go in Peace!* countless people amazed to discover that the consequences in their lives—depression, anxiety, anger, relationship difficulties and/or self-destructive behaviors—were tied to _____. Yet they didn't even realize it until it was pointed out to them. (I know I was one of these people who learned this truth many years ago.) And with this realization came amazement—amazement that other people, beside themselves, were struggling in the same way. Yet, oftentimes we feel isolated and alone. So many people believe that they are alone in their struggles and that no one understands. But this is not the truth. The discovery, of what you are about to learn, encourages each person to learn more about God and to learn about His _____ to unlocking sin deep within his or her heart so that he or she can be set free from the consequences and go in peace. With this in mind, let's look at some of the ways that the sin hidden deep within our hearts affects us today. Because you see, _____ is the beginning of freedom.

To give you a better understanding, let's look at some specific sins. But before we begin, there is one more point I wish to make. In this session, we will be discussing some of the more controversial topics, the issues that most usually choose to avoid such as abortion, sexual immorality and abuse. The reason I address these issues is because many times it is easier to see the consequences directly related to these types of topics. However, if these issues do not directly relate to you, either now or in your past, know that they are only used as examples to give you an understanding of what takes place deep within our hearts when we choose not to deal with the sin hidden within our own hearts. Remember, "for all have sinned and fallen short of the glory of God" (Romans 3:23). With this said, may I encourage you to keep an open _____ and a clear _____ and ask God to reveal to you, if you are struggling with any of the consequences we are about to discuss, what _____ is buried deep within.

First, in regards to abortion: God created all women to love, nurture and protect their children. To have an abortion, a woman must go against how God created her in order to carry through with the traumatic event. When a woman goes against how God created her, there will be _____.

Second, in regards to sexual immorality, although our culture today says that a sexual relationship outside of marriage is acceptable and normal, a person must also go against what God has put within his or her heart in order to carry through with such a relationship. It is interesting to note a passage in Romans concerning the unbeliever:

Even when Gentiles, who do not have God's written law, instinctively follow what the law says, they show that in their hearts they know right from wrong. They demonstrate that God's law is written within them, for their own consciences either accuse them or tell them they are doing what is right.

—Romans 2:14-15, NLT

Instinctively, deep within our hearts, we know right from wrong. We instinctively know that a sexual relationship outside of marriage is immoral. Our consciences confirm to us that: "You shall not commit adultery" (Deuteronomy 5:18, NKJV). You see, God created the sexual union of a man and a woman to be something beautiful. But He prescribed this union to be only within the boundaries of marriage. When the first marriage took place in the Garden of Eden, we learn that: "The man and his wife were both naked, and they felt no shame" (Genesis 2:25). Within the boundaries of marriage there is no shame. However, the moment we step outside of God's boundaries there are consequences. And one of the consequences to sin is _____.

Sometimes it is difficult to see this truth because we have hardened our hearts to what we instinctively know. Therefore, for just a moment, let's consider this truth about sexual immorality from the eyes of a teenager. I have spent many years teaching and discipling teenagers. When you get down to the nitty-gritty and are able to talk openly about this issue, they will honestly share about the _____ they felt after they crossed the line into sexual immorality. They, like Adam and Eve in the Garden of Eden, immediately began to _____ their sin. Think about it: they _____ the truth from their parents, more than likely they _____ about where they had been, and the _____ that came from the possibility of contracting a sexually transmitted disease or pregnancy was almost unbearable. This is just the beginning of the vicious cycle of sin required to cover up the sin of sexual immorality all as a result of the guilt that they felt. In view of this, let's take a look at how the _____ of sin manifested itself in the life of King David after he committed the sin of adultery with Bathsheba. Listen to what he wrote in Psalm 38:4-10:

My guilt has overwhelmed me like a burden too heavy to bear. My wounds fester and are loathsome because of my sinful folly. I am bowed down and brought very low; all day long I go about mourning. My back is filled with searing pain; there is no health in my body. I am feeble and utterly crushed; I groan in anguish of heart. All my longings lie open before you, O LORD; my sighing is not hidden from you. My heart pounds, my strength fails me; even the light has gone from my eyes.

The guilt from David's sin affected him physically, emotionally, mentally and spiritually. And, dear beloved, even though we don't like to admit it, the guilt of _____ sin, which is hidden in the depths of _____ hearts, affects us as well. As we take a look at King David's life consider this question: *How does the guilt of sin manifest itself in your life?*

1. Physically: David described that there was no _____ in his body and that even the strength had failed him. Likewise, it's important for us to realize that sin can cause _____ consequences in our lives.

2. Emotionally: David described the intense feelings he was experiencing because of his guilt. He said that his guilt had _____ him like a burden that was too heavy for him to bear. In the same way, even though we try to deny the sin we have hidden deep within our hearts, it too becomes a _____ too heavy for us to bear.

3. Mentally: David described how his heart pounded and that all day long he went about mourning. In this case, He was describing both the _____ and _____ he was experiencing because of his sin. How many of us also struggle with anxiety and depression because of the _____ that is hidden deep within our hearts? (Now, it's important to know that not all depression is attributed to sin. There are actually three different causes of depression. These three causes can be physical issues, grief issues and/or sin issues. But in my many years of working with women and teens, I have seen that sin hidden deep within a person's heart is the greatest cause or it can actually intensive the other two causes. See appendix 2 for more information.)

4. Spiritually: David wrote, "Even the light has gone from my eyes" (Psalm 38:10b). His fellowship with God had been _____ because of his actions. Why do we think that we will not reap the same consequences for our sin? Remember, "Whatever a man sows, that he will also reap" (Galatians 6:7; NKJV).

The Consequences of Sin

So let's return to our portrait of the Sinful Woman for a moment. I believe that the Sinful Woman was reaping some of these same consequences in her own life. Look how she approached Jesus. She went up to Him from behind—in timidity and humility. She was filled with _____ and knew that she was not worthy enough to approach Him from the front, or even to talk to Him for that matter.

What brought her to the place where her life seemed out of control? What caused her to be weary and burdened? Why did she crave the rest that Jesus spoke about? Was it sin inflicted upon her by another which caused her hurt and pain and led her to make wrong choices for her life? Or was it self-inflicted sin? She was known as the Sinful Woman. Obviously there were sinful issues manifesting themselves in her life that others saw.

We all live in a sinful world, and most of us will not make it through unscratched and unharmed. Whether the hurt and pain is self-inflicted or inflicted by another, it can affect us to the depths of our innermost being. If this hurt is not handled in the manner in which God intends, it can and will wreak havoc in our lives.

You see, whether the sin is self-inflicted or inflicted by another what we do with the _____ within our own _____ as a result of that _____ is what will set us apart. It is important to learn, when hurt is not handled in the manner God intended, it will turn into anger, which in time will turn into bitterness, which will turn into a bitter poison that will _____ your whole life. This _____ is what is fueling the depression, the anxiety, the outbursts of anger or any of the other consequences you are suffering in your life.

During my many years of working with women, and even men for that manner, I have seen over and over again the consequences that have taken place in people's lives because of the infection that was occurring _____ within their _____. Now, before we take a look at these consequences in greater detail, I want to make one point clear. This point especially applies for those who are not struggling with self-inflicted sin, but sin inflicted by another. Perhaps the issue you are dealing with is something as traumatic as rape or abuse. If so, it is important to realize that you were sinned _____, that it was out of your control, and that what happened to you was _____ your fault. However, during my many years of discipling, I have found that the same consequences _____ apply in the life of a person who was sinned against as in the life of a person whose sins were self-inflicted.

I wondered about this and asked God, *Why do I see the same consequences in people's lives when they were the ones who were sinned against? Where are those consequences coming from?* The Lord taught me through His Word that the consequences occurring in the life of a person who had been sinned against were stemming from an _____ deep within that person's _____, just as was the case with the person whose sins were self-inflicted. With this in mind, it is important to ponder this question: *When did the sin first enter the heart of the person who was sinned against?*

To answer this question, we need to again remember that _____ not handled in the manner God intended will turn into _____, which in time will turn into _____, which will turn into a bitter _____ that will infect our entire lives. For this reason, each of us must be aware of the sin that is in our _____ hearts. Even though the anger may be justifiable (such as in the case of rape or abuse), if we do not handle it in the manner God intended, it is _____. It is this sin in the depths of our hearts that causes the consequences. Take a look at what Paul says in Ephesians 4:26:

> "In your anger do not sin:" Do not let the sun go down while you are still angry.

With this in mind, we can now take a closer look at the _____ consequences of sin.

1. _____—Many people suffer from some form of guilt following a _____ issue in their lives. Remember how King David described his guilt.

16

"My guilt has overwhelmed me like a burden too heavy to bear" (Psalm 38:4). Is that how the Sinful Woman felt? Is that why she threw caution to the wind and went to find Jesus at Simon's house?

2. _____—Many people will _____ to cover up the guilt that they feel. Or they will try to _____ others or a situation for their _____ actions. They may even have great sounding arguments, as a means of _____ what they know is wrong. Jeremiah warns: "'Although you wash yourself with soda and use an abundance of soap, the stain of your guilt is still there before me,' declares the Sovereign Lord" (Jeremiah 2:22). Although we may _____, we cannot hide from God by trying to _____ our sin through lying, blaming or justifying our actions. He sees everything; He knows everything.

3. _____—"Cover their faces with shame so that men will seek your name, O Lord" (Psalm 83:16).

In the case of abortion: Many women feel as if they have a _____ light on their forehead flashing the word "abortion, abortion" anytime the subject of abortion comes up. In fact, many women share that when they go to the doctor for their gynecological check up, they never answer the question honestly on the doctor's paperwork concerning how many times they have been pregnant because of the _____ they _____ feel.

In the case of child abuse: Many people have shared with me that when they were children they were afraid to tell their parents or someone they trusted because of the _____ they felt even though they knew something _____ had happened to them.

In the case of abuse: Many women, and even men for that matter, stay in abusive relationships and pretend that everything is perfectly normal to avoid the _____ of admitting the _____ of what is really taking place. In fact, in the case of verbal and/or emotional abuse, many people will stay in this type of abusive relationship because they begin to believe the lies of the abuser and they are _____ of their so-called failings.

4. _____ and/or _____—The person avoids places or people which remind them of the hurtful event. Furthermore, the person will _____ any feelings he or she may have concerning the subject. As a matter of fact, the person will _____ the channel on the radio or television if the subject with is hurtful is being addressed.

In the case of abortion: The woman _____ groups or activities where abortion may be discussed. She may go out of her way to _____ driving past the clinic where the abortion took place. In fact, if the subject of abortion comes up in a conversation, she will _____ away or _____ out what is being said.

In the case of abuse: The person _____ places and people which remind him or her of the abuse. In fact, a common statement I hear over and over again by a person who was sinned against is: *I was abused, but it was _____ big deal.* (If you were sinned against, and you are still trying to convince yourself that it was no big deal then know that it _____ a big deal. Allow God to do the deep heart work that needs to be done to set you free.)

"If we say that we have fellowship with Him and yet walk in the _____, we lie and do not practice the truth. . . . If we say that we have no sin, we are deceiving ourselves, and the truth is not in us" (1 John 1:6,8).

5. _____—Many people struggle with depression. This depression can last for years or until the person deals with the _____ cause of the depression. "For your arrows have pierced me, and your hand has come down upon me. . . . I am bowed down and brought very low; all day long I go about mourning. . . . I am feeble and utterly crushed; I groan in anguish of heart" (Psalm 38:2-8).

6. _____—When exposed to something that reminds a person of a traumatic event the person may experience a _____ response such as a rapid heartbeat, difficulty breathing and/or extreme anxiety.

In the case of abortion or even an unplanned pregnancy: It is not uncommon for the woman to feel _____ around other pregnant women or around infants. In fact, many post-abortive women struggle with _____ feelings when they become pregnant again, even if the child was planned.

In the case of rape or abuse: Many times those who have been through such a traumatic event struggle with _____ and _____ if they think they are in an unsafe place.

7. _____ and/or _____—"Then the man and his wife heard the sound of the Lord God as he was walking in the garden in the cool of the day, and they hid from the Lord God among the trees of the garden. But the Lord God called to the man, 'Where are you?' He answered, 'I heard you in the garden, and I was _____ because I was naked; so I hid'" (Genesis 3:8-10).

In the case of abortion: Many women choose abortion out of _____. For a teenager, she may choose abortion because she is _____ to tell her parents. For a single woman, she may be afraid of what people will think of her if they found out she was pregnant. Or a couple may choose abortion because they are _____ that they cannot afford to raise a child. Or afraid it will change their lifestyle.

In the case of child abuse: Many people have shared with me that when they were children they were _____ to tell their parents or someone they trusted about what had happened to them because they were _____ they would get in trouble. Deep within they knew it was wrong, yet because of their age they couldn't comprehend that they were not responsible; that it was out of their control and not their fault.

In the case of spousal abuse: Many people will stay in an _____ relationship, and even put their children at risk, out of fear and insecurity.

For everyone: It's important to know and understand that "God has not given us a spirit of fear, but of power and of love and of a sound mind (2 Timothy 1:7, NKJV).

8. _____—The person may dream about things that _____ them of the sin, the hurt or the traumatic event. Listen to how Job describes the dreams he was having as a result of the traumatic events he was going through: "I think, 'My bed will comfort me, and sleep will ease my misery,' but then you shatter me with dreams and terrify me with visions" (Job 7:13-14, NLT).

In the case of abortion: A common dream that many have experienced is about babies or small children who are in danger and the person is _____ to help them.

In the case of abuse, rape or a traumatic event: The person may dream that he or she is in _____. A common dream I hear many describe is that someone is chasing the person with a knife.

Many times, the person has a difficult time falling or staying asleep. Nightmares can be a _____ for depression and/or anxiety.

9. Anniversary _____—These are usually experienced subconsciously, deep within a person's innermost being. The person is _____ that he or she feels depressed or sad at the same time of year, every year, because it is the anniversary of the traumatic event. Although the person does not connect the two together—the depression with the traumatic event—deep within his or her innermost being the two _____ connected. Now although Jeremiah was aware what was going on, listen to how he described it: "I remember my affliction and my wandering, the bitterness and the gall. I well remember them, and my soul is _____ within me" (Lamentations 3:19-20).

In the case of abortion: The woman is unaware that she feels depressed or sad at the same time of year because it is the anniversary of the abortion or what would have been the birth month of the aborted child. In fact, in working at a crisis pregnancy center, I frequently counseled women who came in for pregnancy tests around the _____ date of their aborted baby. For example: the woman would share that she had an abortion six months prior when she was three months along which total nice months—full term. Most of the women who came in for testing were not pregnant, though deep in their hearts they desired to be. Not one of these women ever made the connection of the anniversary reaction.

In the case of abuse or rape: The person is _____ that they feel depressed or sad at the same time of year because it is the anniversary of the traumatic event.

19

For everyone: If you struggle with depression and/or anxiety, begin to be aware if the depression or anxiety happens at the same time of year, every year. You may then discover that the reason for the depression or anxiety is _____ to a deep heart hurt or a traumatic event in your life. Knowledge is the beginning of freedom. Many times, anniversary reactions are a _____ for depression and/or anxiety.

10. _____—In fact, they are better described as _____ memories. The person tries to push these memories away, but they are there, ever _____, waiting to return when the person least expects them. Listen to how King David describes them, "How long must I wrestle with my thoughts and every day have sorrow in my heart?" (Psalm 13:2). Certain things may _____ unwanted and disturbing memories when the person least expects them. These things may be something as innocent as a song, a flower, a smell or even a type of clothing; yet they bring back unwanted memories. Disturbing memories not dealt with in the way God intended can be a trigger for depression and/or anxiety.

11. _____—Sometimes amnesia is seen in the case of multiple abortions, sexual abuse or a traumatic event, but it is extremely rare. When something horrendous happens to a person it is usually not easily forgotten.

    In the case of abortion: The woman loses _____ of how many abortions she has had. Or the woman may have forgotten details of the abortion. However, it is not essential to remember everything. God in His infinite wisdom will allow the woman to remember what needs to be remembered for her healing.

    In the case of abuse: The person may remember only fragmented details of the abuse. In some _____ cases, the person has no recollection of the abuse whatsoever.

    For everyone: It's important to understand that as believers we are never to seek ways of trying to remember what has taken place in the past. Do not join in the world's way of thinking and allow yourself to be hypnotized. As stated above, _____ there is something that you need to remember, God in His infinite wisdom will bring anything that you need to know back to your memory in His perfect timing. Anything outside of His timing can be _____. So relax and trust God.

12. _____—The person may struggle with outbursts of anger. The person realizes that their anger is _____ or _____, but he or she does not know where it is coming from or how to stop it. The person frequently expresses feelings of _____ or _____ towards his or her spouse, children or loved ones. God's Word warns about this type of anger: "And 'don't sin by letting anger _____ you'" (Ephesians 4:26, NLT).

13. _____—The person may be overprotective of themselves and/or loved ones, especially if the person has children. The person may feel as if someone is out to get them and therefore he or she is always on the _____. Listen to how King David described this in the book of Psalms. "My heart is in anguish within me, the terrors of death assail me. Fear and trembling has beset me; horror has overwhelmed me. . . . I would hurry to my place of shelter, far from the tempest and the storm" (Psalm 4:8).

14. _____ and/or _____—The person may be controlling, without realizing it, as a means of _____. He or she may try to manipulate events so that his or her life will never again _____ out of control. Many times, it's all a means of protection or self-preservation. Listen to how King David describes some who were trying to control and manipulate events concerning him. Psalm 38:12 describes it this way. "Those who seek my life set their traps, those who would harm me talk of my ruin; all day long they _____ deception."

15. Difficulty _____—The person experiences an inability to _____ on one thing for too long. He or she may often feel _____ and may even have difficulties in making _____—even simple ones. Here is an interesting verse, "He has scattered those who are proud in their inmost thoughts" (Luke 1:51).

16. Unable to _____ Self—For those dealing with self-inflicted sin, many times, they feel as if they are unable to forgive themselves. They may know and understand that God has forgiven them, but they _____ as if they are unable to forgive themselves. It's much like what King David wrote after his sin of adultery with Bathsheba. "For I know my transgressions, and my sin is _____ before me" (Psalm 51:3).

17. Diminished _____—The person loses interest in things that were important to him or her before the traumatic event happened. Example: school, career, hobbies or church. Listen to what Jeremiah described in Lamentations 3:18: "So I say, 'My splendor is gone and all that I had hoped from the Lord.'" The person can even lose interest in _____ relationships.

   In the case of abortion: Many times the relationship with the father of the baby is impacted, especially if the woman feels as if he was pushing her to make this decision. For a couple that is married and chooses abortion, divorce is common. And for a daughter who feels as if her parents talked her into the abortion their relationship will be _____ affected.

   In the case of abuse: For a woman who was raped or abused (emotionally, physically and/or sexually by a man), many times relationships with men, in general, will be impacted.

18. _____ Difficulties—"My friends and companions avoid me because of my wounds; my neighbors stay far away" (Psalm 38:11). Many who are struggling with an unhealed sin issue in their lives erect _____ barriers around themselves so that others will be unable to _____ them. Some ever go so far as to erect the barriers so others may not _____ them. They withdraw in their relationships and reduce their communications with others. They find that they do not want to talk about their lives or how they feel. In fact, many times, they cannot even _____ how they are feeling. Deep inside they feel as if they do not deserve to be married or to have children, and therefore, they may _____ healthy relationships and friendships to reinforce their feelings of unworthiness. If this is the case, the person may even end up in an abusive relationship. (See appendix one, "Profile of an Abuser" for more information.)

19. Self-_____ Behaviors—For those who choose not to forgive themselves, or for those who feel they deserve punishment, they will oftentimes struggle with self-destructive behaviors. These are any type of behaviors that have a _____ affect on a person's life and can include actions such as over-eating, over-sleeping, over-cleaning, over-spending or over-anything else. They can also include the opposite, such as under-eating, under-sleeping, under-cleaning or under-anything else. Many people develop eating disorders such as _____ and/or _____, while others turn to _____ and/or _____ as a means to numb their deep heart hurt. Abuse of prescription drugs can also fall into this category. Some even go so far as to _____ or _____ themselves just to feel something or as a means of punishing themselves. Others turn to _____ or _____ to justify the hurt they have endured. Other self-destructive behaviors include _____ thoughts and/or attempts.

    Look at this interesting passage from Ezra's prayer concerning Israel's disobedience in intermarrying those God commanded them not to marry.

    > What has happened to us is a result of our evil deeds and our great guilt,
    > and yet, our God, you have punished us less than our sins have deserved.
    >
    > —Ezra 9:13

    Ezra realizes that his people, the Israelites, didn't get what their sins deserved. Instead they received God's grace. But he goes on to say in his prayer:

    > . . . . Shall we again break your commands and intermarry with the people
    > who commit such detestable practices? Would you not be angry enough
    > with us to destroy us, leaving us no remnant or survivor?
    >
    > —Ezra 9:14

    Isn't that crazy? It's almost as if Ezra is saying: *Perhaps Lord, if we again break your commands and intermarry with those you forbid us to marry, then you would zap us. Then you would give us the punishment we deserve.*

We can be such fickle people. Deep inside we know we deserve punishment for our sins. And when we _____ not to accept what Jesus Christ did on the cross for us, we too can make choices to destroy ourselves.

Do Not Be Deceived

Did you see any of these consequences in your life? Well, it's time to stop deceiving ourselves. The following exercise lists all the consequences we just talked about. As we read each consequence, put a checkmark next to any one that you have seen in your own life. It doesn't matter how frequently you have struggled with it—put a checkmark if you have ever experienced the consequence in your life. Are you ready? Let's take a look.

The Consequences of Sin

- ○ Guilt
- ○ Shame
- ○ Depression
- ○ Anxiety
- ○ Fear or insecurity
- ○ Nightmares
- ○ Anniversary reactions
- ○ Bad memories
- ○ Rage or outburst of anger
- ○ Overprotectiveness
- ○ Control and manipulation
- ○ Unable to forgive self
- ○ Diminished interest
- ○ Relationship difficulties
- ○ Self-destructive behaviors (such as anorexia or bulimia, cutting or harming yourself, promiscuity or homosexuality, drugs and/or alcohol, or suicidal thoughts).

Have any of these consequences been a part of your life? If so, allow these consequences to bring you to the foot of the cross. Kneel at Jesus' feet, just as the Sinful Woman did. In the same way that God used the consequences of sin in her life to draw her to Him, He uses the consequences in our lives to cause us to want His help. As the psalmist wrote, "Cover their faces with shame so that men will seek your name, O LORD" (Psalm 83:6).

God truly can use the consequences that we suffer as a result of our sin to draw us to Him. He wants to free us completely so that we can go in peace just like the Sinful Woman did after she went to Jesus. Remember the words of the apostle Paul:

> Do not be deceived; God is not mocked; for whatever a man sows, that he will also reap. For he who sows to his flesh will of the flesh reap corruption, but he who sows to the Spirit will of the Spirit reap everlasting life.
>
> —Galatians 6:7-8; NKJV

Do not be deceived any longer. Do not continue to sow to the sinful nature, the flesh, by holding on to the hurt, pain, anger and bitterness any longer. Instead, do you desire to find rest for your soul? Do you want to be like the Sinful Woman and go in peace?

The Sinful Woman deeply desired what Jesus had to offer. Because of this she threw caution to the wind and entered the Pharisee's house. She realized the ridicule and reaction she would receive from those present, but that paled in comparison to the rest her soul so deeply craved. Something she had never found anywhere else in all her life.

You too can accept so gracious a gift of rest!

How we can learn from this woman! All we need to do is to come to Jesus in humility, with a _____ and _____ heart. Don't be like Simon. Don't think that the things you are struggling with are all a result of someone else's actions. In fact, when Jesus said, "Therefore, I tell you, her _____ sins have been forgiven—for she loved much. But he who has been forgiven _____ loves little" (Luke 7:47). Jesus was making the point that Simon was forgiven little, not because he had _____ sin than the Sinful Woman did, but because Simon didn't believe he needed to be forgiven. He didn't believe he was a sinful man. He was _____ himself. And thus he never asked God for forgiveness. Therefore, he was forgiven little. What a shame—to stand in Jesus' presence and miss one of the most precious gifts He has to give.

Let's not make the same mistake. Our only way to be restored, to be healed, to receive joy and peace is to recognize the sin hidden deep within our own hearts. I believe the Sinful Woman recognized this truth about herself and she chose to do something about it. She chose to go to Jesus to find rest for her soul. And she chose to lay the burden of her sin at His feet. We too have the same choice.

Come, kneel at the feet of Jesus, just like the Sinful Woman did, and confess your sin—even the sin hidden in the depths of your heart that you think no one can see—the sin of hurt, pain, anger and bitterness which were not handled in the manner God intended, and have, therefore, turned into a bitter poison.

Ask God to prepare your heart for the truth. Ask Him to show you the root of whatever you are struggling with—the fear, anxiety, depression and so forth. Ask Him for the strength to continue to turn the pages. He wants you to be honest with yourself so that you can be set free and *go in peace!*

Assignment

FOR WEEKEND WORKSHOP:

Take a short break and then move onto the next session.

FOR WEEKLY BIBLE STUDY:

Read chapter five titled "Do Not Be Deceived" in the book _Go in Peace!_ There is an interesting assignment you will find in this chapter that you will begin here and complete at a later time. Don't miss it. You will be blessed! After reading the chapter and doing the assignment spend a quiet time with the Lord and as you do complete the following exercises.

1. What was the most interesting aspect of this session?

   _____
   _____
   _____

2. Were you surprised to discover that the consequences you may be dealing with are directly related to what is taking place in the depths of your own heart?

   _____
   _____
   _____

3. Pray and ask God to show you the root of what is causing the consequences in your life so that you will be prepared for the next two sessions.

   _____
   _____
   _____

4. Which verse(s), within this session, spoke the deepest to your heart? And why?

   _____
   _____
   _____

TAKE EVERY THOUGHT CAPTIVE

*We demolish arguments and every pretension
that sets itself up against the knowledge of God,
and we take captive every thought
to make it obedient to Christ.*

2 CORINTHIANS 10:5

Arguments and Pretensions

*I*n the last session, we saw how God's Word shows us that there are consequences to our sin. In addition to this, when our sin is horrendous, the consequences will be greater and we will have a more difficult time coping with them. Of course, none of us like consequences, so we will always try to find ways of not having to deal with them. In other words, we have fine sounding arguments and wonderful pretensions. The word "pretension" comes from the word "pretense" which means a claim; one not supported by fact; a mere display; for show; in fact, it can even mean, an attempt to attain a certain condition.[1]

Psychologists will often describe these fine sounding arguments and wonderful pretensions as "defense mechanisms," and they can include suppression, rationalization, denial and reaction formation. Those who embrace this type of teaching will tell you that once you recognize that you are using these defense mechanisms, they can help you move on with your life.

However, in studying God's Word over the years and seeking Him for guidance on this issue, He clearly showed me that this is just another form of sin—plain and simple sin—that goes all the way back to the Garden of Eden. Dear beloved, I do not want to lead you astray by giving you any false teaching. As the apostle Paul teaches:

> See to it that no one takes you captive through hollow and deceptive philosophy, which depends on human traditions and the basic principles of this world rather than on Christ.
>
> —Colossians 2:8

You must know the truth if you are to be completely healed by God's love, grace and mercy. Therefore, it is time to rely on Christ, just as the Sinful Woman did, so that you can be set free and go in peace. God's Word teaches that it is time to stop pretending and stop having these fine sounding arguments which in reality just sets themselves up against the knowledge of God in your life. Listen to His Word:

> We demolish arguments and every pretension that sets itself up against the knowledge of God, and we take captive every thought to make it obedient to Christ.

—2 Corinthians 10:5

Before we begin, I want to help you demolish the arguments and pretensions that have perhaps been set up against the knowledge of God in your life. You see many times, we try to convince ourselves that the hurt and pain caused by another in no way affects us. Or we even try to convince ourselves that the hurt and pain caused by our *own* choices have no negative affect upon our lives. And we try to pretend that we have it all together by laying false claim to whatever is easiest to accept as a means of not having to deal with what is truly taking place in the depths of our own hearts. Yet, in spite of this, our lives are out of control and we struggle with the issues we saw in the previous session.

It is only by demolishing and destroying these arguments and pretensions that we can then take every thought captive in order to make them obedient to Christ. Remember what we learned in the last session? Whether the sin is self-inflicted or inflicted by another what we do with the _____ within our _____ hearts is what will set us apart. This is what will cause us to live with arguments and pretensions within our own hearts, or, on the other hand, be set us free so that we can go in peace just like the Sinful Woman did.

Therefore, it is important to be honest with yourself as we study this session. Remember, _____ not handled in the manner God intended will turn into _____, which in time will turn into _____, which will turn into a bitter _____ that will infect our entire lives. For this reason, each of us must be aware of the _____ that is in our own _____. I will say it again, even if the anger may be justifiable (such as in the case of rape or abuse), if we do not handle the hurt, pain, anger and bitterness in the manner God intended, it is _____. It is this sin in the depths of our own hearts that causes the consequences.

This is why God does not want us to hold on to the hurt any longer. He wants us to deal with the painful things in our past so we can move forward. Because you see, if what is in our _____, is affecting us _____, then it's not really in our _____. And the consequences we discussed in the previous session will continue to go on for _____ until we are ready to take every thought captive and make it obedient to Christ. Jesus came to set us free, and freedom can be found in His Word. So let's go back to the Garden of Eden to see where the root of sin began.

Note to the Leader: Read Genesis 2:15 to 3:13 out loud from the Bible.

The Root of Sin Began in the Garden

I so enjoy true love stories, and in this passage we find the first wedding in history. In fact, in reading Genesis 2:25 we learned that "the man and his wife were both naked, and they felt no shame." Remember what we learned in the last session? Adam and Eve had no shame because at this point there was no sin in their lives. In the same way, when we are in God's perfect _____, there is no guilt and no shame in our lives. However, the moment we step out of His will, we will experience both guilt and shame and—even worse—many other _____.

Now all good love stories have a villain and in this case the villain was the crafty serpent, who said to Eve, "Did God really say, 'You must not eat from any tree in the garden?'" (Genesis 3:1). The enemy always takes the truth of God's Word and _____ it just enough to cause us to _____.

The drama continues. Eve ate the forbidden fruit and then gave some to her husband, Adam, who also ate the fruit, even though he knew it was forbidden. Watch what happens the moment they chose to do that which they knew they were not to do:

> Then the eyes of both of them were opened, and they realized they were _____; so they sewed fig leaves together and made _____ for themselves. Then the man and his wife heard the sound of the LORD God as he was walking in the garden in the cool of the day, and they _____ from the LORD God among the trees of the garden. But the LORD God called to the man, "Where are you?" He answered, "I heard you in the garden, and I was _____ because I was naked; so I _____.
>
> —Genesis 3:7-10

Adam and Eve's sin caused them to feel shame and they "realized they were naked" (Genesis 3:7b). Their _____ was laid bare before God. Then, to cover their sin, they "sewed fig leaves together and made coverings for themselves" (Genesis 3:7c). They immediately _____ the consequences of the sin they had _____. Adam told God, "I was afraid because I was naked; so I hid" (Genesis 3:10b). Do you see the consequences of guilt, fear and avoidance in what Adam described? Because Adam was _____ to deal with the consequences of his sin, he tried to _____ the truth and _____ from God.

But this story is not yet over. There is no happy ending for this love story in the Garden of Eden—at least not for a few thousand years. As you read the following passage, take a moment to ask God to reveal to you any areas of your life where you may be saying the same types of things that Adam and Eve said:

> And [God] said, "Who told you that you were naked? Have you eaten from the tree that I commanded you not to eat from?"
>
> The man said, "The woman you put here with me—she gave me some fruit from the tree, and I ate it."
>
> Then the LORD God said to the woman, "What is this you have done?" The woman said, "The serpent deceived me, and I ate."
>
> —Genesis 3:11-13

Did you see how both Adam and Eve tried to place the _____ on anyone but themselves? They both _____ responsibility for their actions and tried to _____ from the consequences. But God knew that they needed to _____ with their sin immediately. In the same way, dear beloved, we must not try to hide from the consequences of our sin by pushing away our guilty thoughts, or by being afraid of dealing with the hurtful issues, or by avoiding the truth of our sin buried deep within our hearts. The longer we _____ to deny feelings or actions associated with the hurtful issues in our lives, the longer we will _____ the consequences of our sin.

With this in mind, let's take a moment and take turns to read out loud the following verses to learn more about this important truth.

Listen to my prayer, O God, do not ignore my plea; hear me and answer me. My thoughts trouble me and I am distraught.

—Psalm 55:1-2

Search me, O God, and know my heart; Try me and know my anxious thoughts; And see if there be any hurtful way in me, And lead me in the everlasting way.

—Psalm 139:23-24, NASB

Morning, noon, and night I plead aloud in my distress, and the LORD hears my voice.

—Psalm 55:17, NLT

The lamp of the LORD searches the spirit of a man; it searches out his inmost being.

—Proverbs 20:27

I the LORD search the heart and examine the mind, to reward a man according to his conduct, according to what his deeds deserve.

—Jeremiah 17:10

Behold, You desire truth in the innermost being, And in the hidden part You will make me know wisdom.

—Psalm 51:6, NASB

Test me, O LORD, and try me, examine my heart and my mind; for your love is ever before me, and I walk continually in your truth.

—Psalm 26:2-3

"For I know the plans I have for you," declares the LORD, "plans to prosper you and not to harm you, plans to give you hope and a future."

—Jeremiah 29:11

According to God's Word, we learn that it is vitally important to ask the Lord to search our hearts and minds. But what happens when we _____ or _____ to take our thoughts captive and to make them obedient to Christ?

> Ruin and misery mark their ways, and the way of peace they do not know.
>
> —Romans 3:16-17

> In his pride the wicked does not seek him; in all his thoughts there is no room for God.
>
> —Psalm 10:4

> O LORD, don't rebuke me in your anger! Don't discipline me in your rage! Your arrows have struck deep, and your blows are crushing me. Because of your anger, my whole body is sick; my health is broken because of my sins. My guilt overwhelms me—it is a burden too heavy to bear. My wounds fester and stink because of my foolish sins. I am bent over and racked with pain. My days are filled with grief. A raging fever burns within me, and my health is broken. I am exhausted and completely crushed. My groans come from an anguished heart. You know what I long for, Lord; you hear my every sigh. My heart beats wildly, my strength fails, and I am going blind. My loved ones and friends stay away, fearing my disease. Even my own family stands at a distance.
>
> —Psalm 38:1-11, NLT

> How long must I wrestle with my thoughts and every day have sorrow in my heart? How long will my enemy triumph over me?
>
> —Psalm 13:2

The enemy will continue to triumph over you until you are ready to take your thoughts captive and make them obedient to Christ. Are you ready to stop wrestling with your thoughts and having sorrow in your heart? Do not be afraid. Remember, Jesus said, "If you hold to my teaching, you are really my disciples. Then you will know the truth, and the truth will set you free" (John 8:31-32). In view of this, let's learn from God's Word so that we can hold to His teaching to be able to find the peace we are seeking.

Inmost Being

In Psalm 139:13a, David writes an interesting statement, "For you [God] created my inmost being." I believe that God created our inmost being as a hole in the depths of our heart that can only be filled by a right relationship with Him. This means more than just having a saved relationship—although that is important, for we must be saved to get to heaven. Rather, what I mean by a _____ relationship is that God truly wants to be our everything. He wants to meet with us daily and have an intimate relationship with us. I believe that it is in the depths of our heart, in our innermost being, where God meets with us.

You see, we have both _____ thoughts (thoughts we are aware of at a specific moment) and _____ thoughts (thoughts that we are not aware of consciously). In a sense, our subconscious thoughts are hidden. We cannot consciously keep every thought we have in the part of our mind where we are aware of them continually—if we did, we would be on _____. Therefore, we store many of our thoughts in our subconscious mind.

Now, the words "conscious" and "subconscious" are relatively new to our society. The word "conscious" first appeared in the 1600s,[2] while the word "subconscious" first appeared in the 1800s.[3] In view of this, the Bible being written way before this time, it does not use the word "subconscious," but it does refer to our _____ being.

In studying the term "inmost being" we will discover that in biblical language it is believed that the inmost being (sometimes also referred to as *heart* and *kidneys*) is the center of the human spirit, from which spring our emotions, our _____, our motivations, our courage and our _____.[4] This is what God tests and examines when He searches a person. This is why God's Word warns:

> Above all else, guard your heart, for it affects everything you do.
>
> —Proverbs 4:23, NLT

So let me explain it to you this way. Look at the following verse that is repeated twice in God's Word:

> The words of a gossip are like choice morsels; they go down to a man's inmost parts.
>
> —Proverbs 18:8; 26:22

This describes an interesting truth. When someone says or does something to hurt us deeply, we can't stop thinking about it. We keep replaying the words or hurtful acts over and over again in our _____. Then, when we can't stand it any longer, we _____ that hurt deep within our hearts, deep within our inmost beings. It is as if we had swallowed it. And once we have swallowed it, we think it is gone away. We think that we are over the hurt, and so we _____ to move on with our lives. Unfortunately, stuffing the hurt only gives a _____ to the enemy, thereby giving him a way to triumph over us.

Strongholds

Now let's go back to our theme verse for this session, and as we do, let's read the prior verse as well.

> The weapons we fight with are not the weapons of the world. On the contrary, they have divine power to demolish strongholds. We demolish

arguments and every pretension that sets itself up against the knowledge
of God, and we take captive every thought to make it obedient to Christ.

—2 Corinthians 10:4-5

As we continue to stuff the hurt and pain, the guilt and shame deep within our inmost beings, we give the enemy a _____. There, deep within, the hurt and pain
begin to fester and decay into an unhealthy anger. Look again at what God's Word says
concerning anger:

> "In your anger do not_____:" Do not let the sun go down while
> you are still angry, and do not give the devil a _____.

—Ephesians 4:26-27

In view of this, let's look at some of the ways we give a stronghold or a foothold to the
enemy. As we do, we will be comparing the human viewpoint known as "defense mechanisms" with the biblical viewpoint of what took place in the Garden of Eden the moment
Adam and Eve chose to sin to see how these fine sounding arguments and wonderful pretensions compare to our own lives.

1. Cover—Suppression

Because of Adam and Eve's sin there was _____ which they tried to
_____ as we saw in Genesis 3:7. With this in mind, let's look at what it
means to *suppress* or to *cover*. The word "suppression" means the "_____
exclusion of unacceptable desires, thoughts, or memories from the mind."[5] In other
words, the person consciously covers or pushes away any negative or painful thoughts
or feelings as they begin to surface. I call it the Scarlett O'Hara theory. Have you ever
seen the movie *Gone with the Wind*? One of Scarlett's famous lines whenever she was
in a difficult situation, which she said throughout the movie was, "I'll think about
that tomorrow." So in reality, suppression is just a fancy word for _____
our guilt, shame and nakedness.

In the case of abortion: Many women will admit that they had an abortion, but
they will _____ admit their negative or painful thoughts and/or feelings
concerning the abortion.

In the case of abuse: Many abuse victims will _____ and
_____ the person who abused them because of the shame and/or insecurity that they feel.

In the case of child abuse: Many parents have asked me, *why was my child so
afraid to tell me?* The answer—the child felt either too much _____ or
too much _____ to reach out for help.

According to Dan Allender in his book *The Wounded Heart* "Suppression of
truth requires enormous energy and the symptoms of 'chosen forgetfulness' will be
_____ and _____."[6] Anniversary reactions, depression, anxiety

33

and/or nightmares are just a few of the common consequences for the person using suppression as a means of covering up what is taking place deep within their inmost being.

According to *Webster's Ninth New Collegiate Dictionary* some of the definitions for the word "cover" are: to guard from attack; to afford protection; to hide from sight or knowledge; to conceal something illicit, blameworthy or embarrassing from notice.[7]

> At that moment, their eyes were opened, and they suddenly felt shame at their nakedness. So they strung fig leaves together around their hips to _____ themselves.
>
> —Genesis 3:7, NLT

There are many different types of sin. So what type of sin is being committed here? The intentional _____ of our shame and nakedness from our _____ thoughts as a means of not having to deal with the _____ issue of what is really taking place deep within our hearts, deep within our inmost being. But there is hope. Look at this wonderful verse. "Then I acknowledged my _____ to you and did not _____ up my iniquity. I said, 'I will confess my transgressions to the LORD'—and you forgave the guilt of my sin" (Psalm 32:5). It is time to stop covering up our sin.

2. **Blame—Rationalization**
Because of Adam and Eve's sin they tried to blame someone other than themselves, as we saw in Genesis 3:11-13. Let's look at what it means to *rationalize* or to *blame*. The word "rationalization" means "to provide plausible but _____ reasons for [our] conduct."[8] This is just a politically correct word for _____. In other words, the person provides plausible or logical _____ for their decision to sin, while at the same time _____ the truth.

In the case of abortion: The woman provides _____ reasons for the abortion while denying the _____ reasons. For example: *I was too young to have a baby. I couldn't afford to raise it. It's just a fetal tissue mass.* When in reality, instead of admitting the truth: *I was afraid. I was selfish.* For the woman who is still trying to rationalize and blame others or the situation for her decision to abort, to _____ abortion is _____ will be very difficult for her. As Michael Mannion in *Abortion and Healing: A Cry to Be Whole* writes, "To give her a cop-out, an escape from dealing with the reality of what she has done will not help her. The reality of what she has done must be named and understood if true reconciliation is to take place."[9]

In the case of abuse: The person continues to _____ a situation or person for _____ actions. In other words, the victim mentality becomes a way of life for him or her without the person even realizing it.

Adam and Eve both _____ someone other than _____ for their own actions. The word "blame" means to put the responsibility for a _____ done on someone or something other than ourselves.[10] Look once again at what Adam and Eve said:

> The man said, "The woman you put here with me—she gave me some fruit from the tree, and I ate it" . . . The woman said, "The serpent deceived me, and I ate."
>
> —Genesis 3:12-13

Adam _____ both the woman and God for his actions, while Eve _____ that the serpent had deceived her.

There are many different types of sin. So what type of sin is being committed here? Every time we provide plausible but untrue reasons for our conduct, it is the same as _____ and _____ a situation or a person for our _____ actions. This is a sin to God. In fact, one of the Ten Commandments says: "You shall not give _____ testimony against your neighbor" (Exodus 20:16). Whenever you lie or blame another for your own actions you are giving a false testimony.

3. Hide—Denial

Because of Adam and Eve's sin they tried to _____ from God and the truth, as we saw in Genesis 3:8-10. Let's look at what it means to be in *denial* or to *hide*. The *Collins English Dictionary* defines "denial" as follows: "A psychological process by which painful truths are _____ admitted into an individual's consciousness."[11] Another definition for denial is a "refusal to _____ the truth or reality of our behavior and consequence on ourselves and others."[12] In other words, denial is just a six-letter word for _____. When we choose _____ to admit the truth to ourselves, we are hiding, just as Adam and Eve did. They hid from God and the truth.

In the case of abortion: For a woman to have an abortion, it requires a great deal of _____. Before the abortion, she begins to convince herself that there is not a baby in her womb, but simply a product of conception or a fetal tissue mass. After the abortion, the woman continues to _____ her real feelings concerning the procedure.

In the case of abuse: Many who were abused use denial as a means of _____ from the hurt. I cannot even tell you how many times I have heard a person say, *I was abused, but it was no big deal.*

In the case of wrong choices: Many people use denial to hide from the _____ that their _____ have hurt themselves or others. They deny that the hurt, pain and anger deep within their hearts, which has become infected, have brought consequences to themselves and/or others.

Many who are in denial do not see the need for _____. As believers, we are very good at hiding behind God's Word and declaring ourselves healed. We deny what is really taking place deep within our hearts, deep within our inmost beings. Instead of dealing with the deep heart hurt, we claim we are forgiven or that we are a new creation in Christ. It is true—you _are_ forgiven and you _are_ a new creation in Christ—however, if what is in your _____ is still affecting you _____, then it is not truly in your past. It must be dealt with today in the manner God intended.

Adam and Eve both tried to hide from God on account of their sin. The word "hide" means "to conceal for shelter or protection; to keep _____; to turn away in _____ or _____; to remain out of sight; to seek protection or to _____ responsibility."[13]

> Then the man and his wife heard the sound of the LORD God as he was walking in the garden in the cool of the day, and they _____ from the LORD God among the trees of the garden.
>
> —Genesis 3:8

What type of sin is being committed here? The sin of hiding from both God and the truth of what is really taking place in the depths of your heart by _____ to admit this truth or accept responsibility. First John 1:8 says: "If we _____ to be without sin, we _____ ourselves and the _____ is not in us."

4. Afraid—Reaction Formation

Because of Adam and Eve's sin they were afraid as we saw in Genesis 3:10. Let's look at the comparison of _reaction formation_ and being _afraid_. Now this particular defense mechanism—reaction formation—is a bit harder to describe, but basically it is just an important-sounding word for being _____. A definition of "reaction formation" is as follows: "If two motives are antithetical [the direct opposite] to each other, the system [meaning the person] may respond by doing all it can to build up the strength of one [motive], usually the more acceptable one, so that the other motive is safely contained."[14] Perhaps the best way to explain this _____ or reaction formation in layman's terms is by giving examples.

In the case of abortion: A woman who has had an abortion may become either _____ pro-choice or _____ pro-life.

For the woman who becomes strongly pro-choice, it is safer for her to believe this point of view and try to _____ others to have an abortion than it is to admit the truth. By doing so, she can better _____ her own decision to abort her child. Admitting that abortion is wrong _____ too much, and she is afraid of how she may react emotionally if she admits this to herself. By holding on to this point of view (that there is nothing wrong with a woman choosing to have an abortion) the other motive (admitting that abortion is wrong) is safely contained. Therefore, the woman will do everything she can to build up the _____ of one point of view (being pro-choice) so that she does not have to deal with the other point of view (abortion is wrong) all out of _____.

On the other hand, reaction formation (or fear) can cause many post-abortive women who have not received full healing to become strongly pro-life. This woman adopts this position to _____ for the life of her baby. She comes to believe that if she can save *just one* baby from being aborted or save *just one* woman from going through what she went through, she will be set free from her hurt and pain. Her _____ is to build up the strength of one point of view (being pro-life to atone for her sin) so she will not have to deal with the other point of view (that abortion is wrong and she deserves punishment for her sin). This is not to say that her thinking is correct—God's Word teaches that all we have to do is confess our sins and He is faithful to forgive us.[15] At that moment, we are set free from the punishment we deserve. I am just pointing out the motivating factor—the underlying _____—that is within the depths of her heart.

Unfortunately, if this woman has not been fully healed by the Lord, she can do more _____ than _____. It is because of this very issue that a local crisis pregnancy center in my town requires all post-abortive women who desire to be counselors to attend a post-abortion workshop, even if that woman _____ to have been healed over this issue in her life.

In the case of abuse: Many, because of their _____ or _____, will make excuses or cover up for an abuser instead of admitting that there is a problem. Remember the definition of reaction formation: If two motives are _____ each other, a person will respond by doing everything he or she can to build up the strength of one particular motive—the one most _____ to that person—so that he or she can _____ the other motive. In this case, it is easier for a woman to build up the strength of the motive that there is no problem—that he is not an abuser—than it is for her to _____ with her own fear and insecurity. Many times, the woman will even allow the abuse to continue to herself and/or her children to keep this fear and insecurity safely contained. Do you see how reaction formation is just a fancy word for being afraid?

In the case of sexual abuse or rape: The person may become protective of self in overt ways. Or the direct opposite, the person may become sexually promiscuous or enter into the homosexual lifestyle.

For the person who becomes protective of self, he or she may try to be unattractive through his or her manner of dress and/or behavior. In fact, for a woman who has been sexually abused or raped she may put on weight, dress unattractively or even put on masculine behavior as a means of _____. The underlying motivating factor in this woman's life is fear.

On the other hand, reaction formation (or fear) can cause a person who was raped or sexually abused to become sexually promiscuous or homosexual. The person choses this path as a means of coping with what happened to him or her. In fact, many times it is an issue of _____ because the underlying motivating factor is _____. It is better to be in control of the situation and _____ this lifestyle than to deal with the issue of abuse—all the hurt and pain—because of the fear of the _____. The person is afraid of how he or she may react if the truth were admitted.

Let me give you a couple of examples. Many women who were sexually abused as a child turn to the homosexual lifestyle as a means of _____ from the opposite sex. They are reacting out of their desire to be loved, but also out of _____—women are _____. Also, many who have been sexually abused by someone of the same sex, as a child or a teenager, turn to the homosexual lifestyle. By turning to this lifestyle it helps to _____ the abuse they suffered. For many, they felt out of control during the act of abuse. But now, by their _____ choices, they relive what happened to them by choosing this lifestyle. By holding on to this point of view (that homosexuality is a normal way of life) the other motive (I need to deal with the hurt and pain within my heart over this issue) is safely contained. I'll say it again; it is a means to control. But it is important to know that the _____ of control is always fear and insecurity.

There is another factor that sometimes gets all mixed up in this issue. God created our bodies to respond to sexual stimulus. When this takes place, even in an act of abuse, this does not mean that deep down inside a person must be promiscuous or homosexual. It means that the body was responding to how it was created. Unfortunately, a human being stepped out of God's will and misused this precious gift. If this is something that you struggle with, please do not let the enemy continue to have a stronghold in your life over this issue. Continue to work though this Bible study to learn how to be set free.

The word "justify" means "to prove or show to be just, right or reasonable."[16] When a person enters into a lifestyle of homosexuality or becomes promiscuous as a means to justify what happened to him or her, the person is trying to make what happened be just, right, reasonable or _____ deep within his or her heart. Usually this happens because the person does not know how to deal with the deep hurt in any other manner. Many times, deep within, the person is _____ that if he or she begins to _____ with the hurt and pain it may be _____. Instead of dealing with the problem, it's safer and easier to enter into a lifestyle of promiscuity or homosexuality all as a means to control and to keep the fear of the unknown safely contained.

Also, for the person whom the abuse is more recent, he or she may be afraid of the unknown of what will happen if the truth were told. Soon the fearful thoughts begin: *The police may be called, I might have to testify, the person who harmed me* _may do something even worse to me._ The worry is endless. Because of this they will _____ dealing with the issue. Thus the underlying motivating factor for the choices this person is making is _____.

Adam and Eve both made wrong choices to hide from God because they were afraid. The word "afraid" means, "feeling fear, or feeling worry about the possible _____ of a particular situation."[17]

> He answered, "I heard you in the garden, and I was _____ because I was naked; so I hid."
>
> —Genesis 3:10

What type of sin is being committed here? The sin of allowing fear to _____ your life, causing you to continue to hide from God and the truth. God wants you to be _____ with yourself. He wants you to run to Him with your fears and insecurities. He desires truth in your innermost being—not lies, denial and deception. As King David declared: "Behold, You [God] desire truth in the innermost being, and in the hidden part You will make me know wisdom (Psalm 51:6, NASB).

Demolish Strongholds

The Lord examines all of our thoughts, and I believe that when we continue to cover the hurt or deny that we have any hurt, pain or sin in the depths of our inmost being, He will try to get us to look at these things. He does so through dreams (nightmares), disturbing thoughts, anxiety, depression, outbursts of anger and overprotectiveness, to name just a few means. The Lord wants to set us free. He wants to unshackle the cord of sin that holds us fast. In His love, He tries to get us to deal with the hurt and the pain because He is a jealous God and does not want to share the place He created within us—our innermost being—with anyone or anything else.

If there is sin in the depths of our innermost being, this will _____ us from God. Listen to what the prophet Isaiah warned:

> Surely the arm of the LORD is not too short to save, nor his ear too dull to hear. But your iniquities have separated you from your God; your sins have hidden his face from you, so that he will not hear.
>
> —Isaiah 59:1-2

This is why I believe His Word says:

> Blows and wounds cleanse away evil, and beatings purge the inmost being.
>
> —Proverbs 20:30

> For he wounds, but he also binds up; he injures, but his hands also heal.
>
> —Job 5:18

God wants to heal your heart in the depths of your innermost being so that He can meet with you. But it is only by purging these wounds deep within, by looking at the _____ issues in truth, that you will be _____ and _____. It is time to stop having fine sounding arguments and wonderful pretensions.

> The weapons we fight with are not the weapons of the world. On the contrary, they have divine power to demolish _____. We demolish _____ and every _____ that sets itself up against the knowledge of God, and we take captive every thought to make it obedient to Christ.
>
> —2 Corinthians 10:4-5

It is true what the psychologists teach; we suppress, rationalize, deny and use reaction formation because in reality we cover, blame, hide and are afraid of the deep hurt that is within our hearts. But for those who follow the world's way of thinking, many times the psychologists, therapists and counselors neglect to teach the next most important truth. That truth is that as long as we cover, blame, hide and live in fear, we lie to ourselves and the truth is not in us. Thus, we live in _____ and will never live in _____. Unless we learn to take every thought captive and make it obedient to Christ in the manner that He intended.

Adam and Eve both tried to cover their shame and nakedness. They tried to shift the blame by denying responsibility for their actions. They both tried to hide from the consequences of their sin. And because of this, they were afraid. But God, in His love, knew that they needed to deal with the consequences of their sin _____. The longer we try to deny feelings or actions associated with our sin, the longer we will reap the consequences. Until we stop trying to cover our shame, blame others, hide from the responsibilities, and be afraid of the outcome, we will never be healed for we are living with arguments and pretensions deep within our hearts.

It is only by admitting the ugly facts and by taking responsibility for our own actions that we can truly find peace. Remember, "God demonstrates His own love toward us, in that while we were still sinners, Christ died for us" (Romans 5:8, NKJV). What arguments and pretensions have you set up in your life? Be bold enough to be honest. Confess your sin to both yourself and to God. Never forget: "If we confess our sins, He is faithful and just to forgive us our sins and purify us from all unrighteousness" (1 John 1:9, NKJV). When you are bold enough to admit the truth, you will be taking steps towards true peace deep within your heart, deep within your inmost being. Continue to work through this Bible study so that you can learn practical ways to take your thoughts captive and give all the hurt, pain, anger and bitterness to God, once and for all, so that you can truly *go in peace*.

Assignment

FOR WEEKEND WORKSHOP:

Take a short break and then move onto the next session.

FOR WEEKLY BIBLE STUDY:

Read chapter six titled "Take Every Thought Captive" in the book *Go in Peace!* Although the chapter is closely related to this session you will find a different perspective which can help to reinforce what you are learning. After reading the chapter spend some quiet time with the Lord and as you do complete the following exercises.

1. What was the most interesting aspect of this session?

   _____

   _____

   _____

2. Which verse(s), within this session, spoke the deepest to your heart? And why?

   _____

   _____

   _____

3. Spend a quiet time with God and ask Him to show you what fine sounding arguments and wonderful pretensions that have perhaps been set up against the knowledge of God in your life. In other words, what is the root of what is taking place in the depths of your heart? What is the root of the depression? What is the root of the anxiety? What is the root of the fear and/or insecurity? What is the root issue(s) of whatever we addressed in the last session?

   _____

   _____

   _____

4. Make a list of any that God puts upon your heart. This will prepare you for our next session.

   _____

   _____

   _____

5. Remember, He loves you more than you know!

   _____

   _____

   _____

Deprived of Peace

I have been deprived of peace. . . .
I remember my affliction and my wandering,
the bitterness and the gall.
I well remember them, and my soul is downcast within me.
LAMENTATIONS 3:17A,19-20

The Downcast Soul

Are you deprived of peace? Can you relate to what Jeremiah wrote in the book of Lamentations? Is your soul downcast within you? Many people who have an un-healed sin issue in their life cry out to God. Over and over again, they ask God to forgive them for their terrible sin, yet they still do not feel free—their peace has not been restored. Why is that? Have you ever pondered the reason why you are deprived of peace?

Let me suggest that there are other sins wrapped up in the hurt package. We learned in session two about the consequences of our sin—depression, anxiety, outburst of anger, to name just a few. And in session three we learned how we give the enemy a stronghold in our lives as we cover our sin, blame others, hide from the truth and are afraid of the outcome because, in reality, we are just living with fine sounding arguments and wonderful pretensions. Now it is time to look honestly at the other sins wrapped up in the hurt pack-age which may be stuffed deep within our inmost beings. In fact, Jesus said of the Sinful Woman, "I tell you, her _____ sins have been forgiven" (Luke 7:47).

As sinful people, we also have many sins that require forgiveness. If we are not will-ing to truly admit that these sins exist, our souls will be _____ because our relationship with God will be _____. Listen to Isaiah 59:1-2:

> Surely the arm of the LORD is not too short to save, nor his ear too dull
> to hear. But your iniquities have separated you from your God; your sins
> have hidden his face from you, so that he will not hear.

Our sin _____ us from God. When we have unconfessed sin in our lives, it is as if a _____ has been built between God and ourselves. God did not build the wall—we did—and we are the ones who must tear it down. So, what other _____ do we have that are wrapped up in the hurt package? To uncover these, I am going to share with you some tough verses. Remember that it is only when we come to truth in our lives and see it for what it is that we can be set free and go in peace. Let's look at what Isaiah goes on to write:

For your hands are stained with blood, your fingers with guilt. Your lips have spoken lies, and your tongue mutters wicked things. No one calls for justice; no one pleads his case with integrity. They rely on empty arguments and speak lies. . . . We look for justice, but find none; for deliverance, but it is far away.

—Isaiah 59:3-4,11b

Perhaps I can illuminate what Isaiah is saying here by adding the following insights. "For your hands are stained with blood, your fingers with guilt" refers to our sinful _____. "Your lips have spoken lies, and your tongue mutters wicked things" refers to our sinful _____ when we declare our fine sounding arguments. "No one calls for justice; no one pleads his case with integrity" refers to our _____ the events in our _____, and sometimes even _____ the _____ of what really happened. "They rely on empty arguments and speak lies" refers to our sin as we try to deceive _____ into believing our own _____ as we try to make ourselves appear good with our wonderful pretensions.

It is true; many of our hands are stained with blood, our fingers with guilt. But what lies have we spoken? What case did we not plead with integrity? Remember, hurt not handled in the manner God intended will turn into anger, which in time will turn into bitterness, which will turn into a bitter poison. Dear beloved, it is important to be _____ with yourself. Is there someone, maybe in your family or a loved one, with whom you are still _____? If abortion is an issue in your life, perhaps it is the person who talked you into the abortion or forced you to go through with it? Perhaps it was the baby's father, or your own mother? If abuse is an issue in your life, perhaps you are still angry with the person responsible for the abuse. Or perhaps you are angry with your parents because they were not there to protect you. No matter what the issue is, honestly search your heart: With whom are you _____? Is it your father, your mother, your sister, your brother, your friend, your spouse or your abuser?

Again and again I see people who have hurt and anger locked and guarded tight in a box deep within their innermost being. The hurt and anger is often locked up so tight that they don't even realize it is there. In fact, if you are like the many I have worked with, you might even be arguing with me right now, especially if this person is someone in your family with whom you love deeply. The sad part is, as long as you have arguments and pretensions you won't even realize that the feelings are there. But it is important to know that until you unlock the anger deep within your inmost being and place it at Jesus' feet—just like the Sinful Woman did—you will be deprived of peace.

Let me explain what I mean about this anger. It's as if we have taken our case to court, but the case was not pleaded with integrity. As Jon Courson states:

[This is] not a legal court on earth, nor an eternal court in heaven. Your sins, my sins were forgiven, praise the Lord; never more to be remembered by Him. So what court? It is the court that takes place in your own

44

_____. You build a case daily, you bring in new witnesses, you gather more evidence, you build this case against _____, against _____, against _____. You build this case; it's in your mind. . . . It grows bigger. You hold the court case over and over and over again [as you replay the event in your mind] and here's the kicker—every time you hold court in your mind, you _____! The other guy _____ wins. *You always win!* You always conclusively conclude, I'm right, they're wrong."[1]

The sad part is that even though in your mind you have won, you are still the one in _____. Your empty arguments offer you no justice, and your pleadings have no merit. The walls you built in your relationships are made of prison bars and shackles, including the _____ you built between yourself and God. Listen to what Charles Spurgeon has to say, "Rest assured, dear hearer, that you will never attain to a well grounded freedom by trying to make your sins appear _____."[2] Even the sin of hurt and anger hidden in the depths of your being that you think no one can see. God sees all! As Proverbs 20:27 states:

> The lamp of the LORD _____ the spirit of a man; it searches
> out his _____ being.

God sees all that is within your heart—your anger towards your mother, your father, your sister, your brother, your spouse, your friend, or whomever else (and yes, you may even be angry at God) deprives you of peace. This anger will continue to deprive you until you give it all to Jesus, just like the Sinful Woman did. This is true even if you were sinned against.

Perhaps you were raped or abused. Perhaps you were hurt deeply by someone or something that was completely out of your control. The important point to understand is that the hurt and anger _____ within your innermost being is something over which you _____ have control. You have a choice! You can _____ to give the anger to God so that you will know and understand that you are forgiven and set free, or you can _____ to hold on to the anger and be deprived of peace. The choice is yours! But I must warn you: If you choose to hold on to the anger, it will cause all the consequences we talked about previously to continue in your life.

Let me share a story with you. In one of our *Go in Peace* workshops, there was a woman who continued to blame everyone around her for pushing her toward having an abortion. No one stood by her side and told her to keep the baby. She cried and shared how she wanted her baby, but everyone was urging her to make the decision to have the abortion. She felt out of control and hopeless. We taught her that it was time to stop blaming others for her decision.

I know how much that hurts, but blaming is an empty argument. Remember, we can no longer offer "empty arguments and speak lies" (Isaiah 59:4). For those of us whom abortion is an issue, each one of us _____ the ultimate decision to have the abortion. In almost every case, no one drugged us or tied us to the table. We walked into the abortion clinic of our own will and went through with the procedure—even though we may have felt as if our hands were tied—we were the ones who walked into the clinic that day. In view of this truth, we must take _____ for our _____. We can no longer place the blame on another, as Adam and Eve tried to do. After we _____ what we did, we must then take our hurt and anger toward others to the feet of Jesus, just as the Sinful Woman did. It's time to let go of the other sins that are wrapped up in the hurt package.

The woman in the *Go in Peace* workshop made the decision to be honest with herself. She decided to take her hurts and her anger to the foot of the cross. About two weeks after the workshop, she came to see me. She was so excited. She shared how she had found letters that she had written to the father of the baby and how in one of those letters she had written, "We really have to talk serious about this baby business. I don't think I'm going to have it, but it is up to you." As she read that letter she finally took responsibility for her part in the decision. Remember what we learned about in session three concerning reaction formation: If two motives are opposite each other, a person will respond by doing everything he or she can to build up the strength of one particular motive—the one most acceptable to that person—so that the other motive is safely contained. Although there were two conflicting motives within her heart—the desire to keep her baby and the choice to abort it—over the years as she held court in her mind and built up the one motive (the more acceptable one) she wasn't being totally honest with herself. Although in her mind she had won, she wasn't pleading her case with integrity. And thus her sins were many, causing her to serve a prison sentence. It wasn't until she unlocked the chamber that held the hurts and anger, and in doing so, admit her part in the decision to abort her child that the prison doors were thrown open and she was set free.

Deprived of Peace

In view of this freedom that Jesus Christ offers, let's learn a little bit more about being deprived of peace so that we can be set free. Let's take a moment to look at the issue of anger and how it keeps us in bondage. Remember that in Ephesians 4:26-27, the apostle Paul tells us _____ to sin in our anger:

> "In your anger do not sin": Do not let the sun go down while you are still
> angry, and do not give the devil a foothold.

Notice that Paul does not say that we cannot be angry; rather, he says that we must not _____ in our anger. God has created us with emotions, but He also knows that holding on to anger over a period of time will _____ us and cause _____.

Being angry over time will cause an _____ deep within our hearts—deep within our inmost beings—that will cause all the _____ we learned about previously. Worst yet, this infection of sin in our hearts _____ separate us from Him. God is a _____ God and He wants nothing to separate us from the intimate relationship He desires to have with us. In view of this, we are called to deal with our anger _____—the same day, before the sun goes down. In fact, we are to search our hearts each night before we go to sleep. Look at what the psalmist wrote:

> In your anger do not sin; when you are on your beds, search your hearts
> and be silent. Offer right sacrifices and trust in the LORD.
>
> —Psalm 4:4-5

Let me explain what happens if we choose _____ to follow God's Word concerning our hurt, pain and anger. Each night that we go to sleep and do not deal with our hurt and anger in the manner God intended, we will _____ it into our inmost beings where it will begin to _____. Many times, we are hurt and angry toward someone we have to be around all the time, but because we care for him or her (or have to live with that person or work with him or her), we stuff the hurt deep inside so we can cope and move on with our lives. Thus we choose _____ to deal with the problem, and so it festers deep inside and becomes _____. Later, when we least expect it, the consequence of our sin—our sin of stuffing hurt, pain and anger—suddenly manifests itself in an outburst of anger. Unfortunately, these outbursts of anger are not usually directed toward the person with whom we are truly angry, but at someone else, usually someone we love deeply (usually our children or our spouses or another family member or a friend).

God knows that anger not _____ with in the manner He intended will turn into _____ deep within a person's heart which will eventually turn into a bitter poison. Listen to His Word:

> Make every effort to live in peace with all men. . . . See to it that no one
> misses the grace of God and that no bitter root grows up to cause trouble
> and defile many.
>
> —Hebrews 12:14-15

> Make sure there is no root among you that produces such bitter poison.
>
> —Deuteronomy 29:18b

Do you have a bitter _____ within you, hidden deep within your innermost being, that produces _____ in your household and in your life? Then come today and kneel at Jesus' feet just like the Sinful Woman did. Ask Him to show you the bitter root which has turned into a bitter poison. Once He reveals it, leave it there at His feet. For this reason, let me teach you a tangible way to do that which He is calling you to do.

Search Your Heart

It is time to take a moment to sit at Jesus' feet and ask Him to help you unlock the hurt, pain and anger that is hidden deep within your innermost being. Remember that He is gentle and humble in heart. He is the Prince of Peace, and He wants to unshackle the chains that hold you fast. But it's your choice to make the decision to be _____ with yourself and _____ the truth. He loves you so much that He gives you a free will. It's time to decide to trust in God and let go of the hurt, the pain and the anger.

It's time to choose to give up your rights and follow Jesus. When you do, He will meet you there and, best yet, He will set you free so that you can go in peace!

For this reason, I want to teach you a _____ way to touch and see your hurt, pain and anger as you make it obedient to Christ. There was a woman who once said to me, "Giving my anger to the Lord is not tangible." What she was saying was that she could not touch or see the anger as she gave it to the Lord. It was just in her imagination, and therefore it seemed unreal. What she said to me was true. In fact, the definition of "tangible" is "able to be touched."[3] Something that is _____ tangible is _____ to be touched. I think this is what most people struggle with when they are told to take the hurt, pain and anger captive and make it obedient to Christ. In view of this, I want to teach you a practical way to touch and see your anger. I want you to spend some time alone with God, search your heart and write a letter. Begin by asking Him to reveal any hurt, pain and anger that you have stuffed deep within your heart. Honestly pray the following verse:

> Search me, O God, and know my heart; test me and know my anxious thoughts. See if there is any _____ way in _____, and lead me in the way everlasting.
>
> —Psalm 139:23-24

It is interesting to note that the word "offensive" in this passage can also be translated as "hurtful," "wicked" and "grievous." Think about this for a moment. As you have stuffed your hurt, pain and anger in your heart, have you allowed it to become so _____ to yourself that it has become not only _____ to God but also _____ and _____ to Him? In Ephesians 4:30-31, Paul says:

> Do not grieve the Holy Spirit of God, with whom you were sealed for the day of redemption. Get rid of all bitterness, rage and anger.

If that doesn't convince you to let go of your anger, then consider this: according to *Strong's* concordance, one definition of the Hebrew word for "offensive" is "_____."[4] An idol is anything you put before God or in place of God. Is it possible that you have allowed the hurt, pain and anger to become an idol in your life? Remember, God is a jealous God, and He does not want to share His rightful place in your heart with anyone or anything. When you choose to hold on to hurt, pain and anger, it can become a disgusting idol that you _____ and _____ within your heart.

After you have prayed the above verse in Psalm 139, ask God to unlock the hidden chambers of your heart and reveal any offensive way in you that has become an idol in your life. Next, begin to write whatever He puts on your heart. Use the letter as a tangible _____ to unlock the anger that you have hidden deep inside. Address the letter to whomever God puts on your heart, and begin to write whatever comes to your mind.

Remember that this letter is between you and God _____—no one else will ever see it. So do not hold back! And it's important to know that you may need to write more than one letter. One time when I was teaching about this tool at a retreat, a woman came up to me after the quiet time and said, "I just wrote 26 pages, and I've been set free!"

Let me share one more interesting story with you to show how easily we can deceive ourselves about the anger in our hearts because we don't want to let it go. Plus this story is a great example to show you that it doesn't matter how big the hurt may be. It doesn't have to be a huge hurt like rape or abuse—it can be a small hurt or even a perceived hurt—but what we do with the hurt is what will either _____ us or set us _____.

When my daughter was about to begin her freshman year of high school, we moved to Bulgaria in Eastern Europe to become missionaries. My daughter was excited about the move. Six months later, however, I began to see some of the consequences we talked about in session two in her life. Now, I knew that she didn't have a major deep heart hurt as a result of abuse or something tragic in her life, so I didn't know where these consequences were coming from. I encouraged her to pray and ask God what was going on deep within her heart, but there was no change. The consequences continued, and even began to get worse.

I realized that it was time to teach my daughter how to get her heart right with God. We spent a few hours together, and I taught her everything that you have now learned up to this point. I then instructed her to take a quiet time with the Lord and ask Him to search her heart. I told her to ask God if she was angry with someone and, if so, who it was.

I explained to her that she was more than likely angry with her dad or me. Many times, the hurt, pain and anger we feel is directed at someone we love deeply. It's part of life. Regardless of whether it is intentional or unintentional, we will be hurt by those we love. And because the person we're angry with is someone we love deeply, we try to deceive ourselves into believing we are not angry with him or her. It gets confusing between the feelings of love and the anger.

I think my daughter thought I was crazy, but I encouraged her and told her that it was OK for her to be honest with herself. I told her to write whatever God put on her heart, as the letter was going to be between her and Him only. After she completed the letter, I asked her if God had shown her anything. Was there someone with whom she had been angry? She smiled and said yes. I giggled and asked her if I was the one she had been angry with. Again, she smiled and answered with a big *yes*. I then asked her if God had shown her why she was angry. Once again, she said yes. She said that the reason that had been revealed to her when she wrote the letter was so strange that it surprised her. It was something she would never have guessed. She said that she had been angry at me because I had *made* her move to Bulgaria! Isn't that amazing? She had wanted to move to Bulgaria. She had been excited about this grand adventure. Yet months later, she was angry about it. Why?

While we were living in Bulgaria, our youth pastor back in California encouraged the youth group to send e-mails to the Fresonke girls to encourage them while they were on the mission field. Unfortunately, most of the e-mails included stories from the group about all the activities that had been going on, such as trips to Disneyland and to the beach. Life in Bulgaria isn't that exciting, and soon my daughter was feeling that life was passing her by. As she continued to think about these things and dwell upon them something happened deep within her heart. Soon the truth that she had been excited about moving to Bulgaria changed to feeling that I had *made* her move. As she held court in her mind, she even changed the facts!

Do you see how even the smallest _____ can turn into something _____ if it is not handled in the manner that God intended? If we don't bring our hurt, pain and anger to Him, we soon find ourselves caught dealing with all the consequences we discussed previously. And we don't even realize it is happening, because we _____ ourselves and the _____ is not in us.

This is why I want to encourage you to have a quiet time with the Lord. Ask Him to search your heart and to see if there is any offensive way in you deep within your inmost being. As you do this, do not hold anything back—including tears! If you begin to cry, just let the tears flow, because it means that God is washing your heart. If you stop the tears, you will _____ what God is _____ trying to say to you.

Let's go back to the story of the Sinful Woman for a moment. Let me paint the picture. The Sinful Woman entered the courtyard of Simon's house filled with shame, but in her heart she knew that Jesus was her only hope. She approached Him from behind. She was afraid to come into His presence, but she knew that Jesus was the only one who could set her free.

In those days it was customary to recline on a couch, at the table, with your legs tucked off to the side and back. Weeping bitterly she began to wet the feet of Jesus with her tears. In humility and brokenness, she bowed down and began to wipe His feet with her hair. She kissed them and poured perfume on them. Look how this scene is described in the *New Living Translation:*

> Then she knelt behind him at his feet, weeping. Her tears fell on his feet, and she wiped them off with her hair. Then she *kept* kissing his feet and putting perfume on them.
>
> —Luke 7:38, emphasis added

According to Ralph Earle in *Word Meanings in the New Testament*, in the original language in which this passage was written, "The three Greek verbs [in verse 38] are the imperfect tense—_____."5 In other words, she *kept* wiping His feet with her tears, she *kept* kissing His feet, and she *kept* anointing them with perfume. Her tears just *kept* falling as she knelt at His feet and opened her heart to Him so that He could do His gentle surgery. She knew that He was the only one who could set her free.

Dear beloved, won't you come and kneel at His feet and allow Him to do the same in your life? Take this quiet time. Allow Him to reveal to you the ugliness that is found within your heart. Write whatever He puts on your heart. In fact, if you are honest with yourself you just may be surprised at what is hidden deep within.

Now, I want to stress that this letter is _____ to be mailed. If you were to mail it, in most cases it would only cause more hurt and pain. Therefore, this letter is between you and God _____ and is just a _____ to allow you to uncover any hidden hurt, pain or anger inside of you—to see if there is *any offensive way* locked deep within your heart.

After you write the letter, the next step is to offer right sacrifices and trust in the Lord by giving the anger to God. Remember what David says in Psalm 4:4-5:

> In your anger do not sin; when you are on your beds, search your hearts
> and be silent. *Offer right sacrifices* and trust in the LORD (emphasis added).

According to God's Word, you are not to let the sun go down while you are still angry, and you are to _____ right sacrifices and trust in the Lord. You can do this in a _____ way by destroying the letter as you offer the hurt, pain and anger to God as a right _____. One of my favorite ways to do this is by burning it in a fireplace. A dear friend of mine once shared that after she burned her letter, she felt the Lord impress the following verse on her heart:

> It is a burnt offering, an offering made by fire, an aroma pleasing to
> the LORD.

> —Leviticus 1:13b

If there is no fireplace available, just tear the letter into tiny little pieces. If you are feeling creative, you can even put some of the little pieces into a helium balloon and offer the anger as a right sacrifice to God by letting go of the balloon and watching it rise to Him. Burning, tearing or sending the letter up in a helium balloon is another visual and tangible way of giving the hurt, pain and anger—*the hurtful, offensive, wicked and grievous way*—to God once and for all.

After many years of discipling people, I have seen that those who are brave enough to be honest with themselves and take a step of faith by going through this exercise come to a place in which they truly know and understand that they are forgiven and set free. Those who choose _____ to write the letters, or choose _____ to give the anger to God, continue to struggle with all the consequences we discussed previously for years to come. The choice is yours! Which will it be: forgiven and set free, or afflicted with consequences for years to come and being deprived of peace?

This exercise is so freeing to me that I continue to do it whenever I feel the need. Although what I have taught you has become a way of life for me, and can usually be handled through prayer, whenever I realize that I am dwelling and brewing on something that is not pleasing to God, I write out a letter to help me discover what is really taking place deep within my heart. I want to encourage you to take every thought captive and make it obedient to Christ. The moment that you do, "you will know the _____, and the truth will set you _____" (John 8:32). So, what are you waiting for? Do it! Let it go so that you may *go in peace!*

Assignment

FOR WEEKEND WORKSHOP:

Find a quiet place and complete numbers one through four. *Leader's Note:* If there is a fireplace have everyone burn their letters before moving onto the next session.

FOR WEEKLY BIBLE STUDY:

Read chapter seven titled "Deprived of Peace" in the book *Go in Peace!* Although the chapter is closely related to this session it is good to read it to have the material sink deeper within your inmost being. God wants to do a deep heart work. After reading the chapter spend a quiet time with the Lord and as you do complete the following exercises.

1. Write Psalm 139:23-24 at the top of a blank sheet of paper?

    _____
    _____
    _____

2. Ask God to reveal to you any hurtful, offensive, wicked or grievous way in you that you may have hidden deep within. Is there someone who hurt your deeply? Is there someone with whom you are still angry?

    _____
    _____
    _____

3. Write the letter(s) of hurt, pain and anger as a visual and tangible tool to see what you have stuffed and hidden deep within your heart.

    _____
    _____
    _____

4. Then offer the letter(s) which contain your hurt, pain and anger to God so that you will finally know without a doubt that you are forgiven and set free. Offer the anger to Him by burning, tearing or sending the pieces of the letter up in a helium balloon. Do not hold onto it any longer. Let it go—once and for all.

    _____
    _____
    _____

FORGIVENESS IS NOT AN OPTION

Be kind and compassionate to one another,
forgiving each other,
just as in Christ God forgave you.
EPHESIANS 4:32

Bitter Poison

*N*ow that we have learned how to give the hurt, pain, and anger to God so that we will no longer be deprived of peace, it is time to discover another important aspect to our walk with Christ. As you may recall, hurt not handled in the manner God intended will turn into anger, which in time will turn into bitterness, which will turn into a bitter poison, which will infect every aspect of our lives. So although we learned how to deal with our hurt, pain and anger it is now time to learn about the bitterness and bitter poison. Because the bitter poison is also known as unforgiveness.

Lamentations 3:19-20 warns about this bitterness:

> I remember my affliction and my wandering, the bitterness and the gall. I
> well remember them, and my soul is downcast within me.

In the original Hebrew, the word "bitterness" in this verse comes from the word "wormwood," which was a bitter herb that the Hebrew people considered _____.[1] Just as our bitterness stuffed deep within our inmost being will become poisonous, and in time will cause our souls to be downcast within us, if we don't learn how to give it to God once and for all. It is also interesting to note that in the original Greek of the New Testament, the word "bitterness" can mean extreme wickedness, a bitter _____ which produces a bitter fruit, and even bitter hatred.[2] This is why I believe God's Word warns us to make sure there is no root among us that produces such bitter _____.[3]

The only way for us to get rid of this unforgiveness—this bitter poison—is to _____ how to forgive others. In the Greek, the word "forgive" can be translated as "to _____ go, to give up, [and] to keep _____ longer."[4] In other words, it's time for us to not only let go of the hurt, pain and anger we learned about in the last chapter, but also to _____ up the bitterness and unforgiveness. It's time to keep these things no longer and move on with our lives.

In view of this, it is time for us to let go of every aspect of the wrong that has been done to us, so that we can lay down the bitterness and unforgiveness at the feet of Jesus just like the Sinful Woman did. It is time for us to forgive so that we too can go in peace, because if we do not learn how to deal with our unforgiveness we will soon be back to where we were at the beginning of this Bible study. Listen to what God's Word warns in Acts 8:23:

> For I see that you are full of bitterness and captive to sin.

If we choose _____ to let go of the bitterness and unforgiveness we will be captive to _____. This is not where we want to be! Ephesians 4:31a clearly states what we need to do:

> Get rid of all bitterness, rage and anger.

In view of this truth, let's discuss what Jesus taught about forgiveness, because He wants us to become victorious in this area of our lives. He wants us to be set free from all the consequences and be more than conquerors over this issue of bitterness and unforgiveness. And He wants us to be at peace with God!

In Matthew 6:15, Jesus prayed:

> But if you do not forgive men their sins, your Father will not forgive your sins.

Jesus' prayer warns that if you and I are unwilling to forgive others, our own hearts are in no condition to ask God the Father to forgive us.[5] Think about it: If we are unwilling to forgive others, what right do we have to ask God to forgive our sins? God knows that unforgiveness will destroy you and me. He knows that unforgiveness in our hearts will cause us to harden our hearts. That is why, dear beloved, forgiveness is not an option. That is why, as we learned in the last chapter, it is time for us to let go of not only the hurt, pain and anger, but also the bitterness. For this reason, it might be a good idea to look at what forgiveness is and what forgiveness is not, so that we can completely forgive the person who hurt us.

What Forgiveness Is

We will begin by looking at seven aspects of what forgiveness is.[6]

1. Forgiveness is _____ after God's forgiveness of us. Because God has forgiven you and me, we need to forgive others. In other words, we are called to be _____ of God. In Ephesians 4:32–5:1, Paul admonished:

   > Be kind to one another, tenderhearted, forgiving one another, as God in Christ forgave you. Therefore be imitators of God, as beloved children.
   >
   > —ESV

2. Forgiveness is a step of _____. We are to take every thought captive—even thoughts of unforgiveness—and make them obedient to Christ. Otherwise,

we are living in disobedience to God. Remember what the apostle Paul teaches in 2 Corinthians 10:5b:

> We take captive _____ thought to make it obedient to Christ.

3. Forgiveness is leaving the _____ to God. If we make plans to get even with someone, we are only letting that person _____ to hurt us. It is similar to what Proverbs 26:27 warns:

> Whoever digs a pit will fall into it, and a stone will come back on him who starts it rolling.
>
> —ESV

In Romans 12:19, Paul also warns:

> Do not take _____, my friends, but leave room for God's wrath, for it is written: "It is mine to avenge; I will repay," says the Lord.

4. Forgiveness is _____. In Matthew 18:21-22, Peter came up to Jesus and asked Him:

> "Lord, how often shall my brother sin against me, and I forgive him? Up to seven times?" Jesus replied, "I do not say to you, up to seven times, but up to seventy times seven."
>
> —NKJV

According to Jewish teaching, a person was to forgive an offender four times. Peter, though more generous with his willingness to forgive up to seven times, was still setting a limit beyond which he did not need to forgive. When Jesus said, "seventy times seven," He was telling Peter that he should forgive without _____.[7]

5. Forgiveness is a _____ issue. In Luke 17:3-4, Jesus said:

> Pay attention to yourselves! If your brother sins, rebuke him, and if he repents, forgive him, and if he sins against you seven times in the day, and turns to you seven times, saying, "I repent," you must forgive him.
>
> —ESV

You may have heard it said that you do not need to forgive someone if he or she does not repent—in other words, if the offender does not come to say that he or she is sorry. However, it is important to realize that just because the verse says *if he repents, forgive him*, it does _____ say that if the person doesn't repent, we don't forgive him or her. We cannot add what we like to God's Word. But what we can learn from this verse is that forgiveness is a *heart issue*. We must have a heart that is always _____ to forgive.

In Psalm 86:5a, David writes:

For You, Lord, are good, and _____ to forgive.

—NKJV

If we are to model our forgiveness after God's forgiveness of us, we must also be _____ to forgive. In other words, we cannot hold a grudge against a person just because he or she has not repented or asked for our forgiveness. Or we cannot hold onto our unforgiveness just because that person is gone or we will never see them again. If we are holding onto grudges and unforgiveness, the truth is not in us. We are just living by excuses and blaming others for our unwillingness to forgive. In other words, we are living in _____ with our fine sounding arguments.

We need to remember that before we repented and asked God to forgive us for our sins, He still loved us and was waiting to say, "You are forgiven!" He was _____ to forgive the moment we repented. We must therefore have hearts that have already done the deep work of forgiveness by letting go of the hurt and are _____ and _____ to say, "I forgive you." It is only then that we will have no unforgiveness in our hearts, because we have already let it go and given it to God. In Mark 11:25, Jesus explained it this way:

And when you stand praying, if you hold anything against anyone, forgive him.

6. Forgiveness is a _____. In his book *From Forgiven to Forgiving*, Jay Adams states, "When our God forgives us, He promises that He will not remember our sins against us anymore. That is wonderful!"[8] When we are forgiven, God treats us as if we had never sinned. Again, if we model our forgiveness after God's forgiveness, we will also _____ to treat the person who has wronged us as if he or she had never hurt us. Proverbs 19:11 shares a proverb to live by:

A man's wisdom gives him patience; it is to his glory to overlook an offense.

7. Forgiveness is for our _____ sake. We need to forgive the offender for our own sake. Ignoring this fact will cause us to dwell in the pit of despair. Listen to what God said in Isaiah 43:25:

I, even I, am he who blots out your transgressions, for my _____ sake, and remembers your sins no more.

If God blots out our sins for His own sake, then this must be best for us as well. Forgiveness may or may not _____ the other person, but it will _____ us!

What Forgiveness Is Not

Now that we have looked at what forgiveness is, let's look at seven aspects of what forgiveness is not. It is important for us to know this distinction, because sometimes we can get feelings and emotions all wrapped up and confused when dealing with this issue. It's important to know, dear beloved, that we are not to live by feelings, but by the truth of God's Word.

1. Forgiveness is not a _____. Forgiveness is not something you or I _____ like doing, but rather a step of obedience to Christ. As Jay Adams states, "Unlike modern discussions of forgiveness, there is _____ in the Bible about 'feelings of forgiveness' or 'having forgiving feelings' towards another."[9]

    Let me give you an example. During World War II, Corrie ten Boom and her family hid Jews in their home. When they were discovered, they were arrested and put in a German concentration camp, where many of Corrie's family died. After World War II, God used Corrie to share His love with many who were hurt during the war. One of her main messages was about forgiveness.

    After one particular meeting, an SS officer from the camp where Corrie and her sister Betsie had lived came up to Corrie and said, "Isn't it wonderful! Jesus has washed away my sins." He then reached out his hand and asked Corrie for forgiveness. Corrie did not have it in her heart to forgive. She did not *feel* like forgiving. In fact, she felt just the opposite. But she was obedient and asked God to give her the strength to forgive the man. "I can do all things through Christ who strengthens me" (Philippians 4:13, NKJV).

    Corrie later stated that though she prayed for strength, her right hand remained limp by her side. She just couldn't bring herself to shake the hand of the man who had once stood by mocking, while she and her sister were forced to strip off their clothes and enter the shower room. "I can't do it, Lord," she said. "Don't ask me for this; it's too much." Her thoughts were angry and hurtful, yet she realized that she herself had demanded such an action from others who had suffered during the war. "Forgive your enemies," she had told them.

    "Then help me, Lord," Corrie prayed. "I can't do it on my own." As she prayed, she suddenly felt power rush along her arm and generate warmth and forgiveness for the man who stood before her. Even now, he was eagerly shaking her hand. God had answered her prayer and provided.[10] Even though Corrie did not *feel* like forgiving the SS guard, she took the step of obedience, and God was faithful.

    Dear beloved, if you and I wait until we _____ like forgiving, it will never happen. If we continue to hold on to our bitterness and unforgiveness we will again be _____ the consequences we learned about in session two of this Bible study and our lives will be out of control and captive to _____ because of the bitter poison we are _____ to keep.

Do you really want that to happen? Remember, forgiveness is not a feeling. For this reason, we need to _____ God to give us the _____ to forgive, just like Corrie did. When we do, we will discover that we truly are strong in the Lord and more than conquerors. In 1 Corinthians 13:4-5, Paul explains it this way:

Love is patient, love is kind. . . . it keeps no record of wrongs.

2. Forgiveness is not holding onto _____. The word "grudge" means "a feeling of deep-seated _____ or ill will."[11] In Hebrew, the word "grudge" means "to _____."[12] However, as we discussed at the beginning of this session, the word "forgive" in the Greek of the New Testament can actually be translated "to let go, to give up, [and] to keep no longer"—which is the exact _____ of keep. We just discussed how forgiveness is not a feeling. It is time to let go of any and all wrong feelings associated with our deep heart hurts. It is time to let go of any and all grudges that we may be hanging on to. Leviticus 19:18 says it clearly:

Never seek revenge or bear a grudge against anyone, but love your neighbor as yourself. I am the LORD.

—NLT

3. Forgiveness is not necessarily _____ why we were hurt. In *Forgive and Forget*, Lewis B. Smedes notes, "We will probably never understand why were hurt. . . . Understanding may come _____, in fragments, an insight here and a glimpse there, _____ forgiving. But we are asking too much if we want to understand everything at the beginning."[13] In the Bible, a man named Joseph suffered incredible betrayal and hurt at the hands of his brothers. However, when he later reflected on all that he had been through, he told his brothers:

You intended to harm me, but God intended it for good to accomplish what is now being done, the saving of many lives.

—Genesis 50:20

4. Forgiveness is not _____ the bad behavior. Forgiveness is sometimes confused with accepting a person's wrongful actions. However, there is a _____ between loving a person and accepting that person's bad behavior. Forgiveness is not an acceptance of destructive, bad behavior, but _____ to love the person regardless of his or her behavior. We learn this example from God, who loves us but He does not _____ our _____ behavior. Even though we hate the person's bad behavior—the sin—we are still called to love the sinner and forgive him or her for the hurt he or she has caused. In Ephesians 4:32, Paul states:

Be kind and compassionate to one another, forgiving each other, just as in Christ God forgave you.

5. Forgiveness is not _____ something wrong or unpleasant. To "tolerate" means "to put up with something or somebody unpleasant."[14] We do not have to _____ or put up with something wrong or unpleasant when we _____ a person for the hurt he or she has caused. For example, imagine there was a man who lived on your block who had sexually assaulted you. He was arrested and sent to jail. Years later he was released and moved back into the house on your block. You had, through Christ's love, forgiven him years before for the hurt he caused you. But now you notice him inviting a young teenager (about the age you were when the assault happened) into his house. You would never _____ or _____ that kind of behavior. The man should be held _____ for the wrong he does, and you would _____ another from suffering the harm that you suffered.

In Luke 23:41a, one of the criminals who hung on a cross next to Jesus said:

> We are punished justly, for we are getting what our deeds deserve.

The criminal realized that he deserved the punishment for his crime. It is good that there were people around who did not tolerate his criminal activity.

6. Forgiveness is not _____. Jay Adams states, "The Bible never commands '_____ and _____.' This is one of those old, unbiblical statements by which people often try to guide their lives that is utterly incorrect. If you try to forget, you will fail. In fact, the harder you try the more difficult you will find forgetting."[15]

Some people get confused by passages in Isaiah and Jeremiah in which God states He promises to forgive our sins and remember them no more.[16] But "forgetting" is not the same as "remembering no more." Adams states, "Obviously, the omniscient [all-knowing] God who created and sustains the universe does not forget, but He can [choose to] 'not remember'. . . . To 'not remember' is simply a graphic way of saying, 'I will not bring up these matters to you or others in the future. . . . I will never use these sins against you.'"[17] The apostle Paul wrote:

> But one thing I do: forgetting what lies behind and straining forward to what lies ahead, I press on toward the goal for the prize of the upward call of God in Christ Jesus.
>
> —Philippians 3:13b-14, ESV

"Forgetting what lies behind" does not mean that we will fully forget the hurt that another has caused us—especially if the hurt was horrendous, as in the case of rape or abuse. But we can _____ to let it go and leave it behind. Then, we can move forward because we have not allowed that hurt to destroy our lives any longer. The choice is ours! God sets a wonderful example of this in Jeremiah 31:34b when He states:

> For I will forgive their wickedness and will remember their sins no more.

7. Forgiveness is not an _____. God knows that unforgiveness will destroy us. This is why forgiveness is not an option. So what do we do, beloved? We do what God's Word commands us to do:

> Bear with each other and forgive whatever grievances you may have against one another. Forgive as the Lord forgave you.

> —Colossians 3:13

The Key to Forgiveness

Many of us desire to be rid of our unforgiveness but have no idea how to go about it. For years, we have held on to our bitterness, which has now turned into the bitter poison of unforgiveness. Although we are tired of it, the unforgiveness is comfortable to us, much like an old security blanket. However, we can discover the _____ in _____ to let go of the unforgiveness in our lives by once again listening to what Jesus said:

> But I say to you who hear, love your enemies, do good to those who hate you, bless those who curse you, _____ for those who mistreat you. . . . Be merciful, just as your Father is merciful.

> —Luke 6:27-28,36, NASB

Remember, beloved, you and I need to model our lives after Christ's life. Praying for those whom we have bitterness and unforgiveness against is the _____ that will set us free and enable us to go in peace. As we see from the life of Jesus, even as He was being crucified He prayed over and over again.

> Then Jesus said, "Father, forgive them, for they do not know what they do."

> —Luke 23:34a, NKJV

The tense of the verb "said" indicates that Jesus repeated this prayer. As the soldiers nailed Him to the cross, He prayed, "Father, forgive them." When they lifted the cross and placed it in a hold in the ground, He prayed, "Father, forgive them." As He hung on the cross between heaven and earth and heard religious people mocking Him, He repeatedly prayed, "Father, forgive them."[18] We, too, need to pray like Jesus prayed.

If there is bitterness and unforgiveness in your heart, Satan, will use this as a stronghold in your life. He will shoot fiery darts aimed at the poisonous infection of bitterness and unforgiveness. When this happens, use prayer as a weapon to extinguish the fiery darts. Every time you are reminded of the past hurt, instead of dwelling and brewing on all the thoughts and feelings associated with it, _____. Pray just as Jesus taught:

Pray for those who _____ you.

—Luke 6:28, NASB

Or, as the *English Standard Version* puts it:

Pray for those who _____ you.

No matter how horrendous the hurt you suffered, God calls you to let it go so that you may go in peace! If the person who injured you is not saved, pray for his or her salvation. If the person is saved, pray for him or her to draw closer to God. Now, it is true that you will not _____ like praying this prayer. You may feel like Jonah felt—he did not want God to spare the Ninevites. You, too, may not want those who have caused you pain to be forgiven. However, forgiving that person is a step of _____, not a feeling.

I have learned over the years that every time I was reminded of a past hurt, the key was to pray for the person who hurt me. As I was obedient to pray for that person, _____ came. Soon, I came to a point where I realized that whenever I thought of the person who hurt me, I really was praying from my heart for his or her salvation or for that person to draw closer to God. When this happened, I knew that the forgiveness in my heart was complete.

In 2 Corinthians 10:4, Paul teaches:

The weapons we fight with are not the weapons of the world. On the contrary, they have divine power to demolish strongholds.

Use _____ as a mighty weapon to _____ the stronghold of bitterness and unforgiveness in your life.

Before moving on to the next chapter, write a letter of forgiveness to the same person or persons to whom you wrote the letter(s) of anger. This time, the letter must be one of _____, not anger. Even if all you can do is write, "So and so, I forgive you" that is okay. Remember dear beloved, forgiveness is not an option. It is a step of obedience, not some big gushy feeling. It is all right if you don't *feel* like forgiving. Just do it! Just let it go! You can do all things through Christ who strengthens you, because you are more than a conqueror.

After you write the letter, _____ it, because God wants you to keep your forgiveness. As you forgive others and live your life according to His Word, you will be at peace with God and be all that He intends you to be. Once you take this step of obedience and forgiveness, you will *go in peace!*

Assignment

FOR WEEKEND WORKSHOP:

Find a quiet place and complete numbers one through five before moving onto the next session.

FOR WEEKLY BIBLE STUDY:

Read chapter eight titled "Forgiveness Is Not an Option" in the book *Go in Peace!* Although the chapter is the same as this session it is good to re-read it at your own pace so that you can take the time to think about the points that are important to you. God wants to do a deep heart work. After reading the chapter spend some quiet time with the Lord and as you do complete the following exercises.

1. Write Luke 23:34 at the top of a blank sheet of paper.

   _____

   _____

   _____

2. Ask God to give you the strength to forgive those who have hurt you.

   _____

   _____

   _____

3. Write the letter(s) of forgiveness as a visual and tangible tool to the same person(s) whom you wrote the letter(s) of hurt and anger.

   _____

   _____

   _____

4. Find a place to keep these letter(s) because God wants you to keep your forgiveness.

   _____

   _____

   _____

5. Read Philippians 4:13.

   _____

   _____

   _____

THE WEAPONS OF VICTORY

*The weapons we fight with
are not the weapons of the world.
On the contrary,
they have divine power to demolish strongholds.*
2 CORINTHIANS 10:4

The Battle

Now let's go back to our story of the Sinful Woman. Remember the scene? I believe she heard Jesus speaking to a crowd, pleading with them to come and find rest for their souls. As she was going about her daily routine she found something she was seeking. Here was a man who spoke with authority, "Come to me" (Matthew 11:28a). Here was a man who spoke with compassion, "All you who are weary and burdened" (Matthew 11:28b). Here was a man who spoke with promise, "And I will give you rest" (Matthew 11:28c). More importantly, when He spoke these words they resonated within her entire being. She was one who desired what He offered. But imagine the battle that must have been taking place within her heart—her feelings of unworthiness and failure raging within. Imagine the spiritual battle taking place in the heavenly realm as Jesus spoke these words. Imagine what you would feel if it were you walking through the marketplace that day and heard Jesus' words.

Let me share with you what I mean about the spiritual battle. Let's look at Ephesians 6:10-12 to get a heavenly perspective.

> Finally, my brethren, be strong in the Lord and in the power of His might. Put on the whole armor of God, that you may be able to stand against the wiles of the devil. For we do not wrestle against flesh and blood, but against principalities, against powers, against the rulers of the darkness of this age, [and] against spiritual hosts of wickedness in the heavenly places.
>
> —NKJV

So you see, our struggle is not against flesh and blood. In other words, our battle is not against our loved one, or a family member, or a co-worker, or a neighbor, or whomever you are struggling with, but in reality, at times it is against what is taking place within the spiritual realm. This is why God's Word calls us to put on the whole armor of God so that we may stand against the wiles of the devil.

For this reason, let's learn about who this devil is and how he operates so we can understand his wilily ways. In Scripture, the devil has many different names. Perhaps the one that most know him by is Satan. In Hebrew, the word "Satan" literally means "_____"[1] ("the devil" in Greek carries the same meaning),[2] for he accuses you day and night before the throne of the King.[3] Satan also means "_____,"[4] or "one to contend with." He is the archenemy of God and contends with him, and for this reason he is your _____ as well.

Satan is compared to a _____[5] and a roaring _____.[6] He is known as the god of this age,[7] for he is the unseen power behind all _____ and _____. Perhaps his most effective disguise, however, is that he masquerades as an _____ of _____.[8] In other words, this guy is extremely dangerous.

But the good news is: he is a _____ being, not an *eternal* being like our God. He is _____ in his knowledge and is not *all-knowing* like our Savior. He is _____ in his activity and is not *all-powerful* like our Lord. He is even _____ in that he can only be in one place at one time—not *omnipresent (every-where-present)* like our King.

Notice the word that is repeated in this description of Satan: limited. Satan has _____, and you should never forget that fact. Do not make him into something bigger than he is, for that is just what he would like you to do. However, to live your life as if he does not exist is also playing into his hands. Either of these two extremes can be _____ to your walk. In view of this, the true knowledge of who he is and how he operates is of strategic importance. And though he is limited, he has been given authority over the earth from the time of the fall. Thus, another name he has been given is the _____ of this _____.[9]

You may be wondering how, if Satan is limited, he is able to accomplish so many things in different parts of the world. Remember what Paul says in Ephesians 6:12:

> We do not wrestle against flesh and blood, but against principalities, against powers, against the rulers of the darkness of this age, [and] against spiritual hosts of wickedness in the heavenly places.
>
> —NKJV

Who are these principalities, powers, rulers and spiritual hosts? They are Satan's cohorts. There is a vast army of fallen angels (also known as demonic beings) that assist Satan in his attacks against _____ and against _____. In the book of Revelation, John states that when Satan rebelled against God, he took one-third of the angels with him.[10] Daniel states that these fallen angels struggle against God's angels for control of the affairs of nations.[11]

Now, I do not believe that Satan, or any of his cohorts, can read your mind. Remember, he is a _____ being and is limited in his power. However, I do believe that he can read your _____ language—he can _____ your words and even _____ your actions. He studies you to find ways to keep you shackled and chained. That's why Paul says in Ephesians 4:26-27:

> "In your anger do not sin": Do not let the sun go down while you are still angry, *and do not give the devil a foothold* (emphasis added).

This is why it is so vitally important for you to continually take your thoughts captive—especially the hurtful, painful, angry thoughts—and make them obedient to God. For if you do not, Satan, or one of his many cohorts, can gain a _____ and use these things _____ you.

Let's think about this for a moment. Have you ever tried to imagine what it must be like in the spiritual realm? There is an interesting verse I want to share with you.

> For He shall give His angels charge over you, To keep you in all your ways.
>
> —Psalm 91:11, NKJV

In fact the *New Living Translation* states it this way:

> For he will order his angels to protect you wherever you go.

Humor me for a moment. Since the enemy can see what is taking place in the spiritual realm and we know from the verse above that God sends his angels to protect us. What do you think Satan does when he sees the Lord assign an angel to look after us? I think, he too, assigns a fallen angel to watch us. I imagine the spiritual realm, at least concerning angels assigned to us, to be much like the cartoon where there is a good angel on one shoulder and a fallen angel on the other.

This fallen angel, although he cannot read our minds, can read between the lines on the words we speak and he can read our body language. Now think about this for a moment. What if that fallen angel was there when we were hurt? What if he saw another's sin against us? Do you think he will not use that hurt against us if we haven't yet given it to God in the manner that He intended? Ephesians 6:16 says:

> Above all, taking the shield of faith with which you will be able to quench all the fiery _____ of the wicked one.
>
> —NKJV

In view of this, you need to be _____ with the spiritual armor that God has given to you so that you can fight the good fight. Because I believe that when we haven't given something to the Lord the enemy will _____ fiery darts at us. He is hoping that the fiery darts will take hold and start a wild fire within our _____. He is hoping to set up a _____ in our lives.

And I believe that even if we have dealt with a past hurt, pain or anger the enemy will even shoot his fiery darts hoping to get us to take it all back _____. Therefore, you must be prepared for this _____. It is a battle in the spiritual realm; a battle to keep you shackled and chained, a battle to keep you from becoming all that God created you to be.

But God is a good God. And He understands this spiritual battle. For this reason, He has made a way for us to be _____. In view of this, let's take a look at each piece of this spiritual armor. Remember, "The weapons we fight with are not weapons of the world. On the contrary, they have divine power to _____ strongholds (2 Corinthians 10:4).

The Weapons

Therefore, let's learn about the weapons we can fight with. Ephesians chapter 6 goes on to say:

> Therefore take up the whole armor of God, that you may be able to withstand in the evil day, and having done all, to stand. Stand therefore, having girded your waist with truth, having put on the breastplate of righteousness, and having shod your feet with the preparation of the gospel of peace; above all, taking the shield of faith with which you will be able to quench all the fiery darts of the wicked one. And take the helmet of salvation, and the sword of the Spirit, which is the word of God; praying always with all prayer and supplication in the Spirit, being watchful to this end with all perseverance and supplication for all the saints.
>
> —Ephesians 6:13-18, NKJV

So let's learn about each piece of armor so that we can fight the good fight and be victorious. This way the enemy will no longer have a stronghold in our lives.

1. The _____ of Truth—The first piece of armor, which represents the Word of God, is the *belt of truth*. When you gird your waist with the truth, you allow the Word of God to govern your _____ and _____. This is why it is so important for you to read God's Word on a _____ basis—so that you will be able to make _____ and _____ choices. The belt of truth must fully surround, encircle and encompass every aspect of your life, just as a normal belt would. As God's Word fully _____ every aspect of your being and you begin to make wise choices, you will discover true victory in your life.

   Let me give you an example of making wise choices based on God's Word. Say that Satan shoots his fiery darts at you and you begin again to dwell on the hurt, pain, anger or bitterness of your past situation. But then you immediately remember what you learned in this Bible study, and instead of _____ on the hurt and the pain, you _____ to "pray for those who mistreat you" (Luke 6:28, NASB). That is what having your waist girded with the belt of truth is all about. Isn't that cool! That's how easy it is. You allow God's Word to fully encircle this aspect of your life.

2. The _____ of Righteousness—The next essential piece of armor is the *breastplate of righteousness*, which _____ the _____. Proverbs 4:23 warns:

    Above all else, guard your heart, for it affects everything you do.

    —NLT

    Remember, it is in your heart—in the depths of your innermost being—where God wants to meet with you and whisper His plans for you. As you meet with Him, you move the truth of His Word from your _____ to your _____ so that you can make _____ choices. When you choose to believe in your heart and make decisions _____ on His truth instead of your feelings and desires, you will be wearing the breastplate of righteousness.

    Let me give you an example of a practical way to put on the breastplate of righteousness. Say that you are a single young lady and that all of your life you were told that you were a mistake. One day, a guy walks up to you and asks you for a date. You think, *He's sort of a loser, but no one else will ever ask me out.* So you accept the date. In this instance, you made a decision _____ on your _____ and _____ and not on the truth of God's Word. Thus, you were _____ wearing the breastplate of righteousness.

    Now let's say the same thing happens and the guy asks you out on a second date. Your thoughts start going in the same direction, but all of a sudden you think, *Wait a minute—I'm the daughter of the King of kings. God loves me, and He knows the plans He has for me.* So you turn down the date, because you know the truth is that God has someone better for you (if you are to marry). In this case, you made a decision _____ on the _____ of who you are in Christ—the daughter of the King of kings—and thus you moved the truth from your head to your heart. That is what it means to put on the breastplate of righteousness.

3. The _____ of Peace—The next piece of armor is the *sandals of peace*. Peace is only achieved by learning to take every hurtful and angry thought _____ and making it _____ to Christ. This is what will _____ you from the disabling wounds that are inflicted in life and what will keep Satan from _____ up strongholds. Once you make it a _____ to take the hurtful and angry thoughts captive, you will walk forward in peace, and *your feet will be shod with the preparation of the gospel of peace.*

    In other words, as you walk worthy of your calling by making wise choices with your thoughts, you will be a light unto God and reflect His glory. Actions speak louder than words, and people will watch how you live. Sometimes, your life will be the only _____ they will ever read. Thus, as you take your thoughts captive and walk forward in peace, you will prepare the way for others to come to know Christ.

People will _____ what you _____. This is what it means to have your feet shod with the preparation of the sandals of peace. You are _____—you did the deep heart work to be a cleansed vessel—and thus can be a light to those who are watching no matter what is taking place in your life.

I have seen this happen on many occasions. One time, a young woman I knew went through *Go in Peace!*, and it so impacted her life for the better that people started to notice the change in her. Soon her mother came to me and said, "I saw such a change in my daughter that I asked her what had happened. She told me that she was being discipled by you through *Go in Peace!* I want what she has. Will you disciple me too?" Pretty soon, the amazing work that God was doing within their hearts impacted their whole family. Praise the Lord!

4. The _____ of Faith—Another important piece of armor is the *shield of faith*. As you begin to live your life based on the truth of God's Word, Satan will attack you in an attempt to destroy your _____ and your _____ with God. He will shoot his fiery darts at you and try to provoke you to take _____ all the hurt, pain, anger and bitterness that you have given to God. Satan hopes that these fiery darts will hit their target, burst into flames, and start a wildfire within your _____ that will be almost impossible to extinguish. It is your _____ in God that will give you the confidence to live your life _____ on the truth of His Word and resist Satan's attacks. It is your _____ in God that will _____ these fiery darts and give you the strength to walk worthy of your calling.

Hebrews 11:1 defines "faith" as "being sure of what we hope for and certain of what we do not see." Having faith means trusting God and His promises.[12] Therefore, when you begin to worry about everything around you—just _____! As the prophet Isaiah states:

> You will keep in perfect peace him whose mind is steadfast.
>
> —Isaiah 26:3a

Instead of focusing on everything that is causing you to worry, or all the hurt, pain, anger and bitterness, pick up the shield of _____ and stay _____ on God and His Word. When you decide by faith to keep your mind steadfast on God and His promises instead of the fiery darts that Satan shoots your way, you will be using the shield of faith effectively.

5. The _____ of Salvation—The next piece of armor is the *helmet of salvation*. As a believer, you are called to protect your _____. Satan wants to destroy your _____ life, and he will do this by playing on your feelings and desires in an attempt to hold your mind _____. Many times, your thoughts will trigger your desires, and your desires will trigger your _____.

Therefore, if you do not protect your mind—and especially what you choose to think about or dwell on—you will allow Satan to influence you to make _____ and _____ choices. It is important to remember that sin includes not only your wrong _____ but also your wrong _____.

In Philippians 4:8, Paul provides the _____ to using the helmet of salvation effectively in order to protect your mind and your thought life:

> And now, dear brothers and sisters, let me say one more thing. . . . Fix your thoughts on what is true and honorable and right. Think about things that are pure and lovely and admirable. Think about things that are excellent and worthy of praise.
>
> —NLT

These are the types of things on which you are to _____ and _____. If something is _____ true, honorable, right, pure, lovely, admirable, excellent and worthy of praise, you should _____ be thinking about it—and especially _____ be dwelling on it! You must keep your thoughts away from anything that _____ your mind. If you begin to think on discouraging, disgusting and/or polluted things, it is time to _____ your thinking. This may take some practice at first, and you may have to change your thinking _____ of times a day, but as you do, you will be wearing the helmet of salvation.

6. The _____ of the Spirit—The next piece of equipment in the believer's arsenal is the *sword of the Spirit*. Like the belt of truth, it also represents the Word of God, but there is an important distinction. In the New Testament, there are two Greek words used to describe the Word: logos and rhema. "Logos" speaks of the general _____ of the Word, which represents the belt of truth. "Rhema," on the other hand, speaks of _____ words or phrases. It is the piercing, double-edged sword of the Spirit that defines specific _____ and allows you to apply these truths when Satan attempts to attack you. It is more than a general knowledge of the Word of God; it is a _____ weapon that is meant to yield the truth of God's Word in _____ situations to help you overcome temptations—even temptations to dwell on hurt, pain, anger and bitterness. As mentioned previously, just because you gave something to God doesn't mean you won't be hurt _____ or desire to take an old hurt back _____. This is why it is vitally important to read God's Word daily and to memorize _____ verses. You need to know how to use this incredible weapon.

    Psalm 119:11 holds the key to effectively using the sword of the Spirit:

    > I have hidden your word in my heart that I might not sin against you.

    Therefore, a great passage to memorize (in fact, the best you have learned so far) to help you avoid the temptation to dwell on something unpleasing to God is Psalm 139:23-24:

Search me, O God, and know my heart; test me and know my anxious thoughts. See if there is any offensive way in me, and lead me in the way everlasting.

As you take the time to _____ God's Word, you will actually be hiding it within your heart. Then, when you find yourself in a situation where you are being tempted, God will bring His Word to your memory. All of a sudden, a verse will come to you that will be applicable to that specific situation. When you take _____ based on God's Word, you will be using the sword of the Spirit effectively.

7. The Weapon of _____—The final weapon in the believer's arsenal is *prayer*. This is perhaps one of the most important weapons that you can use to remain victorious. Through prayer, you can continue to give all the hurt, pain, anger and bitterness, including any unforgiveness, to God and _____ against any other fiery dart that Satan tries to send your way. Through prayer, you can also receive God's strength, guidance and _____ to walk worthy of your calling in _____ situation. However, you have to make the choice to use the weapon. As Charles Spurgeon wrote, "Look upward, and let us weep. O God, You have given us a mighty weapon, and we have permitted it to _____."[13] Prayer is a top-secret weapon with which God has equipped you for battle, so don't allow it to rust. Use it every time you find yourself in a situation that you need God's strength, guidance and wisdom.

The Victory

Let's conclude by looking at the story of the Sinful Woman once again to see how we can use the weapons of victory to our advantage. Remember, it was earlier in the day that Jesus taught the following to a crowd:

> Come to me, all you who are weary and burdened, and I will give you rest. Take my yoke upon you and learn from me, for I am gentle and humble in heart, and you will find rest for your souls. For my yoke is easy and my burden light.
>
> —Matthew 11:28-30

As I mentioned, I believe that the Sinful Woman was present and heard these words of Jesus. This message spoke to the depths of her heart, and she became single-mindedly focused. She picked up the *shield of faith*, without even realizing it, and chose to do what Jesus was calling her to do. He said, "Come!" and she _____, knowing that He was her only _____. She chose to use the *sword of the Spirit* all the way to Simon's house as she battled all the _____ in her _____ and _____. Imagine the fiery darts of unworthiness, guilt and shame that Satan was firing at her, yet the craving to receive rest for her soul drove her to stay focused on Jesus' words. Without realizing it, she was using the *shield of faith* in the manner in which

God intended. By faith, she chose to throw caution to the wind and ignore the fiery darts. She chose to run to Simon's house in spite of all the conflicting emotions raging within her, because her soul craved the rest that Jesus spoke about.

It was when she chose to obey God's Word that the Lord met her there and performed one of the most amazing events in her life. Many times, God does the same thing in our lives—He calls us to walk the walk according to His Word and _____ He meets us there. The principals of His Word are simple, but that does not mean they are _____ to do. We must _____ by faith to be single-mindedly focused on the Word of God. We must _____ by faith to pick up the weapons of victory. We must _____ by faith to fight the good fight so that we may be set free. God loves you more than you know. And He has equipped you for battle so that you can *go in peace.*

Assignment

FOR WEEKEND WORKSHOP:

Take a short break and then move onto the next session.

FOR WEEKLY BIBLE STUDY:

Read chapter nine titled "The Weapons of Victory" in the book *Go in Peace!* Don't miss reading this chapter. Although this chapter is similar, it is different as well. It will give you more insight into Satan, his cohorts, and better yet, God. After reading the chapter spend some time with the Lord and as you do complete the following exercises.

1. What was the most interesting aspect of this session?

    _____

    _____

    _____

2. Which Scripture passage spoke the deepest to you heart? And why?

    _____

    _____

    _____

3. Have you equipped yourself with the armor of God? If not, why not?

    _____

    _____

    _____

4. Are you reading God's Word daily so as to have the belt of truth on?

    _____

    _____

    _____

5. Do you have the breastplate of righteousness on by making decisions based upon the truth of God's Word and not on your feelings or desires?

_____
_____
_____

6. Do you have the sandals of peace on by taking the hurtful, angry thoughts captive and making them obedient to Christ moment-by-moment?

_____
_____
_____

7. Are you using the shield of faith to quench the fiery darts of the enemy?

_____
_____
_____

8. Do you have the helmet of salvation on by protecting your thought life?

_____
_____
_____

9. Do you have the sword of the Spirit ready at a moments notice by memorizing key verses and passages?

_____
_____
_____

10. Are you effectively using the weapon of prayer to fight the good fight?

_____
_____
_____

11. What can you do to better equip yourself with the armor of God?

_____
_____
_____

A Broken and Contrite Heart

*The sacrifices of God are a broken spirit;
a broken and contrite heart.*

Psalm 51:17a

The Place of Repentance

Note to Leader: Before you begin this session read the story of the Prodigal Son found in Luke 15:11-24 out loud.

The story of the Prodigal Son is a beautiful picture of what takes place between God, the Father, and ourselves the moment we confess our sin and return to Him. He is there waiting with open outstretched arms. Throughout the previous sessions I pray that you have noticed that an element of repentance was woven within each issue. As you learned about the Sinful Woman you became aware of the sin in your own life, bringing you to the place of repentance. Then as you confronted your fine sounding arguments and wonderful pretensions and admitted the truth concerning the hurt, pain and anger hidden deep within your heart, this too brought you to the place of repentance. As you took the step of forgiveness by praying for those who mistreated you there was an element of repentance in your heart as you prayed that prayer. And as you equipped yourself with the weapons of victory and refused to allow the enemy to entice you to take back again—all the hurt, pain, anger and bitterness—there was an element of repentance woven within.

Still repentance is such an important issue that I would be remiss if I did not address it deeper. Therefore, let's learn more about the issue of repentance. Perhaps King David wrote it best when he penned these vivid words.

> Create in me a clean heart, O God, and renew a right spirit within me. . . .
> The sacrifices of God are a broken spirit; a broken and contrite heart.
>
> —Psalm 51:10,17a, ESV

So let's return to our story of the Sinful Woman for a moment. Do you remember the way in which she approached Jesus? She desired what King David wrote about. She too wanted God to create in her a clean heart and renew a right spirit within her. She was broken and had a contrite heart. By "contrite," I mean that she was _____ for her past sins and _____ to avoid future sin.[1] That's why she went to Jesus. She knew He was the only one who could give her the rest her soul so deeply craved. As she did this, she had _____. But what exactly does repentance mean?

According to Ralph Earle in *Word Meanings in the New Testament*, "The Greek noun *metanoia* [in English, "repentance"] literally means 'a _____ of mind.' It is more than emotional sorrow, which too often does not produce any change of life. Rather, it is a change of _____, or _____, towards God, sin and ourselves. Deep repentance involves a real turnabout in life."[2] Deep repentance involves a _____ life. We see this in the Sinful Woman's case. She entered the room broken and weeping, but left with peace and faith in a Savior.

Dear beloved, God loves you so much that He desires the same for you. He wants you to _____ of your sin, which means to _____ your _____, change your _____ and change your _____. Let me give you an example. Prior to God healing my broken heart, I was pro-choice, meaning I believed that abortion was a woman's choice and that nothing was wrong with a woman making such a decision to abort her baby. Of course, I had great reason to take this position, for to believe otherwise was just too painful to bear. It would have meant that I had to admit that what I had done was wrong.

Yet God, in His timing and love, showed me the error of my ways. Just as His Word teaches, it is God's kindness that leads us toward repentance.[3] Once I understood the truth, I had to repent of my ways and change my mind. So I changed my viewpoint and now, of course, I am pro-life. (By this point, I am sure you figured that out!)

The Elements of Repentance

As I began to seek God, I learned that according to the *New Unger's Bible Dictionary*, repentance contains _____ essential elements.

1. "First, a genuine _____ towards God on account of _____."[4]

    Let me give you a couple of examples to better explain this element of repentance. For someone in jail he may say, *I'm sorry I got caught and ended up in jail.* But, he is _____ sorry for what he has done. He is just sorry he got caught. This is not _____ sorrow towards God on account of his sin. Instead it is the sorrow of the world which according to God's Word this type of sorrow leads to death. Listen to 2 Corinthians 7:10:

    > For godly sorrow produces repentance leading to salvation, not to be regretted; but the sorrow of the world produces death.
    >
    > —NKJV

    Many of the issues I have written about have caused you hurt, pain and sorrow. But they were necessary _____ which you needed to _____ so that God could truly _____ your broken heart. So I join with the apostle Paul when he wrote:

Even if I caused you sorrow by my letter, I do not regret it. . . . I see that my letter hurt you, but only for a little while—yet now I am happy, not because you were made sorry, *but because your sorrow led you to repentance. For you became sorrowful as God intended* and so were not harmed in any way by us.

—2 Corinthians 7:8-9, emphasis added

This is exactly what happened for me. When I looked closely at how a baby is knit together in the mother's womb and learned what God's Word said about the baby in the womb, I had a genuine sorrow toward God on account of my sin. I pray that you too, dear beloved, have the same kind of _____ sorrow towards your sin. If so, you have accomplished the first element of repentance.

Is your heart broken over the issue of sin in your life? Well, that's a good thing, because repentance causes your heart to _____. That's what King David was writing about when he wrote: "The sacrifices of God are a broken spirit; a broken and contrite heart" (Psalm 51:17a, ESV). But, as way of encouragement, God can _____ your _____ heart if you give Him all the _____.

Give God all the pieces, even the pieces that contain your sorrow, the ones that you have kept locked up tight because they hurt too much. There is an old Yiddish proverb which says: "There is nothing more _____ than a broken _____."

2. The second element of repentance is to _____ your sin as God _____ it. In other words, you have to have "an inward _____ to sin necessarily followed by the actual _____ of it."[5] The word "repugnance" means to have a strong _____ or _____ for something.[6] If you look in a thesaurus for other terms to use in replace of "repugnant," you will find the words "repulsive" or "disgusting" among the list.[7]

Think about this for a moment. In the case of abortion, you only have to look at what an abortion actually is to feel repugnance for it. Knowing the medical facts of abortion and how an abortion is performed it is repulsive and disgusting. With the knowledge I now have, I find it amazing that abortion is even allowed by human intelligence. In America, the abortion industry calls the baby a "product of conception" or a "fetal tissue mass," or some other dehumanizing term. The abortion industry is trying to make such a disgusting and repulsive thing appear to be not so ugly, thereby encouraging people to believe the _____ that it is not a baby. However, when you search God's Word, you will know the _____. I pray that you, dear beloved, have joined me in this second element of repentance by feeling repugnance and repulse for this sin.

There is another aspect to this second element. Remember that repentance means you have "an inward repugnance to sin necessarily followed by *the actual _____ of it*."[8] In other words, if you have truly repented of the sin of abortion, then you can no longer be pro-choice. Remember the definition of "contrite"? It not only means to be remorseful for past sin but also to be _____ to _____ future sin.

In the case of holding on to past hurts and anger: As we see the ugliness within our hearts, the way that God sees that ugliness, we too can achieve this second element of repentance—that inward _____—necessarily followed by the actual _____ of it. As we forsake our sin we choose to let go of the hurt, pain, anger and bitterness. Plus we continually choose to fight the good fight by refusing to take it back again.

But just in case you need a _____ word picture to help you be repulsed and disgusted by the _____ of holding on to hurt, pain, anger and bitterness, including any unforgiveness, let's look at an interesting verse.

> All of us have become like one who is unclean, and all our righteous acts are like filthy rags.
>
> —Isaiah 64:6a

According to the *NIV Study Bible* the term "filthy rags" refer to "the _____ a woman uses during her _____, a time when she is 'unclean.'"[9] In other words, as the verse says, "all of us have become like one who is unclean [when we choose to hold on to or take back again all our hurt, pain, anger and bitterness], and all our righteous acts [in other words, our fine sounding arguments and wonderful pretension] are like filthy rags [like the cloths a woman uses during her menstrual period]."

Now if that doesn't cause you to be repulsed and disgusted by the sin of holding on to hurt, pain, anger and bitterness, or taking it back again, I don't know what will. But it is important to know that this is how God sees your sin. Your sin is like filthy rags, (like the clothes use during a women's menstrual cycle) in the sight of God. That's why He doesn't want to meet with you in the depth of your inmost being when your heart is unclean. Listen to how this concept is described in the book of Ezekiel.

> Son of man, when the people of Israel were living in their own land, they defiled it by their conduct and their actions. Their conduct was like a woman's monthly uncleanness in my sight.
>
> —Ezekiel 36:17

Filthy Rags! Our actions and conducts of holding on to the hurt, pain, anger and bitterness are like filthy rags to the King. When you truly think about it—how _____!

3. The third element of repentance we will discuss in a later session. Until then, you need to ask yourself if is there something that God is putting on your heart for which you need to repent. If so, come and kneel at Jesus' feet, just like the Sinful Woman did, so you can go in peace.

Change Your Ways

It's time to _____ your _____. It's time to change your _____. And it's even time to change your _____ by resolving to avoid future sin. In Matthew 3:8, John the Baptist warned the religious leaders of his day to "produce _____ in keeping with repentance." Likewise, in Acts 26:20, Paul states that he "preached [to the Jews and Gentiles] that they should repent and turn to God and _____ their repentance by their _____." Dear beloved, you cannot change the _____, but you can change the _____!

"Repentance" means to change your mind and change your life by your actions. In fact, as a repentant person, you are _____. You could compare your life to a drama. The person you played in act one (the bad guy) is not the same person you are today. Paul, with wisdom inspired by God, wrote:

> One thing I do: Forgetting what is _____ and straining to-
> wards what is _____, I press on toward the goal to win the
> prize for which God has called me heavenward in Christ Jesus.
>
> —Philippians 4:13b-14

So press on toward the goal. In fact, the next time Satan reminds you of your past, you remind him of his future! (According to the book of Revelation Satan will be thrown into the lake of burning sulfur and be tormented day and night for ever and ever.)

You have learned, you have grown, and you have matured. Praise the Lord! You are a new creation in Christ. As Paul again states:

> Therefore, if anyone is in Christ, he is a new creation; the old has gone,
> the new has come!
>
> —2 Corinthians 5:17

In view of this marvelous truth, as you choose to live your life in the manner God intends and as you choose to change your ways so that you can become all that God created you to be, you will *go in peace!*

Assignment

FOR WEEKEND WORKSHOP:

Find a quiet place and complete numbers one through four.

FOR WEEKLY BIBLE STUDY:

Read chapter ten titled "A Broken and Contrite Heart" in the book *Go in Peace!* Don't miss reading this chapter. Although this chapter is similar, it will reinforce what you just learned. Plus it is important to read it at your own pace so that you can take the time to ponder what you are learning. After reading the chapter spend some time with the Lord and as you do complete the following exercises.

1. What was the most interesting aspect of this session?

   _____

   _____

   _____

2. Which Scripture passage spoke the deepest to you heart? And why?

   _____

   _____

   _____

3. Pray and ask God if there are any filthy rags still hidden in the depth of your heart. Is He showing you any? If so, get rid of them by letting them go.

   _____

   _____

   _____

4. Write a letter to God. This letter does not need to be anything specific, just write whatever is on your heart. Some people write a letter of repentance, others write a letter of thanksgiving for the freedom they now feel in their hearts. Write whatever comes to mind and as you do may your heart be set free as you *go in peace!*

   _____

   _____

   _____

THE PRICE IS PAID

*And He Himself bore our sins in His body on the cross,
so that we might die to sin and live to righteousness;
for by His wounds you were healed.*

1 PETER 2:24

Amazing Love!

This truth is truly the most amazing love in all the universe. It is a love which has the ointment to heal your broken heart. It is a love which has the power to set you free from anything you may be struggling with. And it is a love which has stood the test of time to help you become all that God created you to be. In fact, this love is so amazing that I would be remiss if we were to overlook it. For this reason, we are going to take a look at the final eighteen hours of Christ's life.

When I originally wrote this curriculum and began to put the chapter *The Price is Paid* in workbook form I felt the Lord impress upon my heart not to do this. Instead, I was to leave the chapter from the book *Go in Peace!* in its original format. For this reason, I have included the chapter here. We are going to read it together as you either follow along or close your eyes and listen with your heart as this chapter of love is read to you; whichever way helps you to more fully understand the message of love that God wants you to grasp. As we do this, I want to encourage you to imagine yourself there. When Jesus is in the Garden of Gethsemane imagine the night crickets and the soft snores of His disciples. When He is led through the streets of Jerusalem imagine the clanking of the soldiers' armor. When He is hung on the cross picture yourself standing there alongside of Mary, His mother, and the others. What would you be feeling? What would you be thinking? Are you ready to learn about the most amazing love in all the universe?

Note to Leader: Either read out loud "The Price is Paid" which is found below or follow along as I read it. You can do this by visiting my web page at www.cheriefresonke.com. Click on "Blog" and in the search box type "The Price is Paid" to find the reading.

The Price is Paid

Over the years I have heard many people say, "I know and understand that God forgives me for my sins, but I cannot forgive myself." What these individuals are truly saying in making such a statement is that Christ did not pay a large enough price for their sins. Do you *feel* as if you cannot forgive yourself? Do you *feel* as if your sins are so reprehensible that they are unforgiveable? If so, you need to understand that Jesus paid the price and that the price He paid is sufficient! The apostle Peter states this clearly:

> He Himself bore our sins in His body on the cross, that we might die to sin and live to righteousness; for by His wounds you were healed.
>
> —1 Peter 2:24, NASB

It is by Christ's wounds, dear beloved, that you and I have been healed and set free from our sins. However, what you are struggling with is normal. Not that it is right or good, mind you, but it is normal. As the apostle Paul states:

> Even when Gentiles, who do not have God's written law, instinctively follow what the law says, they show that in their hearts they know right from wrong. They demonstrate that God's law is written within them, for their own consciences either accuse them or tell them they are doing what is right.
>
> —Romans 2:14-15, NLT

It is your conscience that is accusing you and causing you to *feel* as if your sins are unforgiveable, because deep down you know right from wrong. God's law is written deep within your heart, and because of this truth you know deep within your innermost being that your sins deserve punishment. In fact, because God's law is written within your heart, you know that "the wages of sin is death" (Romans 6:23, NLT). As the writer of Hebrews states:

> [God's] law requires that nearly everything be cleansed with blood, and without the shedding of blood there is no forgiveness.
>
> —Hebrews 9:22

Yet God made a wonderful way for you and I to be set free from the penalty of sin. In Romans 6:23, Paul goes on to say:

> For the wages of sin is death, but the free gift of God is eternal life through Christ Jesus our Lord.
>
> —NLT

With this in mind, it is important to learn and understand the price that Christ paid for your sins, for it is in understanding and accepting God's gift that you can be set free and get to the place where you can forgive yourself. In view of this, let's learn more about the One who paid the price. In Philippians 2:8, Paul writes:

> And [Christ] being found in appearance as a man, he humbled himself and became obedient to death—even death on a cross!

It was love that sent Jesus Christ to the cross—a love so deep for you, a love so deep for me. I want you, dear beloved, to feel, touch and grasp just how deep and immeasurable this love was that Christ had for you. I want you to see, hear and picture the most important event in all of history—the death and resurrection of our Lord and Savior, Jesus Christ—and know without a doubt that the price He paid for you and for me is sufficient!

I am not going to go into a theological debate or discuss the prophetic significance of Christ's sacrifice. There are numerous books and volumes written on those subjects. But I do want to paint a picture of the sacrifice that Jesus endured for our sins. He took the punishment we deserved and paid the price so we could be set free. For this reason, it is my prayer that you will come to an understanding of the love that Jesus poured out on the cross for you and me. And, better yet, that you will comprehend that the physical cost of that sacrifice was sufficient to pay the price for your sin both now and forever more.

In *The Cross of Jesus*, Warren Wiersbe writes, "On Sunday evening, February 19, 1882, Charles Haddon Spurgeon opened his message with these words: 'On whatever subjects I may be called to preach, I feel it to be a duty which I dare not neglect to be continually going back to the doctrine of the cross. . . .' Unless we go back to the cross, we can't go forward in our Christian life."[1] David Hocking, a Bible teacher, adds, "I do believe at some point in a Christian's life he should study the details of what happened in the suffering and torturing of Jesus Christ. No man has ever endured what He endured."[2]

The problem for many of us is that we have heard the story of the cross so often and we know it so well that it has lost some of its punch. As Pastor Jon Courson states, "We think, 'Oh, yeah. He was beaten. He was marred more than any man and eventually nailed to a tree.' But it would do us well, I think, to sometimes take a long walk in the evening or get up early in the morning and consider what Jesus really went through step by step with you on His mind, with you in His heart. . . . willingly walking in to the butchery that bruised and beat Him more than any other man—all for you. [Ponder this truth:] He really did it for me. I was on His mind. I was in His heart when He took those blows, when He felt that pain, when He endured that horrible suffering. It was all for me. It was all for you."[3]

As Weirsbe writes, "It was love that motivated the Father to give his Son to be the Savior of the world (John 3:16; Romans 5:8; 1 John 4:9-10), and it was love that motivated the Son to give his life for the sins of the world (John 15:13)."[4]

> Amazing love! How can it be? That Thou my God should'st die for me!
>
> —Charles Wesley

It was out of a love so deep for you and for me that God, in His infinite wisdom, devised a plan before the foundations of the world to save us from our sins.[5] As Weirsbe again states, "The cross was a divine assignment, not a human accident."[6] It was a divine assignment of love. Listen to these words of love from Jesus:

> I lay down my life for the sheep. . . . No one takes it from me, but I lay it down of my own accord. I have authority to lay it down and authority to take it up again.
>
> —John 10:15b,18a

81

Jesus willingly laid down His life in love. Weirsbe said it best when he wrote, "The false impression that in his death Jesus was a victim instead of the victor [is not the truth]. . . . Our Lord was not murdered against his will; he voluntarily gave himself to die for us."[7]

Approximately 700 years before Jesus was born, the prophet Isaiah penned a portrait of the Suffering Savior. As the *Halley Bible Handbook* explains, "It begins at [Isaiah] 52:13. [It is] so vivid in detail that one would almost think of Isaiah as standing at the foot of the cross. . . . so clear in his mind that he speaks of it in the past tense, as if it had already come to pass. Yet it was written seven centuries before Calvary. It cannot possibly fit any person in history other than Christ."[8]

Let's take a closer look at the events that led up to Jesus literally laying His life down in love for you and me at the cross. We will begin with the scene in the Garden of Gethsemane. It is interesting to note that "Gethsemane" means oil press. As Courson notes, "In an oil press, olives were crushed, broken, and ground up so that oil might be produced. Scripturally, oil is symbolic of the Holy Spirit. The picture is clear: before the Holy Spirit could be given, Someone had to be crushed and broken. And that Someone was Jesus Christ."[9]

> Then Jesus went with his disciples to a place called Gethsemane, and he said to them, "Sit here while I go over there and pray." He took Peter and the two sons of Zebedee along with him and he began to be sorrowful and troubled. Then he said to them, "My soul is overwhelmed with sorrow to the point of death. Stay here and keep watch with me."
>
> —Matthew 26:36-38

Why was Jesus so overwhelmed with sorrow to the point of death? Because He knew what lay ahead. As Courson explains, "There was far more for Jesus than the physical agony of being crucified in a few hours. Should He go through with this plan to pay for your sins and my sins, He would not only feel the wrath of God poured upon Him as He died in place of us, but His suffering would go much farther and longer than what we could possibly imagine. Jesus didn't suffer for just a few hours on a Friday afternoon. Revelation 3:18 speaks of the Lamb slain before the foundation of the world. In other words, the suffering was eternal and incredible. Jesus understood this, and He could have bailed out in the Garden."[10] But He didn't. Instead, He submitted to the will of the Father and paid this incredible price for your sins and mine.

> Amazing love! How can it be? That Thou my God should'st die for me!
>
> —Charles Wesley

After Jesus asked three of His disciples to keep watch and pray with Him, He walked about a stone's throw away and knelt down to pray. Soon, the three whom He had asked to pray were fast asleep. Meanwhile, Jesus, in agony, pleaded with the Father. Three times He cried out, "Abba, Father. . . . everything is possible for you. Take this cup from me. Yet not what I will, but what you will" (Mark 14:36). Can you hear His cry? Can you hear the crying and pleading of a man so filled with passion as He knelt down and thought of the events to come—as He thought of you and me in love? He is so overwhelmed, in fact, that we read "an angel from heaven appeared to him and strengthened him" (Luke 22:43).

Jesus clearly had a choice—a choice of faith to follow the will of the Father or a choice of the flesh to refuse and say the price was too high. It was a choice that caused Him great distress. As the physician Luke writes, "Being in anguish, he prayed more earnestly, and his sweat was like drops of blood falling to the ground" (Luke 22:44).

According to Dr. Frederick Zugibe, "The sweating of blood, called hematidrosis, is a clinical term because there have been many cases of it. It was first described by Aristotle. Around the sweat glands themselves there are multiple blood vessels in a net-like form."[11] Dr. Robert Beck explains, "It has been shown to occur in great stressful situations. What happens is that around the sweat glands [are] these very fragile capillaries, these are little vessels that only one blood cell can go through at a time, for some reason they rupture and the blood is mixed in with the sweat. Christ did not lose a large amount of blood during this time, but what it does, it makes the skin exquisitely sensitive and very tender to the touch."[12]

Imagine this anguish of love so deep for you and me. Yet Jesus said to the Father, "Not my will, but yours be done" (Luke 22:42b). David Hocking describes the scene like this: "It happened in a moment of great trial and torture as He sweat as it were drops of blood as He felt the agony, says the Bible, of all of the events that would come against Him. The passion of Gethsemane was real and awful because Jesus *knew* what would happen."[13] Out of love, Jesus set His face like flint[14] and walked toward His captors. Can you feel His love with each step He takes—steps of love toward the cross?

It was a man named Judas, one of Jesus' own disciples, who betrayed Him.[15] Imagine one of your closest friends, with whom you had shared the last three years, betraying you. That was what Judas did, and He betrayed His Lord with a kiss![16] Let's pick up the story in the Gospel of John:

> So Judas came to the grove, guiding a detachment of soldiers and some officials from the chief priests and Pharisees. They were carrying torches, lanterns and weapons.
>
> Jesus, knowing all that was going to happen to him, went out and asked them, "Who is it you want?"
>
> "Jesus of Nazareth," they replied.
>
> "I am he," Jesus said. (And Judas the traitor was standing there with them.) When Jesus said, "I am he," they drew back and fell to the ground.
>
> —John 18:3-6

As you picture this scene in your mind, realize that a detachment of soldiers was 600 men! This was a huge group of soldiers who had come to arrest Jesus. When Jesus then says, "I am he," as Courson explains, "Jesus is actually saying, 'I AM,' *Ego Eimi*'—a declaration of deity."[17] Jesus was claiming, and rightfully so, that He was God. But catch the picture. Can you see it? I like the way Courson goes onto to describe the scene: "With torches flying, armor clanking, and swords falling, these guys go down under the sheer power of Jesus' proclamation."[18] The *NIV Study Bible* explains it this way: "They came to arrest a meek peasant and instead were met in the dim light by a majestic person."[19] Do you understand? Jesus was in complete control at all times. He gave up His life willingly out of His immeasurable love for you and me.

After the soldiers got up and brushed themselves off, they stepped forward, seized Jesus and arrested Him.[20] It was at this point that Peter decided to try and save the day. He whipped out his sword and cut off the ear of a servant of the high priest.[21] "Put your sword back in its place," Jesus said to him, "for all who draw the sword will die by the sword. Do you think I cannot call on my Father, and he will at once put at my disposal more than twelve legions of angels?" (Matthew 26:52-53).

As Courson teaches, "A legion being six thousand, Jesus was talking about seventy-two thousand angels at His disposal—quite a force, considering it took only one to wipe out 185,000 Babylonians (2 Kings 19:35). What a glorious day when you learn you don't have to defend Jesus Christ—that He is perfectly capable of defending Himself."[22] At any time, Jesus could have stopped these events from taking place. But He chose not to do so. Why? Because of His love for you and me! He chose to go to the cross out of a love so deep—a love to set you free! Given this, can we not be willing to choose love as well? Jesus made faith choices over flesh choices out of His love for us. Can we offer Him any less?

The disciples deserted Jesus, and He was led alone from the Garden of Gethsemane to stand before Caiaphas, the high priest that year. But remember, as Courson points out, "It was not the chains, the ropes, nor the soldiers which bound Jesus. It was love."[23] It was not the trial, the beating to come or the cross that Jesus was thinking about. He had already set His face like flint when He was led through the city of Jerusalem. He was thinking about you and how much He loves you. He knew this was the only way to set you free from the penalty of your sin.

Jesus was taken first to Annas (who was the former high priest) and then to Caiaphas (who was the son-in-law of Annas).[24] During this time, as Courson goes on to explain, "A meeting of the Sanhedrin was called. The Sanhedrin was the seventy-one member Jewish Supreme Court. From the very outset, however, the trial was illegal, since night meetings of the Sanhedrin were forbidden by Mosaic Law."[25]

> They were looking for false evidence against Jesus so that they could put him to death. But they did not find any, though many false witnesses came forward.
>
> —Matthew 26:59-60

During this illegal trial, "they all condemned him as worthy of death. Then some began to spit at him; they blindfolded him, struck him with their fists, and said, 'Prophesy!' And the guards took him and beat him" (Mark 14:64-65). Can you hear the guards' mockery? Imagine the spit running down Jesus' face. Can you hear their laughing? But there was only silence in reply from the Creator of the Universe. Even though Jesus was blindfolded, He knew exactly who was hitting Him, just as He knew the exact day we first denied His love. Even though He chose to be silent, He knew. In the same way as the palace guards struck Him and beat Him, we struck Him in His heart with our denial of Him in our lives. Can you hear the silence? Can you hear His heart break? He did it for you. He did it for me.

> Amazing love! How can it be? That Thou my God should'st die for me!
> —Charles Wesley

Courson continues, "It was now 5:00 A.M. After a night of agony in the Garden of Gethsemane, an illegal trial by the Sanhedrin, followed by a beating at the hands of the palace guards, Jesus was led before Pontius Pilate."[26] There, as the false accusations were told to Pilate, the Roman governor, Jesus remained silent, just as had been foretold seven centuries earlier:

> He was oppressed and afflicted, yet he did not open his mouth; he was led
> like a lamb to the slaughter, and as a sheep before her shearers is silent, so
> he did not open his mouth.
> —Isaiah 53:7

Christ's very silence in the midst of all the agony, the torture and the mockery fulfilled that prophecy. Pilate was amazed that Jesus did not utter one word in His defense.[27] In Luke's account, we read:

> Then Pilate announced to the chief priests and the crowd, "I find no basis
> for a charge against this man."
> —Luke 23:4

According to Courson, "The uniqueness of Jesus is verified by the fact that Pilate went on record, saying, 'I find no fault in Him'—a finding which has never been disputed by historian or cynic. According to many historian records, Pilate himself committed suicide in Sicily not long after this."[28]

Let's take a break in our depiction of Jesus to look a bit more in-depth at suicide. We read in the Gospel of Matthew that Judas committed suicide by hanging himself.[29] Here, we learn from Courson that according to historical records, Pilate himself committed suicide not long after Jesus' crucifixion. The reason? These two men never grasped the depth of the love that God had for them. Likewise, many sinful folks have struggled with suicidal thoughts, fantasies or attempts because of the overwhelming feelings of guilt they have from their sinful lives.

Judas and Pilate both committed suicide because of their sin. Dear beloved, learn a lesson from these men. They did not take their sin, their guilt and their shame and kneel at Jesus' feet. They did not recognize who He was, nor did they give Him the rightful place in their lives. They denied Christ, even though He stood among them, and tried to carry their burdens all by themselves. We cannot forget that Jesus offered this wonderful invitation:

> Come to me, all you who are weary and burdened, and I will give you rest.
>
> —Matthew 11:28

Jesus came to carry the load. The only way you will be able to fully receive rest from your sin is to understand that the price has been paid, and paid in full!

Jesus stands in your midst. Will you accept the sacrifice He made in love for you, or will you, too, deny Christ though He stands before you? Perhaps you are realizing that you have never bowed your knee before Him. If so, it is not too late. He is waiting with open arms to receive you. When you finish reading this chapter, go back to the chapter titled "Are You Right with God?" and again read those words. Put your faith in Christ to be your Lord and Savior. He paid the price—in full!

Now, as if the beating and the mockery that Jesus had endured were not sufficient, Pilate, as a way to get rid of this problem, sent Jesus to Herod.[30] There, "Herod and his soldiers ridiculed and mocked him. Dressing him in an elegant robe, they sent him back to Pilate" (Luke 23:11). Can you imagine all the suffering Jesus had endured thus far—being sent first here, then there—and all the ridicule and mockery? He endured it for you. He endured it for me.

> Pilate called together the chief priests, other rulers and the people, and said to them, "You brought me this man as one who was inciting the people to rebellion. I have examined him in your presence and have found no basis for your charges against him. Neither has Herod, for he sent him back to us; as you can see, he has done nothing to deserve death. Therefore, I will punish him and then release him."
>
> —Luke 23:13-16

The punishment of which Pilate was speaking was scourging. As Courson describes, "Scourging was brutal. It was done with a Roman instrument of torture called a flagellum—a whip made of twelve or thirteen leather thongs. Lead balls were attached to the end of these thongs and pieces of glass and metal were embedded between the lead balls and the handle. . . . The accused would be tied by his wrists and dangled about a foot off the ground, rendering him helpless to protect himself in any way. Then the beating would begin—usually thirty-nine lashes."[31]

At this point, it's interesting to consider for a moment the nature of the typical Roman soldier. Dr. Beck illuminates their mindset for us: "They are veterans in battle, they know how to kill, they hate the Jews, they hate being in Israel, they hate everything and for them to finally get a hold of somebody and just beat them, is nothing but to their joy."[32] The courtyard was filled with these Roman soldiers. Can you hear them mocking Jesus? Can you see them inciting the soldier with the whip to beat Him as hard as he could? Can you hear them egging him on, saying, "Beat Him! Beat Him!"

So the beating began. Just think of Jesus' extra-sensitive skin from sweating drops of blood. Dr. James Strange describes the flagellum whip the Romans would have used as follows: "When flicked as it were, with considerable strength by the person doing the beating, it actually whips around the body and embeds in the flesh and then when it is pulled out one bleeds profusely."[33] Can you hear the snap of this whip? Can you hear Jesus' intake of breath with each stripe He received for you and each stripe He received for me?

> Amazing love! How can it be? That Thou my God should'st die for me!
> —Charles Wesley

Dr. Beck goes on to elaborate about the damage that would have been done to Jesus' body by the whip: "First, it ripped through the skin, then what we call the subcutaneous tissue, the fatty tissue under the skin. . . . Then they would continue to whip the individual not only on the back, but on the buttock, on the legs, on the feet. . . . They would love to see just shreds of flesh and muscle just hanging. Literally off the back or the back of the legs and also to expose the vertebrae and the ribs. Now the severity of the scourging was according to how long the individual would last. And with Christ they did a severe scourging."[34] Pastor Corson goes onto explain, "At the end of the beating, the accused would be cut down, and his body would fall to the ground, where he would lay in a pool of his own blood."[35]

Can you picture Christ lying there with His stripes of love for you and with His stripes of love for me? He endured this out of love, and it is by His stripes that we are healed.[36] As Courson states, "So brutal was the beating Jesus endured, Isaiah prophesied He would be more disfigured than any man who ever lived.[37] His beard would be plucked; His face would be swollen. The spit of His accusers would be running down His cheeks. He could have called ten thousand times ten thousand angels. But He didn't."[38] Why? Because of His deep love for you and His deep love for me.

> I offered my back to those who beat me, my cheeks to those who pulled
> out my beard; I did not hide my face from mocking and spitting.
> —Isaiah 50:6

Many men died as a result of such a beating. After the scourging, "the soldiers twisted together a crown of thorns and put it on his head. They clothed him in a purple robe and went up to him again and again, saying, 'Hail, king of the Jews!' And they struck him in the face" (John 19:2-3). The Roman soldiers draped this rough cloth robe across Jesus' raw and bleeding back, and in a moment of cruel mockery they fashioned a crown of thorns and pushed it down onto His head.[39] As Dr. Beck explains, "They forced that down through His scalp creating even more bleeding because the scalp itself has a large amount of blood supply. It is very vascular. You cut your scalp and it looks like you cut the major vessel in your body."[40]

I like the way Pastor David Hocking describes this scene: "Many people try to get us to relate to this by having a picture of Jesus on the cross. . . . Often when they have that picture of Christ on the cross, invariably, you see maybe the crown of thorns on Him, with

87

maybe a little blood trickling down, but His face always looks nice. I am sorry—that is not the Bible. Do you understand that Jesus' face was beat up so bad nobody could recognize who He was? And that bloody mess, that pulp, was led out in front of the people by Pilate. . . . 'Behold the man!' It was a mockery."[41] Pilate's statement was a joke! Jesus was marred and beaten beyond recognition. It was impossible to even identify He was a man. Listen to how John describes the scene:

> Pilate went out again and said to them, "See, I am bringing him out to you that you may know that I find no guilt in him." So Jesus came out, wearing the crown of thorns and the purple robe. Pilate said to them, *"Behold the man!"* When the chief priests and the officers saw him, they cried out, "Crucify him, crucify him" Pilate said to them, "Take him yourselves and crucify him, for I find no guilt in him."
>
> —John 19:4-6, ESV, emphasis added

Can you hear the cries of the crowd—the passion with which they yelled? Did our *own* actions of sin yell just as loudly to Christ, "Crucify Him! Crucify Him!"?

Wiersbe writes, "In spite of their [the Jews] careful attention to the study of the Old Testament, the people didn't recognize their Savior and King when he arrived. They mocked him as a prophet and said, 'Prophesy! Who is it that struck you?' They mocked him as a king, putting a robe on him, giving him a scepter, and placing a crown of thorns on his head. They shouted to Pilate, 'We have no king but Caesar!' They laughed at Christ's claim that he was the Son of God. 'He saved others; let Him save Himself if He is the Christ, the chosen of God!'"[42] Let us weigh our *own* actions carefully, lest we make the same mistake that they made.

Jesus endured hours of misery, but the worst of the ordeal was yet to come:

> Finally Pilate handed him over to them to be crucified. So the soldiers took charge of Jesus. Carrying his own cross, he went out to the place of the Skull (which in Aramaic is called Golgotha).
>
> —John 19:16-17

As Dr. John Bonica states, "I can't imagine how a person who was whipped or who was injured in [such] ways would be expected to carry a very heavy load. I would anticipate that the average individual would not be able to tolerate that for more than a few feet."[43] Dr. Strange goes onto explain, "The cross itself is a very heavy timber. . . . the objective is to make it last a long time. The timber is unfinished, it is not lovely, sanded down timber, it is just cut out with adzes so it is quite rough and even injures the skin when it is being carried."[44] Keep this in mind as you read how Luke describes the scene:

> As they led Jesus away, Simon of Cyrene, who was coming in from the country just then, was forced to follow Jesus and carry his cross. Great crowds trailed along behind, including many grief-stricken women.
>
> —Luke 23:26-27, NLT

Imagine the scene. Imagine the people. Imagine the heartbreak. Once the Romans soldiers reached Golgotha, they threw Jesus down to the ground to prepare Him for the cross. They stripped Jesus of His clothing with brutal indifference to the gaping wounds that covered His body. Then, as John relates:

> They crucified him, and with him two others—one on each side and Jesus in the middle.

> —John 19:18

As Courson notes, "Crucifixion was developed by the Persians, today called the Iranians, around the year 1000 BC. Designed to be excruciatingly painful. . . . The Persians considered the ground of their country to be holy, they mandated that a crucified victim be elevated lest his cursing defile it. That is why when a man was crucified he was raised up usually three to four feet off the ground. When the Greeks took over the Persian Empire, they adopted crucifixion. And when the Romans came on the scene, they borrowed it from the Greeks."[45]

Dr. Beck explains, "Now the hand itself cannot support the full weight of the body. But in Greek when they mention [the] hand it also includes the wrist. So the one area that you could drive that nail was either through the wrist or between the two bones which make up the forearm."[46] The Romans pounded the nails quickly into Jesus' hands and feet. Can you hear the hammer hit the nail? Yet not a word did Jesus scream or mutter in pain. Pound, pound, pound . . . in love for you! In love for me!

Dr. Beck goes on to describe the areas of the hands and feet where the soldiers would drive the nails: "There is really not an arterial vessel in this area. . . . But what is there is a nerve called the median nerve. And as they were driving that [nail] through, it would cause the hand to go into a claw-like appearance with immense shooting pain in the hand and up the arm."[47] Dr. Zugibe explains, "If the median nerve is ruptured or injured [this] will cause severe excruciating, burning-like pain. Like lightening bolts traversing the arm into the spinal cord."[48] Can you imagine what Jesus endured in love for you and endured in love for me?

> Amazing love! How can it be? That Thou my God should'st die for me!

> —Charles Wesley

We know from the Gospel accounts that there were four women there at the scene of the cross. As Courson states, "It was not easy for them. It was not easy for Mary to watch her Son convulsing in pain, or for her sister to hear the curses hurled at Him. It was not easy for the wife of Cleophas to see the spit of the crowd running down His face, or for Mary Magdalene to see His blood flowing from His wounds. But these four women, [who loved the Lord and followed Him,] were there at the foot of the Cross, no matter how great the price, no matter how deep the pain."[49] Through it all, these women watched. Can you see the love in their eyes for their Savior? Imagine how you would feel if it were your son being crucified. Can you see the sorrow?

When they had crucified him, they divided up his clothes by casting lots. And sitting down, they kept watch over him there.

—Matthew 27:35-36

And as prophesied in the Old Testament dogs have surrounded me; a band of evil men has encircled me, they have pierced my hands and my feet. I can count all my bones; people stare and gloat over me. They divide my garments among them and cast lots for my clothing.

—Psalm 22:16-18

Can you imagine the pain Jesus endured—a pain so great that He could count all His bones because each one was crying out in a symphony of pain? Can you imagine the shame of hanging on a cross, practically naked, with people looking on in mockery and cruelty, casting lots and dividing up the clothes He wore? Can you see the flies swarming around His body and the vultures circling overhead? Why did He allow it? Out of His deep love for you and out of His deep love for me!

Jesus said "Father forgive them; for they know not what they do."

—Luke 23:34, KJV

Weirsbe writes, "Consider the wonder of the appeal. The tense of the verb 'said' indicates that our Lord repeated this prayer. As the soldiers nailed him to the cross, he prayed, 'Father, forgive them.' When they lifted the cross and placed it in the hole in the ground, our Lord prayed, 'Father, forgive them.' As he hung there between heaven and earth, and heard religious people mocking him, he repeatedly prayed, 'Father, forgive them.'"[50]

Beloved, as He looked upon you and upon me, He cried, "Father forgive them; for they know not what they do" (Luke 23:34, KJV). Imagine the look of love—a love so deep for you and a love so deep for me!

As Jesus hung on the cross, He would have literally had to fight for each breath He took. Jesus was hanging in a position called "inhalation." This is how Dr. Beck describes this torturous position: "Now to exhale He had to first of all flex His arms, in other words bend them, to pull up on those nails. At the same time as He was pulling up He had to push on that nail which was basically the weight-bearing nail. He would slide up the wood, which would again open up His back and wounds. And He would start bleeding again. With each movement the pain was absolutely excruciating."[51]

According to Weirsbe, "Close to the end of his ordeal, Jesus was forsaken by the Father and announced this fact in a loud voice: 'My God, My God, why have You forsaken Me?' (Matthew 27:46). This was the climax of the awful darkness that had shrouded the cross for three hours."[52] God the Father cannot look upon sin,[53] and it was at this point that Jesus became sin for us.[54] He took upon Himself the sin of the whole world—including our sin. Though He was without blemish or any iniquity at all, He took your sins and mine upon Himself. He took the punishment we deserved and literally laid down His life for you and for me. Why? Because of His deep and immeasurable love for us! He offered Himself as the penalty for our sin.

Amazing love! How can it be? That Thou my God should'st die for me!

—Charles Wesley

Then Jesus cried out in a loud voice, "It is finished!" (John 19:30). According to Weirsbe, "In the Greek language in which John wrote his Gospel, this statement was only one word of ten letters—tetelestai. In the Greek, it means, 'It is finished, it stands finished, and it always will be finished.'"[55] *Tetelestai* is a word that was familiar and commonly used in Jesus' day. To a merchant, the word would have meant that the debt had been fully paid. As Weirsbe notes, "Unbelieving sinners are in debt to God and can't pay their bill. Having broken God's law, they are bankrupt and unable to pay (Luke 7:36-50). But Jesus paid the debt when he died for us on the cross. That's what tetelestai means: the debt has been paid, it stands paid, and it always will be paid. When we turn to Christ in faith, our sins are forgiven and the debt is canceled forever."[56] It is interesting to note that the verses Wiersbe references in Luke seven are from the story of the Sinful Woman. The price had been paid!

Soon, Jesus' ordeal was over. As Luke describes the scene:

Then Jesus, calling out with a loud voice, said, "Father, into your hands I commit my spirit! And having said this he breathed his last.

—Luke 23:46

Jesus' parting words prove to us that the Father and the Son are together again. Weirsbe said it best when he wrote, "He was forsaken by the Father that we might never be forsaken by God."[57]

Perhaps the next part of the story is the most inconceivable to me. It shows the depravity of humans in their religious endeavors. Oh, how we can twist up our sins to make them presentable! Courson describes the scene found in John 19:31 this way: "The next day being Passover, the Jews didn't want the bodies left on the crosses. 'Break their legs' the Jews said to Pilate, 'and speed up the death so we can move on with our holy convocation.' Incredible!"[58]

The soldiers therefore came and broke the legs of the first man who had been crucified with Jesus, and then those of the other. But when they came to Jesus and found that he was already dead, they did not break his legs. Instead, one of the soldiers pierced Jesus' side with a spear, bringing a sudden flow of blood and water. . . . These things happened so that the scripture would be fulfilled. "Not one of his bones will be broken," and, as another scripture says, "They will look on the one they have pierced."

—John 19:32-37

Ponder what Courson has to say for a moment: "Not a bone of Jesus was broken. Why is this such a big deal? Because where is the blood continually produced in the body? It's produced in the bone. Therefore, God mandated not a bone of His would be broken ensuring a perpetual and inexhaustible supply of blood. That's why Paul could later declare, 'Where sin abounds, grace abounds yet more' (Romans 5:20).' Truly, the blood of Jesus Christ is sufficient to cleanse you from every sin you have ever committed or will commit. Why? Because not a bone of His was broken."[59]

> In him we have redemption through his blood, the forgiveness of sins, in accordance with the riches of God's grace that he lavished on us with all wisdom and understanding.
>
> —Ephesians 1:7-8

It is the blood that cleanses us. Remember what we talked about at the beginning of this chapter? "Without the shedding of blood there is no forgiveness" (Hebrews 9:22).

According to the *Halley Bible Handbook*, "Jesus was already dead when the spear pierced his side, after being on the cross six hours. Some medical authorities have said that in the case of heart rupture, and in that case only, the blood collects in the pericardium, the lining around the wall of the heart, and divides into a sort of bloody clot and a watery serum. If this is a fact, then the actual immediate physical cause of Jesus' death was heart rupture. Under intense pain, and the pressure of his wildly raging blood, his heart burst open. It may be that Jesus, literally, died of a heart broken over the sin of the world. It may be that suffering for human sin is more than the human constitution can stand."[60]

Jesus died of a broken heart.

Perhaps, just perhaps, dear beloved, His heart did not break because the sin of the whole world was placed upon Him. Perhaps, just perhaps, His heart did not break because He was separated from the Father. Perhaps His heart broke from love—a love so deep for you and a love so deep for me that it literally broke His heart that we forsook His love.

Have you ever loved someone so deeply, but that love was not returned? Did your heart feel as if it would break? Did Christ's heart break because we denied His love?

> He was pierced for our transgressions, he was crushed for our iniquities; the punishment that brought us peace was upon him, and by his wounds we are healed.
>
> —Isaiah 53:5

Amazing love! How can it be? That Thou my God should'st die for me!
>
> —Charles Wesley

Ponder this love over the next week or two when you feel you cannot forgive yourself. Ponder this love over the next month or so when you feel no one loves you. Ponder this love over the next year or so as you choose to live a life pleasing to God. And remember to ponder this love as you walk away from the side of the bridge into a whole new life filled with truth and meaning. He loves you more than you know!

Courson said it best: "According to the Word of God, if you open up your heart to Jesus Christ and believe in His work on the Cross, your sin is gone."[61] There is no reason you cannot forgive yourself. The price is paid!

But the story is not yet ended. In fact, the best is yet to come! At dawn, three women went to the tomb to anoint Jesus' body with spices. "As they entered the tomb, they saw a young man dressed in a white robe sitting on the right side, and they were alarmed. 'Don't be alarmed,' he said. 'You are looking for Jesus the Nazarene, who was crucified. He has risen! He is not here" (Mark 16:5-6a).

> On the evening of that first day of the week, when the disciples were together, with the doors locked for fear of the Jews, Jesus came and stood among them and said, "Peace be with you!" After he said this, he showed them his hands and side. The disciples were overjoyed when they saw the Lord.
>
> —John 20:19-20

The first words Jesus spoke to His disciples after the crucifixion and resurrection were "peace be with you!" Why do we choose to stand in the prison cell when the door is wide open? Accept the gift. The price is paid! He is the One who walked away from an empty tomb. Dear beloved, won't you join Him? Won't you *go in peace!*

Assignment

After reading the chapter "The Price if Paid" spend some quiet time with the Lord and write a letter. This letter is a little different from the other letters you have written, because this is a letter from God. Now, this may seem strange at first request, but if you learn how to do this it can become one of the most awesome things you learn to do because it teaches you how to listen to God. In view of this, grab some paper, find a quiet spot and spend some time with the Lord. Ask Him to open your heart as you listen to His still small voice. Whatever He begins to impress upon your heart write it down.

FOR WEEKEND WORKSHOP:

Since this session is the last session on Saturday evening either complete the letter before going to sleep or get up early in the quiet of the morning and sit a Jesus' feet. Write whatever He impresses upon your heart. Don't be afraid; just try it! You will be blessed.

FOR WEEKLY BIBLE STUDY:

Either write the letter immediately following the session, before the cares of this world get in the way, or find a quiet place and spend some time with Jesus before your next Bible study session.

THE TEMPLE OF THE HOLY SPIRIT

Do you not know that your body is
a temple of the Holy Spirit,
who is in you, whom you have received from God?
You are not your own; you were bought with a price.
Therefore honor God with your body.

1 CORINTHIANS 6:19-20

Guard Your Heart

*N*ow let's go back to our story of the Sinful Woman for a moment. Although God's Word does not tell us what kind of sin she was involved in, many believe that she was a harlot because of the title of her name. Perhaps she was. But what brought her to the place that everyone in her town knew her as the Sinful Woman? Did she have such an infection in her heart, because of all the hurt and pain she may have stuffed deep within? Was she reacting out of those hurts as we saw in session two? Remember, one of the consequences of the infection in a person's heart is self-destructive behaviors which can include sexual immorality. Is that what brought her to the place of being known as the Sinful Woman?

In a previous session you learned that the biblical term "inmost being" (NIV) or "inward parts" (NKJV or NASB), which sometimes is also referred to in the Bible as the word "heart," is the center of the human spirit from which spring your _____, your emotions, your motivations and even your _____.[1] In fact, when researching the word "heart" you will discover that the heart was considered in biblical days to be the center of one's being, including the person's mind, will and emotions.[2] I believe this is still true today. As a matter of fact, I believe that the inmost being is the essence of who a person is. The part of you that will live forever in one of two place. In view of this, we can understand the warning in the book of Proverbs:

> Above all else, _____ your _____, for it affects everything you do.
>
> —Proverbs 4:23, NLT

For many of us, if we are truly _____ with ourselves, our path to destruction and to much of our deep heart hurt began when we _____ to walk outside of

95

God's _____ and instead _____ by our feelings and our desires. Is that what happened to the Sinful Woman? Did she choose to live by her feelings and desires because she did not learned how to _____ her heart? Is it possible that we too make _____ choices with our lives because we too never learned the importance of guarding our hearts?

In view of this, we need to take some time and understand the path that leads to destruction. For if we do not take the time to learn and understand this, we can easily find ourselves back in the pit of despair—back where we were when we began this Bible study. Therefore, let's learn so that we may _____ our hearts. So that we may also be like the Sinful Woman who after meeting Jesus chose to change her life as she held onto His' words:

> Your sins are forgiven. . . . Your faith has saved you; go in peace.
>
> —Luke 7:48,50

Don't Let Your Guard Down

To guard your heart, there are three elements in life that are important to understand. These three elements can cause a constant struggle in your inmost being.

1. Satan thinks up the lie.
2. The world sells the lie by enticing us.
3. Our flesh, when we allow ourselves to be tempted to sin, buys the lie.

Let me explain by going back to the story of Adam and Eve. First, Satan thought up the lie. He whispered to Eve, "You will not surely die" (Genesis 3:4). He does the same thing to us each day, telling us that _____ is not really that bad and will not carry any consequences. Second, Eve _____ that the fruit was _____ to the eye. The world will often try to sell Satan's lies by _____ us and making something look attractive and pleasurable. The world cleverly packages the lie for us to see and then causes us to believe that there is some reason we need what the world is selling. Finally, Eve fell victim to her own fleshly desires when she _____ to give in to the temptation. Pay attention to the wording of Genesis 3:6:

> When the woman _____ that the fruit of the tree was good
> for food and _____ to the eye, and also _____
> for gaining wisdom, she took some and ate it.

In other words, she chose to live by her fleshly desire when she chose to eat the fruit. In the Bible, the word "flesh" sometimes means "the weaker element in [our] human nature."[3] In other words, when we are living by our flesh, we are choosing to make _____ decisions based on our fleshly _____ and _____, not on truth or what we know is right.

In view of this, let's take a look at 1 Thessalonians 4:3-5 for a moment.

> It is God's will that you should be sanctified: that you should avoid sexual immorality; that each of you should learn to control his [or her] own body in a way that is holy and honorable, not in passionate lust like the heathen, who do not know God.

As we think about what we have learned so far, let's discuss a few questions for a moment.

1. If it is God's will for each one of us to avoid sexual immorality, who then thought up the lie that it is acceptable to be sexually active outside of marriage?

_____
_____
_____

2. What are some of the lies that Satan whispers?

_____
_____
_____

3. In what way does the world sell the lie?

_____
_____
_____

4. Why do we, the flesh, buy the lie?

_____
_____
_____

Because of the three elements: (1) Satan, (2) the world and (3) our flesh, we truly do need to guard our hearts, minds and wills. Although our emotions can trigger our thought life, and visa versa, our thought life can trigger our emotions it is important to know and understand that our _____ trigger our _____ and our desires trigger our _____. In view of this, let's follow the downward path to destruction.

The Downward Path—Thoughts ➜ Desires ➜ Actions

1. Thoughts—The definition of the word "thought" means to _____, to give _____ consideration, and it can also mean, the power to _____.[4] Listen to what God's Word says concerning the thoughts of a person.

The LORD detests the _____ of the wicked, but those of the pure are pleasing to him.

—Proverbs 15:26

And Jesus knowing their thoughts said, "Why are you _____ evil in your _____?"

—Matthew 9:4, NASB

For out of the _____ comes evil _____, murder, adultery, sexual immorality, theft, false witness, slander.

—Matthew 15:19, ESV

As we can see from these verses it is our thoughts that lead us astray. And it is our thoughts that trigger our desires.

2. Desires—The definition of the word "desire" is to long or _____ for. It often implies strong intention, as if to _____ something. It even stresses the force of _____ appetite or _____ need.[5] Let's learn what God's Word has to say concerning our desires.

For the time already past is sufficient for you to have carried out the _____ of the Gentiles, having pursued a course of sensuality, lusts, drunkenness, carousing, drinking parties and abominable idolatries.

—1 Peter 4:3, NASB

All of us also lived among them at one time, gratifying the _____ of our sinful nature and following its _____ and _____. Like the rest, we were by nature objects of wrath.

—Ephesians 2:3

Each one of us can struggle with our sinful nature—our flesh. When we choose to _____ upon our thoughts—thoughts which are unpleasing to God—this can trigger our _____ to gratify our sinful nature. It is important to know and understand that our desires can then trigger our _____—our actions down the path of destruction.

3. Actions—the definition of the word "action" is an act of _____; a thing done; a _____; a behavior or a _____.[6] Listen to how God's Word describes a person's heart, and more importantly, pay attention to what God's action will be concerning that person's conduct.

The _____ is deceitful above all things and beyond cure. Who can understand it? "I the LORD _____ the heart and examine the mind, to _____ a man according to his _____, according to what his [or her] _____ deserve.

—Jeremiah 17:9-10

To stress this point a bit further, listen to what the apostle Paul wrote in 2 Corinthians 5:10 and it's important to know that he was writing to believers.

For we must all appear before the judgment seat of Christ, so that each one may be recompensed for his _____ in the body, according to what he has done, whether _____ or _____.

—NASB

The word "recompensed" means to give compensation for, or to make restitution for.[7] In other words, we will be held accountable for our actions and deeds. We will be _____ and _____ for the things done during our lives that God considers to be _____. While on the other hand, we will somehow have to make _____ for or be held _____ for the things done which were _____. (Please don't misunderstand me! This accounting has nothing to do with justification. See appendix 4—The Judgment Seat of Christ—to learn more.)

That's why for me personally I like to keep a short account with God. When I realize that I have blown it, I admit it to myself, I confess it to God and I repent by _____ my ways. And I _____ in my heart *to above all else, guard my heart, for it is the wellspring of life* of which I will be held accountable for.

Yet the moment I repent, God washes me clean. It is as if I had never sinned. Therefore, I don't believe, according to God's Word, that God will hold me accountable for anything I have repented of. The same is true for you! That's the Good News!

The Wellspring of Life

So let's talk more about our hearts. Listen to what the *NIV Study Bible* has to say about the verse we saw in Jeremiah. "The heart, 'the wellspring of life,' in which wickedness must _____ be allowed to take _____."[8] The reason? According to God's Word, "If the root is holy, the branches are too" (Romans 11:16, NASB). Therefore it stands to reason, that if the root is _____, then the branches, every part of our lives, will be _____ as well. This is why it is important to guard our hearts just as Proverbs 4:23 warns:

Above all else, _____ your heart, for it is the _____ of life.

You see, when we guard our hearts, and our hearts are holy, this is where love, joy, peace, patience, compassion, mercy, forgiveness, self-control and anything pleasing to God

99

spring from. As Jesus said, "The _____ man brings _____ things out of the _____ stored up in his heart" (Luke 6:45a). Our hearts are the well-spring of our lives.

But when we do not guard our hearts, and our hearts are unholy and filled with sin, this is where anger, resentment, hatred, cruelty, greed, lust, unforgiveness and anything unpleasing to God spring from. As Jesus goes onto say, "And the _____ man brings _____ things out of the evil stored up in his heart. For out of the _____ of his heart his mouth _____" (Luke 6:45b). You see, in God's economy it's either good or it's evil.

In fact, as we learned previously, Satan will use the evil store up in a person's heart to his advantage. He wants to cause you to stumble and fall. He knows that if he can make you choose a life of habitual sin, it will cause you to fall away from the Lord. For this reason, the enemy (or one of his many cohorts) will whisper lies hoping to mess up your _____ life and he will shoot fiery darts to play upon your feelings and _____ hoping that you will step out and sin with your _____.

Perhaps Billy Graham expressed it best when he said, "A thought enters; we pamper it; it germinates and grows into an evil act."[9]

This is why to God our _____ are just as important as our _____, because He knows that what we allow into our thoughts can become a root deep within our hearts, which can trigger our desires and eventually trigger our actions. This is why Jesus taught:

> "You have heard that it was said, 'You shall not commit adultery.' But I say to you that everyone who _____ at a woman with lustful intent has already committed adultery with her in his _____."
>
> —Matthew 5:27-28, ESV

In view of this, we need to learn to take our thoughts captive, moment-by-moment, and make them obedient to Christ. If our thoughts are not made obedient then our thoughts can trigger our desires, and our desires can trigger our actions. So for most of us, the sin began with the _____ thought or the _____ look.

Now let's go back to the story of Adam and Eve for a moment. Remember Genesis 3:6?

> When the woman _____ that the fruit of the tree was good for food and pleasing to the eye, and also desirable for gaining wisdom, she took some and ate it.

The word "saw," as it appears in the original Hebrew, could actually be translated "to gaze at, to look intently at, to observe, to consider, to learn about, and to give attention to."[10] In view of this, we learn that the _____ began with Eve's _____ life. In fact, the tense of the word "saw" in this verse indicates that it relates "not so much as to _____ occasion, [but] as to a _____ condition . . . frequent repetition."[11] In other words, Eve gazed at the fruit and considered eating it for some time.

When she _____ that the fruit was good, it means she took more than a casual glance—she _____ to gaze at it and then considered and _____ about eating it.

Can you picture the event? Imagine what might have happened. It was a beautiful day in the Garden of Eden. Eve was walking about when all of a sudden the serpent appeared and said, "Hey, Eve, come over here. Check this out." (Loosely paraphrased, of course.) I don't think Eve ate the fruit that day, because the tense of the word "saw" indicates she considered it for some time. Rather, I believe the serpent planted that seed by whispering his lies. That seed became a _____ when Eve chose to start _____ about eating the fruit, when she took the second thought. Each time Eve walked passed the tree in the middle of the Garden, she began to gaze at it a little bit more intently. She _____ that it was pleasing to the eye, which played upon her _____. And then she began to justify her future _____ of eating the fruit as a good thing, because it was _____ for gaining wisdom. The sin began way _____ her actions matched her thoughts.

Do you see how Eve's thoughts triggered her desires—her desires of gaining wisdom? And her desires triggered her actions. The same is true for us: sin begins with the _____ thought or the _____ look. You see the first thought, many times, can actually be just a fiery dart sent by one of Satan's cohorts and the first look could actually be very innocent. As an example, imagine a man just walking down the street and *boom* right in front of his face some sort of pornography. A person has no control over these types of situations. But the second thought or the second look is a _____. The sin takes root when we begin to _____ at something intently or _____ doing wrong. Sin begins to grow in our hearts and in our minds well before any action has taken place. If we don't stop our _____, this can be the beginning of the vicious downward spiral of sin, sin and more sin. So be warned. Be careful about not only what you look at but also what you think about.

Here's an example of how easily our thoughts can get out of control. Let's look at this from a woman's point of view for a moment. Say you stop at the gas station to fill your tank and as you are walking into the station to pay, a nice looking guy walks by. You say "hi" in passing. He replies, "Hi!" and sort of flirts with you. You think, *Wow, he thinks I am cute.* Then you take a second look to see if he is still checking you out. That is the moment where sin comes in. The moment you allow the thought to play on your emotions and your desires, it triggers the action of the second look.

At this point you may be thinking, *Come on, that's not that big of a deal.* However, it is important to recognize that you have a choice when you are in a situation like that—a _____ choice or a _____ choice. The flesh choice is to start thinking about it and dwelling on it, and then possibly taking the second look. While it might seem innocent—*just* a little flirt—and that no harm can come of it, it is still _____. The faith choice is to decide _____ to even allow your thoughts to go there so you don't take the second look and commit a sin. You can pick up your shield of faith to deflect the fiery darts and keep on walking.

Remember that God's Word says to be prepared to "take up the shield of faith, with which you can extinguish all the flaming arrows of the evil one" (Ephesians 6:16). As you choose not to allow your thoughts to run amuck, you are using the shield of faith in the manner God intended. Of course, making this faith choice is not as much fun at that moment, but it is the choice from which you will reap the _____—the blessings of a content marriage, children who are walking with the Lord, and friends who consider you a person of virtue. As for you single ones who may be arguing, *But he could be my future husband,* don't worry. If he is truly the one, God will work it out. Remember, you are the daughter of the King of kings. Your heavenly Father knows exactly whom He has picked for you if you are to marry, so _____ and _____ Him.

Unfortunately, all too often we tend to fall into this trap. We allow our thoughts to run wild, and soon our thoughts trigger our desires—the desire (for those who are single) to be married, the desire (for those who are married) to have a spouse who is caring and kind, the desire (for all of us) to simple be loved for who we are. Those desires, in turn, trigger an action—just a look, just a little flirt. We try to deceive ourselves into believing that flirting is innocent (especially if we are already married).

> Beloved, do not think it strange concerning the fiery trial which is to try you, as though some strange thing happened to you.
>
> —1 Peter 4:12, NKJV

Many married women I disciple deeply desire for their husband to be the spiritual leader in their house. One woman I knew desired this so strongly that the enemy was able to use it to get a foothold in her life. Every day she thought that if only her husband were the spiritual leader in their home, they would be so much happier.

Soon, in all innocence (or so she thought), she began to communicate with a man via the Internet. The things he wrote to her triggered her emotions of having someone interested in her—a new love and a new romance. Then the emotions triggered her desires—the desire of wanting her husband to be the spiritual leader. Before long, she began to compare her husband to the romantic knight in shining armor who was sending her emails—a figure of her imagination with whom her husband could not compare. The woman began to think that her husband would *never* be the spiritual leader in their house, and this desire began to trigger an action—the action of building a friendship with the other man over the Internet, and then setting up a meeting.

Nothing had happened (she justified to herself deep within her heart) except that now she was considering leaving her husband for this man. Notice that the sin did not begin when she went so far as to arrange a meeting. The sin began with the second thought—the thought that perhaps this man would care for her and fulfill the desires of her heart. The sin began in her mind when she allowed the enemy's fiery darts to take root and grow into thoughts of romance and love.

My friend shared with me that this man was a believer and that she just knew in her heart that he would be the spiritual leader she so desired. I told her that this individual could never be the spiritual leader she was seeking. "But you don't know him," she said. "How can you say that?" I replied, "Because if he were, he would have fled from you and left his coat in your hands." (Read the story of Joseph and Potiphar's wife in Genesis 39.) Praise the Lord! My friend broke off the relationship and stayed with her husband.

How many of us began relationships that _____ innocent but quickly went way too far and got out of control? My friend was ready to give up her family and her life for romantic thoughts. This is where the enemy so deceives us. Romantic thoughts never come true when they are outside of God's will. All they will ever be are thoughts—thoughts of _____. Yes, there is pleasure in sin for a short season,[12] but what then? Visitation rights to see your children every other weekend? Remarriage and then, after a couple of years, the same problems you had in your first marriage? A blended family with kids all struggling to fit in? For those of you who are single, this pattern—date one person, dump that person, date another person, dump that person—is a total setup for marriage and divorce, marriage and divorce. Sounds romantic, doesn't it? Were these real-life problems included in your thoughts of love and romance?

Have you ever looked up the definition of "romance"? According to the *Webster's Ninth New Collegiate Dictionary*, it is "a medieval _____ based on _____; a prose narrative treating _____ characters involved in events remote in time or place; something, as an extravagant story or account, that _____ basis in _____."[13] How about the definition of "romantic"? It means "consisting of or resembling a romance; having no basis in fact: imaginary; impractical in conception or plan."[14] It seems as if the enemy has twisted words once again. I know I was surprised at these definitions, and it gets even more interesting if you look up the words "romance" and "romantic" in a thesaurus. Some of the more interesting synonyms suggested in the *Roget's 21st Century Thesaurus* include "_____," "_____," "_____," "crazy," "dreamer" and "_____."[15] I challenge you to look at a thesaurus and check it out yourself.

Our thoughts truly can trigger our desires and our desires can trigger our actions. So let's learn how to take our thoughts captive and make them obedient to Christ so that we can walk in victory.

Create in Me a Clean Heart

King David after he was broken over his sin of adultery wrote:

> Create in me a clean heart, O God, And renew a steadfast spirit within me.
>
> —Psalm 51:10, NKJV

We too can ask God to _____ our hearts from the _____ we have committed through our thought life or even through our actions. Yet not only that, we can join with King David and ask God to give us the power to remain _____ and _____ in everything, including our thoughts. Do not dwell on thoughts that are not pleasing to God. If you struggle in this area, find ways to _____ your mind. Listen to worship music, read God's Word and focus on things that are pleasing to Him. Find ways to nurture good thoughts and get rid of everything that pollutes the mind. This may even mean that you need to clean some things out of your house. Get rid of anything that can trigger impure thoughts. In comparison to the downward path to destruction, let's look at the upward path to life more abundantly.

The Upward Path—Thoughts ➔ Desires ➔ Actions

1. Thoughts—God knows all our thoughts (as seen in Matthew 9:4; 12:25; Luke 11:17). Are all your thoughts pleasing to God? If not, memorize the following verses for encouragement and strength.

> Therefore, holy brothers, who share in the heavenly calling, fix your _____ on Jesus.
>
> —Hebrew 3:1

> Finally, brothers, whatever is true, whatever is noble, whatever is right, whatever is pure, whatever is lovely, whatever is admirable—if anything is excellent or praiseworthy—_____ about such things.
>
> —Philippians 4:8

When you begin to dwell upon thoughts that are wrong, _____ your thinking and dwell upon thoughts that are pure or upon these verses.

2. Desires—We must realize, as the *NIV Study Bible* warns that "to break God's commandments _____ is equivalent to breaking them _____ (as seen in Matthew 5:21-30.)"[16] If we keep God's Word in the right perspective in our lives then we will not allow our desires to be against His will. Inwardly, we will desire to follow His will. Our hearts will be in line with Psalm 40:8:

> I _____ to do your will, O my God; your law is within my heart.

3. Actions—Perhaps Romans 12:2 says it best:

> Don't copy the behavior and customs of this world, but let God transform you into a new person by _____ the way you _____. Then you will learn to know God's will for you, which is good and pleasing and perfect.
>
> —NLT

As you change your thinking, you allow God to transform you into the person He created you to be. Your actions will match what is taking place deep within your heart. As Proverbs 20:11 states:

> Even a child is known by his _____, by whether his conduct is pure and right.

It is as simple as that—guard your heart for it truly does affect everything you do—it affects you, it affects your family, it affects your loved ones and it affects your co-workers. In fact, it affects everyone you come into contact with. As you guard your heart you will *go in peace.*

Assignment

FOR WEEKEND WORKSHOP:

Take a short break and then move onto the next session.

FOR WEEKLY BIBLE STUDY:

Read chapter twelve titled "The Temple of the Holy Spirit" in the book *Go in Peace!* Although portions of the chapter are the same, there is another interesting true story of a woman who allowed her thought life to get way out of control that was not included here. In fact, so out of control that it ended her marriage. My prayer is that her story will encourage you to take control of your thought life so that you can become all that God created you to be. Plus there are some practical ways listed, which weren't included in this Bible study to help you be victorious in this area of your life. After reading the chapter spend some quiet time with the Lord and as you do complete the following exercises.

1. Which verse spoke the most deeply to you in this session? Write it down here.

    _____

    _____

    _____

2. If you have a couple of different versions of the Bible look up Proverbs 4:23 in each and pick your favorite translation. Now, write Proverbs 4:23 here and on a 3x5 card to keep with you. Take time throughout the day to memorize it.

    _____

    _____

    _____

3. Have you been guarding your heart? If so, in what way have you been the most successful? If not, what can you do to better guard your heart?

    _____

    _____

    _____

4. Take some time to close in prayer. Share with God the areas you need to improve on. Remember, He knows everything—nothing is hidden from Him. He just wants you to be honest with yourself. Ask Him to help strengthen you.

_____

_____

_____

BREPHOS

As soon as the sound of your greeting reached my ears,
the baby [brephos] in my womb leaped for joy.
LUKE 1:44

Controversial Debate

When I first began discipling with the *Go in Peace! Biblical Discipleship Curriculum*, if I was discipling someone who had never had an abortion I would think that I should just skip this session. But every time God always impressed upon my heart that all of us, even those whose lives have not been impacted by abortion, need to know the truth that is found within this session. Since abortion is such a prevalent issue in our society there may be a time when someone you know will be considering an abortion. For this reason, we will not skip it because it has the potential to save lives.

As I mentioned in a previous chapter, many who have chosen abortion (even those who follow Christ) believe that abortion is acceptable. One of the main reasons they believe this is because to believe otherwise hurts too much. For many years I also needed to believe that lie, for to believe otherwise was just too painful to bear.

However, for the person whose life has been impacted by abortion, if you wish to lay all of your burdens concerning abortion at the feet of Jesus, then you must look at abortion as God sees it. Remember, the Wonderful Counselor, also known as the Prince of Peace, is always by your side. God, in His infinite wisdom, knew that we would have this controversial debate over this important question and that human life would depend on His answer. So, if you want to know the truth, open your heart and join with me as we take a look at the beautiful story of Jesus before His birth. This story is so awesome that it answers the age-old question, "Does life begin at birth or at conception?"

> In the sixth month, God sent the angel Gabriel to Nazareth, a town in Galilee, to a virgin pledged to be married to a man named Joseph, a descendant of David. The virgin's name was Mary. The angel went to her and said, "Greetings, you who are highly favored! The Lord is with you."
>
> Mary was greatly troubled at his words and wondered what kind of greeting this might be. But the angel said to her, "Do not be afraid, Mary, you have found favor with God. You will be with child and give birth to a son, and you are to give him the name Jesus. He will be great and will be

called the Son of the Most High. The Lord God will give him the throne of his father David, and he will reign over the house of Jacob forever; his kingdom will never end."

"How will this be," Mary asked the angel, "since I am a virgin?"

The angel answered, "The Holy Spirit will come upon you, and the power of the Most High will overshadow you. So the holy one to be born will be called the Son of God. Even Elizabeth your relative is going to have a child in her old age, and she who was said to be barren is in her sixth month. For nothing is impossible with God."

"I am the Lord's servant," Mary answered. "May it be to me as you have said." Then the angel left her.

At that time Mary got ready and hurried to a town in the hill country of Judea, where she entered Zechariah's home and greeted Elizabeth. When Elizabeth heard Mary's greeting, the baby leaped in her womb, and Elizabeth was filled with the Holy Spirit. In a loud voice she exclaimed: "Blessed are you among women, and blessed is the child you will bear! But why am I so favored, that the mother of my Lord should come to me? As soon as the sound of your greeting reached my ears, the baby in my womb leaped for joy. Blessed is she who has believed that what the Lord has said to her will be accomplished!" . . . Mary stayed with Elizabeth for about three months and then returned home.

—Luke 1:26-45,56

I would like to share with you some key points from these verses—points that I pray will confirm to you the truth of God's Word about the sanctity of life from the moment of conception. First, note that the angel told Mary that Elizabeth, her cousin, was going to bear a child and that she was six months pregnant at the time. The child to be born to Elizabeth was John the Baptist, and the child to be born to Mary, of course, was Jesus.

Notice that the passage says, "At that time Mary got ready and hurried to a town in the hill country of Judea" (Luke 1:39). As soon as this miraculous event occurred, Mary got ready and hurried to where Elizabeth lived. Upon hearing Mary's greeting, John the Baptist leaped for joy in Elizabeth's womb. He recognized and honored the life of Jesus in the womb.

At that same moment, Elizabeth was filled with the Holy Spirit and exclaimed to Mary, "Blessed are you among women, and blessed is the child you will bear!" (Luke 1:42). She went on to say, "But why am I so favored, that the mother of my Lord should come to me?" (verse 43). She, too, recognized that Jesus, her Lord, was present.

It is important to remember that Jesus had just been conceived. Judea was about 60 miles away, as the crow flies, from where the angel appeared to Mary. In biblical times, this journey would have taken Mary one to two weeks to travel. Therefore, we can safely say that Mary arrived at Elizabeth's house during the first month of her pregnancy. Mary stayed with Elizabeth for about three months, and then returned home. If Elizabeth was six months along when Mary arrived, then Mary stayed long enough (three months) to see the birth of Elizabeth's child. This, then, is another confirmation of Jesus just being conceived when John the Baptist and Elizabeth recognized and honored Him.

There is one more beautiful illustration that I would like to note. Sharon Pearce writes, "When writing this Gospel, Luke used a single word to describe children, born and unborn."[1] The Greek word he used is brephos. As the following verses illuminate:

> When Elizabeth heard Mary's greeting, the baby [*brephos*] leaped in her womb. . . . In a loud voice she [Elizabeth] exclaimed . . . "As soon as the sound of your greeting reached my ears, the baby [*brephos*] in my womb leaped for joy."
>
> —Luke 1:41-42,44

Luke, who was a doctor, used this same word to describe Jesus after His birth:

> This will be a sign to you: You will find a baby [*brephos*] wrapped in cloths, lying in a manger. . . . So they hurried off and found Mary and Joseph, and the baby [*brephos*], who was lying in the manger.
>
> —Luke 2:12,16

Luke, inspired by God, also used this word to describe other children:

> People were also bringing babies [*brephos*] to Jesus to have him touch them.
>
> —Luke 18:15

Now, I would be remiss in my teaching if I didn't include the words penned in Psalm 139:13-16, which represent some of the most beautiful verses about life before birth in the Bible. King David was truly inspired when he wrote:

> For you created my inmost being; you knit me together in my mother's womb. I praise you because I am fearfully and wonderfully made. Your works are wonderful, I know that full well. My frame was not hidden from you when I was made in the secret place. When I was woven together in the depths of the earth, your eyes saw my unformed body. All the days ordained for me were written in your book before one of them came to be.

Knit Together

In view of this wonderful truth found in God's Word, let's take a look at how God knit us together in our mother's womb.

1. The Moment of _____—From this moment the new life inherits 23 chromosomes from each parent, for a total of 46 in all. This single cell contains the blueprint for every facet of that baby's development—its sex, hair color, eye color, height and

skin tone.[2] From the moment of conception, the knowledge stored in the files of an individual's genetic hard disk is _____ times _____ than the data contained in an entire set of the _Encyclopedia Britannica_.[3] Amazing!

This cell begins to divide at a tremendous rate. One cell becomes two, then the two become four, and then four become eight. At some point, early during this stage of growth, the cells begin to specialize. Some cells begin to form the respiratory system, some the skeletal system, others the nervous system, and on and on. To this day, medical science _____ explain _____ the cells know to begin to differentiate, but there is Someone who does:

> As you do not know the path of the wind, or how the body is formed in a mother's womb, so you cannot understand the work of God, the Maker of all things.
>
> —Ecclesiastes 11:5

2. _____ to _____ Week—The baby develops at an astronomical rate. In the third to fourth week, the baby's heart begins to _____, pumping its _____ blood, not the mother's. This circulation of blood means that the cardiovascular system is the first organ system to reach a functional stage.[4] Eyes, ears, arms and legs have just begun to show, and the foundation for the baby's brain, spinal cord and nervous system are also in place.[5]

3. _____ Week—During the sixth week, the baby's brain begins to function and control movements of the muscles and organs. In fact, brain waves can be _____ and _____.[6] The mother is about to miss her _____ period and has probably _____ she is pregnant.

4. _____ Week—At seven weeks, the baby also acquires the ability to rotate its head and will frequently touch its hand to its face at the same time.[7] Seven-week embryos have been photographed _____ their _____.[8] Isn't that so cute!

5. _____ Week—At eight weeks, the medical term for the baby changes to "_____," which is the Latin word for "young one" or "offspring." At this point, _____ of the organs that are found in a fully developed adult are _____. The fetus' heart has been _____ for more than a month, its stomach is producing digestive juices, and its body even responds to _____, although the mother will not feel movement until the fourth or fifth month.[9] The fetus' diaphragm is fully completed by eight weeks' gestation (_____ have even been observed at this early stage).[10] If you were to view a video of fetal development, you would be able to see that the baby's fingers and toes are fully _____ by this point.

In the brochure *What They Never Told You About the Facts of Life*, Dr. Paul Rockwell describes an event that took place when he was presented with a fetus at approximately this stage of development: "While giving an anesthetic [medicine] for a ruptured ectopic [tubal] pregnancy . . . I was handed what I believe was the smallest human ever seen. . . . This tiny human was perfectly developed, with long, tapering fingers, feet and toes. . . . The baby was extremely alive and swam about the sac approximately one time per second, with a natural swimmer's stroke."[11]

6. _____ Month—During the third month of development, the fetus' _____ become evident,[12] and its _____ also begin to develop.[13] If the mother goes to the doctor, she can now _____ the baby's _____. The fetus now sleeps, awakens and exercises its muscles. It can turn its head, curl its toes, open and close its mouth and make a tight fist with its hand. The fetus breathes amniotic fluid to help develop its respiratory system.[14]

7. _____ Month—By the end of the fourth month, the fetus is now 8 to 10 inches in length and weighs half a pound or more. This is the point at which the mother begins to "_____." The fetus' ears are functioning, and the available evidence suggests that it can even hear the mother's voice and heartbeat as well as other external noises.[15] The mother may be able to _____ the baby _____ at this stage.

8. _____ Month—From the fifth month on, the infant continues to grow and store fat—just growing and waiting for its time to be born. Each stage of development is a part of the _____ of _____—a story that begins at _____ and continues until _____. As the brochure *What They Never Told You About the Facts of Life* goes onto say, "Birth isn't the beginning of . . . life—it's just one _____ in a continuing story. In fact, the baby will continue to develop, just like [it] did in the womb, until [it] reaches the ancient age of approximately twenty-three years!"[16]

Fine Sounding Arguments

Dear beloved, if abortion is an issue in your life, you may be saying to yourself right now, *All of this is fine for her, but she has no idea of the situation I was in at the time. There was no way I could have kept my child.* Believe me, I do know. I had all the same arguments and reasons why I could not have a child at 16. But as I look back, I can see that it would have worked out. God would have provided somehow, either financially for me to raise the child or through providing loving parents who desired adoption. That fact—of being able to look back and see that everything would have worked out—was part of my pain. Why did I do it?

Do you know that there were two inspirational men in the Bible who at one time wished they had never been born? One of these men was the prophet Jeremiah. He states that he wished his mother's womb would have been his tomb:

For you did not kill me in the womb, with my mother as my grave, her womb enlarged forever.

—Jeremiah 20:17

The other man, Job, said the following during an extremely difficult time in his life:

May the day of my birth perish, and the night it was said, "A boy is born!" That day—may it turn to darkness. . . . For it did not shut the doors of the womb on me to hide trouble from my eyes. Why did I not perish at birth, and die as I came from the womb? Why were there knees to receive me and breasts that I might be nursed? For now I would be lying down in peace; I would be asleep and at rest.

Job 3:3-4a,10-13

Imagine if these two men had died in their mother's womb. We wouldn't have the book of Job or the book of Jeremiah (and possibly not even the book of Lamentations, as many attribute that book to Jeremiah as well). Imagine how many lives these two men have touched! God had plans for Jeremiah and Job, just as He has plans for every baby in the womb. It is not God's will to put these children to death. We must remember that nothing is impossible with God!

In Acts 7:18-19, Luke quotes the following from Stephen's speech to the Sanhedrin:

Then another king, who knew nothing about Joseph, became ruler of Egypt. He dealt treacherously with our people and oppressed our forefathers by forcing them to throw out their newborn babies [*brephos*] so that they would die.

Let us no longer throw out our babies in the womb. Many people believe that during the first three months of pregnancy the baby is not truly a life. But, as God's Word and the medical evidence shows, this is not the truth. It is time to let go of our fine sounding arguments, and instead, let us honor life—both born and pre-born—as God honors life.

For those of you who have chosen this abomination and today have realized the error of your ways, please know that our God is a God of mercy and compassion—a God of love and forgiveness. Today, give over the sin of abortion to Him, the God of all creation. Let Him cleanse you from all unrighteousness.

Deep down, every woman knows that abortion is wrong. We were created to love and nurture our children. To have an abortion requires us to go against the way we were created and shut down our God-given maternal instincts. And for every man, you were created to protect your family. For many of us, we have been shutting down those instincts for years. It is time to stop.

The first important step that you must take in regard to your healing is to admit that abortion is wrong. No more excuses. Of course, to admit that abortion is wrong means that you must admit that what you did was wrong. Yes, what *you did* was wrong! This may be difficult and painful to admit, especially if you are able to remember at what stage of development your baby was when it was aborted. As you can see from the scientific evidence, it was not *just* a product of conception or a fetal tissue mass—it was a baby, your baby—your *brephos*.

In view of this truth, let me encourage you to kneel at Jesus' feet just like the Sinful Woman did. As you do, admit the truth to Him, He already knows it. And more importantly, take responsibility for your actions. As you do this, and as you kneel at His feet, listen to His still small voice as He whispers to your heart:

Your sins are forgiven. . . . Your faith has saved you; *go in peace.*

—Luke 7:48,50, emphasis added

Assignment

FOR WEEKEND WORKSHOP:

Take a short break and then move onto the next session.

FOR WEEKLY BIBLE STUDY:

Read chapter thirteen titled "Brephos" in the book *Go in Peace!* Don't miss reading this chapter. Although, in this case this chapter is the same, when we read the curriculum together we read it so fast, therefore, as you read it, take the time to ponder the truth. After reading the chapter spend some time with the Lord and as you do complete the following exercises.

1. What was the most interesting aspect of this session?

   _____

   _____

   _____

2. Which Scripture passage spoke the deepest to you heart? And why?

   _____

   _____

   _____

3. Has the issue of abortion impacted your life in some way? And if so, how?

   _____

   _____

   _____

4. Has this chapter spoke to your heart, is there anything you need to repent of? If so, do so now.

   _____

   _____

   _____

5. Write Luke 7 verses 48 and 50 here.

_____

_____

_____

6. Are you ready to go in peace?

_____

_____

_____

WEEPING MAY LAST FOR THE NIGHT

Weeping may last for the night,
But a shout of joy comes in the morning.
PSALM 30:5b, NASB

A Time to Mourn

Note to Leader: Read Ecclesiastes 3:1-8 out loud before beginning.

In the book of Ecclesiastes, we learn not only that "God has made everything beautiful for its own time (Ecclesiastes 3:11a, NLT), but also that there is a time for everything: "A time to weep, and a time to laugh; a time to mourn, and a time to dance" (Ecclesiastes 3:4, NKJV). Yet, most of us desire that our lives fall only under the categories of laughing and dancing. We shy away from any situation that may cause us to weep or to mourn. Yet grief is a normal part of life, which comes as a result of many different situations. Of course, a normal grief issue is the death of a loved one. But we can also grieve other situations in our lives—divorce, loss of our childhood innocence due to abuse, seeing our dreams shattered, watching those we love make wrong choices, and even issues that are self-inflicted, such as abortion.

We saw this in the Sinful Woman's life. As she knelt weeping at Jesus' feet she was not only broken over the choices she had made in her life, but she was grieving from the depths of her soul as well. Yet it was Jesus who gave her rest and healed her broken heart, just as God's Word gives us both hope and comfort when we run to Him.

You see, dear beloved, grief, like the other issues we have covered in this book—hurt, anger, bitterness and unforgiveness—can also keep us from becoming all that God created us to be.

Therefore, as believers, we need to model our lives after Christ. The prophet Isaiah wrote that Jesus was "a man of sorrows and acquainted with grief" (Isaiah 53:3, NKJV). According to Charles Spurgeon's description of Jesus, "He carried out to the full that. . . . precept, 'weep with those who weep' (Romans 12:15b, NKJV)."[1] We see evidence of this when we read the story of how Mary and Martha mourned the loss of their brother, Lazarus. Scripture tells us that when Jesus saw Mary weeping, "He was deeply moved in spirit and troubled" (John 11:33). In fact, Scripture goes on to tell us that "Jesus wept" (John 11:35).

Jesus came to set us free, and many times freedom is found through tears. In Luke 4:18, Jesus said:

"The Spirit of the Lord is upon me, because he has anointed me to proclaim good news to the poor. He has sent me to proclaim liberty to the captives and recovering of sight to the blind, to set at liberty those who are oppressed.

—ESV

Many of us who have not allowed ourselves to grieve properly are prisoners who have become oppressed by not allowing ourselves the freedom to express our emotions. For years we have kept our emotions under lock and key, so afraid that if we allowed ourselves a moment of grief, we would lose control and never be able to stop crying. Please know, beloved, that it is only by allowing ourselves to grieve that we will unshackle the chains that hold us fast. This is a safe place. The Wonderful Counselor, also known as the Comforter, is here with you now. Jesus promised:

And I will ask the Father, and he will give you another Counselor, who will never leave you. He is the Holy Spirit, who leads into all truth.

—John 14:16-17a, NLT

Jesus was explaining to His disciples that when He would no longer be able to be with them physically, the Holy Spirit would be there for them at all times. Just as He was with them, He is here with you now, teaching you this truth concerning grief. Let's learn.

Grief Poorly Managed

In *Comforting the Bereaved*, Wiersbe and Wiersbe (yes, father and son) write, "Just as it takes time for a broken bone to heal, so it takes time for a broken heart to heal; and the pain can be just as great or greater. . . . Doctors tell us that there is a definite relationship between illness and a grief badly managed. When the emotions do not heal properly, they affect the body and make the grieving person much more susceptible to certain illnesses. . . . Loneliness and depression that are not handled in a mature way will certainly cause long-term problems that may not respond to medicine. Time by itself does not heal a broken heart. It all depends on what people do with time."[2]

In view of this truth, let's take a look at both the physical infirmities and the spiritual infirmities as a result of a grief poorly managed.

1. Physical Infirmities: First, let's look at how the psalmist described his grief.

    My sight is blurred because of my tears. My body and soul are withering away. I am dying from grief; my years are shortened by sadness. Misery has drained my strength; I am wasting away from within.

    —Psalm 31:9b-10, NLT

    God wants us to handle our grief in the manner He intended because grief does _____ us. Depression and anxiety are just two of the _____ infirmities we can have as a result of not managing our grief properly.

2. Spiritual Infirmities: Second, grief poorly managed can also cause us to feel _____ from God, especially if we are _____ with God. Listen to these words from Lamentations 3:1-3,8:

> I am the man who has seen affliction by the rod of his wrath. He has
> driven me away and made me walk in darkness rather than light; indeed,
> he has turned his hand against me again and again, all day long. . . . Even
> when I call out or cry for help, he shuts out my prayer.

In these verses we see how Jeremiah felt separated from God during his time of grief. If we focus on our grief and not on the hope that Jeremiah wrote in the verses that followed these, we can understand why the person _____ praying and reading God's Word. They _____ going to church, and the person may even make choices _____ to God's Word just out of _____.

Stages of Grief

Anytime there is a grief issue in life, you will go through stages of grief. To understand these different stages, we are going to take a look at some of the eloquent verses concerning grief contained in the book of Lamentations. This book of mourning portrays the events of the destruction of the city of Jerusalem and the Temple in 586 BC. This poetic book of the Bible, as the *NIV Study Bible* points out, "poignantly shares the overwhelming sense of loss that accompanied the destruction of the city, temple and ritual as well as the exile of Judah's inhabitants."[3]

According to the *Illustrated Encyclopedia of Bible Facts*, "The Jewish name of this book literally means 'Ah, how!'"[4] The name can also mean, "How?"[5] Our English word "lament" means "to mourn aloud, wail, to express sorrow or mourning, [and] to regret _____."[6] Yes, beloved, it is acceptable to strongly regret the decisions we made in the past. That is part of grieving.

It is believed that Jeremiah was the author of this book. As Wiersbe and Wiersebe state, "The fact that Jeremiah expressed these deep emotions in an inspired book of the Bible would indicate that God expects us to grieve, and that He accepts our expressions of grief."[7] So, using this information as a backdrop, let us compare this book of grief to the normal stages of grief seen as a result of death.

1. Shock: The first stage of grief is _____. Listen to how Jeremiah first described the destruction of Jerusalem in Lamentations 1:1:

> *How* deserted lies the city, once so full of people! *How* like a widow is she
> (emphasis added).

When we compare our grief to a normal grief situation, such as the death of a loved one, we see that asking "how" and "why" is a typical response. The *NIV Study Bible* explains that "how! expresses a mixture of _____ and _____."[8] Wiersbe describes it like this: "There is an emotional numbness when we hear a loved one has died. This is a normal response triggered by the nervous system of the body. It is God's way of anesthetizing the person so that he or she might be able to face the reality of death and handle the difficulties to come. Of course, if this stage lasts too long, it is _____ and will _____ problems."[9]

In the case of abortion: Emotional numbness is a response that allows the woman to get through the first few days and weeks after the abortion. However, many post-abortive women stay stuck there, too afraid to move on to the next stage of grief.

In the case of abuse: Emotional numbness, many times, can be used by the enemy to keep a person in an abusive relationship. The enemy can especially use this response to his advantage the first few times the abuse takes place. The victim is so shock by what happened that they don't take action to end the relationship.

2. Strong Emotions: This next stage is strong emotions. Listen to how Jeremiah describes it:

Bitterly she weeps at night, tears are upon her cheeks.

—Lamentations 1:2

He goes on to describe his own reaction of grieving. Listen to what he writes:

My eyes fail from weeping, I am in torment within, my heart is poured out on the ground.

—Lamentations 2:11a

Perhaps Weirsbe described it best when he wrote, "God made us to _____, and _____ are always in order when there is a _____ heart. The foolish counsel 'Now, don't cry!' is based on both bad psychology and bad theology. Jesus wept, and so did the saints of God named in the Scriptures (Genesis 23:2; 50:1; 2 Samuel 18:33; Acts 8:2). *We are not told that it is wrong to sorrow. We are told that our sorrow should not be hopeless*, like the sorrow of the world (1 Thessalonians 4:13-18)."[10]

Many times we see this counsel given to those who are mourning deeply. This usually happens because most people do not know what to _____ to a grieving person. Just one month after the terrible tragedy of September 11th, I had the opportunity to minister in New York City. At that time the Mayor of New York City was telling the people to get on with their lives, but in reality what they needed to do was to grieve. Most were still in this phase of strong emotions. For those who could not face Ground Zero, Union Square Park became their place to grieve. Daily, people from around the world came to light candles and to place letters, artwork and/or flowers. But under the Mayor's order of getting on with life as normal, park officials came twice daily to pick up and throw away all items of grief. I saw that this only caused more hurt and confusion among the people. This counsel of getting on with life was also the foolish counsel, "Now, don't cry." It causes us to stuff our tears deep within, which only causes more problems later.

In the case of abortion: We see this _____ counsel of "Now, don't cry" at work whenever someone tells a woman who has had an abortion that the problem has been solved and she should "get on with her life."

In the case of abuse: Many times, as the strong emotions erupt for the abuse victim, we see this _____ and _____ counsel of "Don't cry" given by the abuser in statements such as, "Don't cry, it really wasn't that big of a deal." Or, "Don't cry, I'll never do it again. I'm sorry." Yet this can cause the victim to stuff his or her emotions deep within, which will only cause more problems later since the problem as not been dealt with and the heartache as not been grieved.

3. Depression: The stage of grief that follows strong emotions is _____. Listen to what Jeremiah writes on this subject:

> This is why I weep and my eyes overflow with tears. No one is near to comfort me, no one to restore my spirit.
>
> —Lamentations 1:16a

> He has besieged me and surrounded me with bitterness and hardship. . . . He has walled me in so I cannot escape; he has weighed me down with chains. Even when I call out or cry for help, he shuts out my prayer. . . He pierced my heart with arrows from his quiver. . . . and my soul is downcast within me.
>
> —Lamentations 3:5-20

According to Weirsbe, "Sometimes there are even symptoms of _____ problems. If the grief is not fully worked out, it could lead to _____ physical problems."[11] It is true, dear beloved, that we are powerless to change the _____, but we can change the _____! And there is a Friend closer than a brother[12] with whom we can share our deepest hurts.

In the case of abortion: For many, because of the secret of abortion, there is no one with whom they can share why they are depressed. They may have fallen into depression because they cannot change the past and they may feel the need to be punished for what they have done for the rest of their lives.

In the case of abuse: Many abuse victims are ashamed and/or afraid to disclose what is really taking place in their lives. For this reason, they feel _____ and _____ and can fall into depression because their life is not turning out the way they had dreamed and planned.

4. Fear: The next stage of grief is fear. Even Jeremiah states that he felt fear in the midst of his grief:

What I see brings grief to my soul because of all the women of my city. Those who were my enemies without cause hunted me like a bird. They tried to end my life in a pit and threw stones at me; the waters closed over my head, and I thought I was about to be cut off. I called on your name, O LORD, from the depths of the pit. You heard my plea. . . . You came near when I called you, and you said, "Do not fear."

—Lamentations 3:51-57

As Wiersbe goes onto explain, "The bereaved person finds it difficult to _____, to concentrate, and then becomes _____ and _____. Life seems to be falling apart both on the outside and the inside. Sometimes well-meaning people misunderstand what the grief-stricken person is saying or doing, and this only leads to more _____ and disorientation."[13]

In the case of abortion: For the woman who has had an abortion, many of those close to her have no idea what she has been through and therefore do not understand how to help. Again, the woman may be _____ of her reactions if she allows herself to grieve—and, of course, she worries about what others would think.

In the case of abuse: Unfortunately, fear, many times, is the motivating factor of what drives the abuse victim back to the abuser. This is why it is so important for a person who just got out of an abusive relationship to understand that fear is a _____ part of the grief process. If you are in this situation, do not allow the enemy to use this fear against you and cause you to run back to a bad situation. Instead, allow your fear to cause you to run to _____ so that He can heal your broken heart so that you can become all that God created you to be.

5. Guilt: The next stage of grief is _____. Listen to how Jeremiah describes it:

Let him sit alone in silence, for the LORD has laid it on him . . . and let him be filled with disgrace.

—Lamentations 3:28,30b

As Wiersbe writes: "A sorrowing person often has the tendency to blame himself or herself for the death of the loved one. . . . The person blames themselves and feels responsible for the loved one's death and begins to think, "if only this" or "if only that." "This '_____' response is a normal expression of grief: the bereaved person takes all the blame."[14]

In the case of abortion: A woman who is working through the stages of grief over her abortion often feels _____ because she is finally taking _____ for the death of her child. The woman continually plays the scenario over and over in her mind and thinks, *If only I had done things differently.*

In the case of abuse: The person begins to place the blame of the abuse upon themselves. "_____" *I hadn't gone there.* "_____" *I hadn't said or done that.*

6. Anger and Rebellion: Soon, the depression, fear and guilt turn into anger and rebellion. Once again, listen to how Jeremiah describes these same feelings of grief:

> Is any suffering like my suffering that was inflicted on me, that the LORD brought on me in the day of his fierce anger? . . . See, O LORD, how distressed I am! I am in torment within, and in my heart I am disturbed, for I have been most rebellious.
>
> —Lamentations 1:12,20

Wiersbe writes, "Along with blaming himself or herself, the sorrowing person will also blame others. . . . We remember old resentments and negative experiences, and these become a confusing part of our hurt feelings. We can do nothing about the loss of the loved one, and this frustration only creates more _____. Sometimes people show this hostility by blaming God and even saying all kinds of blasphemous things. It is this feeling of _____ and _____ that helps to cause some of the family problems. . . . Death not only creates problems, but it also _____ them."[15]

Delores Kuenning, in her book *Helping People Through Grief*, writes, "It is not uncommon during the grief process to feel anger towards _____. . . . These feelings against God usually add to the problem because we then feel guilty for our anger."[16] Our anger and rebellion _____ us from _____ and enable a bitter root to grow into a bitter poison in our lives. This is why it is so important to learn what Warren Weirsbe writes in *Why Us? When Bad Things Happen to God's People*: "Bitterness only makes suffering _____ and closes the spiritual channels through which God can pour his grace."[17]

Dear beloved, take every thought captive and make it obedient to Christ so that God can pour out His grace in your life. We can do nothing to _____ the past but we can _____ it.

If you have been angry with God take a moment to tell Him; He already knows. Just take a step of obedience and share with Him so that your intimate relationship with Him can be restored. As you do, remember to take a moment and ask God to forgive you for your feelings. He will be faithful to forgive you and restore you.

7. Apathy: The next stage of grief is apathy. "Apathy" means "lack of _____ or _____."[18] We can see this stage of grief in what Jeremiah writes:

> The LORD has done what he planned; he has fulfilled his word, which he decreed long ago.
>
> —Lamentations 2:17a

Weirsbe states, "It seems strange that [anger and] hostility can be replaced by apathy, but this is often the case. 'Nobody understands how I feel. . . . Life is not worth living.' The bereaved person finds it painful to relate to real life and wants to withdraw into his or her own shell and be left alone. Certainly it is _____ for a hurting person to be left alone; but if this withdrawal continues too long, it becomes _____."[19]

8. Adjustment and Acceptance: The _____ stage of grief is adjustment and acceptance. Even Jeremiah described this:

> Because of the LORD's great love we are not consumed, for his compassions never fail. They are new every morning; great is your faithfulness. . . . The LORD is good to those whose hope is in him, to the one who seeks him. . . . For men are not cast off by the LORD forever. Though he brings grief, he will show compassion, so great is his unfailing love.
>
> —Lamentations 3:22-32

Weirsbe describes it this way: "Slowly the person learns to _____ the loss, rearrange his or her life, and comes to grips with reality. This does not mean the total absence of grief, loneliness, or bewilderment; but it does mean that the bereaved person _____ what is happening and is able to _____ with it. . . . There are definite signs when this adjustment is taking place: the bereaved person can openly and easily talk about [the past in the proper place]. . . . The person no longer gives vent to hostility but, instead, seeks for ways to _____ to others when they suffer loss."[20] The person comes to the place where he or she wants to help others and is ready for ministry work.

Grief Properly Managed

Now that we have learned that it is normal and acceptable to grieve, let's explore how we can do so in a healthy manner. One time when I was listening to a radio program, I heard a woman share a story of grief about the tragic death of her son due to an unfortunate accident. The woman stated that though she knew it was important to grieve the loss of her son, it was just as important to God for her to move on with her life. She knew that she couldn't stay stuck in shock or depression for the rest of her life.

So this woman set aside a time each day—literally with a timer—to be alone with the Lord. She would go to her room, close the door and let out all the emotions and feelings associated with her terrible grief. She would share all of her feelings of anger, depression and fear with God and pour out her heart and her tears. Then, after the timer went off, she would get up and go on with her day. Every day she did this, she would deduct one minute from her allotted time to grieve. She used this as a means to get through the normal cycle of grief and still move on with her life so that she could bring glory and honor to God.

There will be times when you will feel depressed or sad. This is normal. When you notice this in your life, take time with the Lord and ask Him to reveal to you the reason for your feelings. When I am feeling blue, I like to find a quiet place and honestly search my heart. I ask God to "search me . . . and know my heart; try me and know my anxious thoughts; and see if there be any hurtful way in me, and lead me in the everlasting way" (Psalm 139:23-24, NASB).

During such times of searching, the Lord might remind you of how an issue associated with abortion or abuse or some other hurtful issue came up recently in a movie or a discussion, and that deep down you are grieving over that matter once again. When this happens, allow yourself to grieve so that you do not become stuck in one part of the normal pattern of grief. It is all right to take time alone and shed a few tears—remember that the problems will develop when you try to stuff everything deep down inside. It is amazing the comfort and release you will feel when you learn to recognize what is really going on and allow yourself time to grieve. As God promises:

> Weeping may last for the night, but a shout of joy comes in the morning.
> —Psalm 30:5b, NASB

Loss of a Child

Many who have had an abortion or lost a baby through miscarriage or stillbirth wonder if their child is in heaven. If you have had these thoughts, it is important to take comfort in knowing the heart of God. He desires that none shall perish.[21] The verses that I find bring the most comfort to me are the ones that describe the death of King David's infant son. Let me give you the background to the story, which is found in 2 Samuel 11–12.

King David had an adulterous affair with Bathsheba, and she became pregnant. David tried to cover his sin of adultery by calling Uriah, Bathsheba's husband, back from war. David thought that if he sent Uriah home for the evening, Uriah would sleep with his wife and later think the child was his own. But Uriah did not go home. He didn't feel that it was right to do so with his men still on the battlefield, so he slept at the entrance to the palace. David, still trying to cover his sin, decided to get Uriah drunk. He figured that this would make Uriah go home for the evening and lie with his wife. But, once again, Uriah did not go home. So King David sent Uriah back to the battlefield. David wrote a letter to the commander of the army and instructed him to put Uriah in the front line, where the fighting was the fiercest. Then the commander was to withdraw, leaving Uriah alone so he would be struck down.

King David was now not only guilty of adultery but also responsible for the death of Uriah—and he did all of this as a means to cover his sin with Bathsheba. After Uriah's death, David married Bathsheba and she bore a son. "But the thing that David had done displeased the LORD" (2 Samuel 11:27, ESV).

Nathan, a prophet of the Lord, was sent to rebuke David for what he had done. Ultimately, King David recognized his guilt and confessed his sin, saying to Nathan, "I have sinned against the LORD" (2 Samuel 12:13, ESV). Nathan explained to David that because his sin had made the enemies of the Lord despise God, his son would die. (We reap what we sow.)

King David's child was ill for seven days. During this time, David fasted and wept and prayed for the child. When the child died, David's servants were afraid to tell him the news. The king had been so distraught while the child was alive that they were concerned he might now do something desperate. David overheard his servants whispering, and he asked if the child was dead. Let's pick up the story:

> And David said to his servants, "Is the child dead?" They said, "He is dead." Then David arose from the earth and washed and anointed himself and changed his clothes. And he went into the house of the LORD and worshiped. He then went to his own house. And when he asked, they set food before him, and he ate. Then his servants said to him, "What is this thing that you have done? You fasted and wept for the child while he was alive; but when the child died, you arose and ate food." He said, "While the child was still alive, I fasted and wept, for I said, 'Who knows whether the LORD will be gracious to me, that the child may live?' But now he is dead. Why should I fast? Can I bring him back again? *I shall go to him, but he will not return to me.*"
>
> —2 Samuel 12:19b-23, ESV, emphasis added

I believe that all children under the age of accountability—whether the parents are saved or not—go to heaven. As we read in Matthew 19:14, Jesus said, "Let the little children come to me, and do not hinder them, for the kingdom of heaven belongs to such as these." These words of Jesus are repeated in three of the four gospels. The only requirement for us to join our children in heaven, as King David stated in 2 Samuel, is for us to have accepted Jesus Christ as our Lord and Savior. Then, at the moment that God takes us home, we will join them there. I am so thankful that we have these beautiful verses in the Bible. God knows there are many grieving parents in this world, and He left us with His comfort in these inspired words.

Let's go back to what we learned about Adam and Eve's sin in the Garden of Eden for a moment. For those of us whose lives have been impacted by abortion, the *covering* of our shame and nakedness (perhaps a pregnancy outside of marriage or the abortion itself), the *blame* (believing others talked us into it), the *hiding* (rationalizing the baby is just a fetal tissue mass) and the *fear* (worry about what others would think if they found out) caused us to depersonalize our children. Our healing cannot continue with this depersonalization. We must realize and admit the baby (*brephos*) was a child. Our child!

Many who embark on this journey to mourn and heal find different ways of comfort. Some who are artistic enjoy drawing or painting a picture of an infant or small children. Others find comfort in writing a poem or a letter to or about their children. (Of course, in saying this I am not suggesting that you are able to talk to the dead. God's Word says this is impossible, as seen in the parable of the rich man and the poor man.[22] But you can write a letter about what you *would* say to your child if you could.) Some have even written songs about a child lost to abortion. Some instinctively know if their child was a boy or a girl, while others desire to know. If you ask, the Lord, in His timing, will reveal to you whether your child was a boy or a girl. Many times, He will even impress upon your heart his or her name.

Many find comfort in tangible ways for healing. One woman, to help her sister heal, purchased two beautiful rose bushes. After completing the *Go in Peace* workshop, she and her sister planted the rose bushes on each side of a memorial plate for the unborn at her church as a way of honoring her lost. I thought it was interesting that the name of the two rose bushes they planted was "peace." What a beautiful memorial to the memory of her children.

There is also a National Memorial for the Unborn in Chattanooga, Tennessee. This memorial is at a facility that, from April of 1975 to May of 1993, was an abortion clinic. God, in His sovereignty, led a small group of believers to pray regularly at this clinic, and when the group discovered that the property was to be sold in bankruptcy court and that the abortionist was planning to buy it, God supernaturally opened the door for the Pro-Life Majority Coalition of Chattanooga to purchase the property. The property was then turned into a memorial for the unborn. As the organization's brochure states, "The National Memorial for the Unborn is dedicated to healing generations of pain associated with the loss of aborted children. On the site where 35,000 babies died, the memory of unborn children is honored."[23]

Now it is time again to spend some quiet time with the Lord. Ask Him to search your heart to see if there is any hurtful way in you. Ask Him if you are grieving a situation in your life that has not been fully dealt with. Ask Him to reveal to you if you are stuck in one part of the normal stages of grief so that you can move onto the adjustment and acceptance stage. Write whatever He impresses upon your heart so that you can *go in peace!*

Assignment

FOR WEEKEND WORKSHOP:

Find a quiet place and complete numbers one through five before moving onto the next session.

FOR WEEKLY BIBLE STUDY:

Read chapter fourteen titled "Weeping May Last for the Night" in the book *Go in Peace!* Although the chapter and the session are similar they are different as well. Plus, do you remember the interesting assignment from the chapter "Do Not Be Deceived" found in the book? (The one in which you made the list of all the things you do when you feel guilty.) Well, in reading chapter fourteen from the book *Go in Peace!* you will be instructed how to complete that assignment. Don't miss it. You will be blessed! After reading the chapter and doing that assignment spend a quiet time with the Lord and as you do complete the following exercises.

1. Which verse(s), within this session, spoke the deepest to your heart? And why?

   _____
   _____
   _____

2. Are you grieving a situation in your life?

   _____
   _____
   _____

3. If so, are you stuck in one stage of grief?

   _____
   _____
   _____

4. What can you do to move onto the adjustment and acceptance stage?

   _____
   _____
   _____

5. Write a letter to God concerning your feelings of grieve. He understands.

   _____
   _____
   _____

YOUR WORTH IN CHRIST

It is because of Him that you are in Christ Jesus,
who has become for us wisdom from God—
that is our righteousness, holiness and redemption.
1 CORINTHIANS 1:30

Someone Special

The Word of God says that from the moment of your salvation you become someone who is very special. To learn more about who you are in Christ we are going to take turns as we read the following list out loud. As we do this, I challenge you to let the truth of who you are in Christ fill your heart. Are you ready?

1. I am loved by God.
2. I am in Christ Jesus.
3. I am complete in Him.
4. I am not a mistake.
5. I am God's workmanship.
6. I am created in the image of God.
7. I am God's beloved.
8. I am saved.
9. I am a citizen of the Kingdom of God.
10. I am a child of God.
11. I am chosen.
12. I am a chosen generation.
13. I am blessed.
14. I am of worth.
15. I am the bride of Christ.
16. I am protected by God.
17. I am forgiven.
18. I am set free.
19. I am victorious.
20. I am more than a conqueror.
21. I am reconciled to God.
22. I am a partaker of His divine nature.

127

23. I am the temple of the Holy Spirit.
24. I am able to stand firm.
25. I am strong in the Lord.
26. I am strong till the end.
27. I am near to Jesus.
28. I am able to sleep without fear.
29. I am promised rest.
30. I am at peace with God.
31. I am justified.
32. I am the righteousness of God.
33. I am a new creation in Christ.
34. I am free from condemnation.
35. I am redeemed.
36. I am redeemed from the curse of the law.
37. I am redeemed from the hand of the enemy.
38. I am washed clean from my sins.
39. I am God's.
40. I am the apple of God's eye.
41. I am dead to sin.
42. I am crucified with Christ.
43. I am sealed with the Holy Spirit.
44. I am the salt of the earth.
45. I am the light of the world.
46. I am called by God.
47. I am an ambassador for Christ.
48. I am always in God's thoughts.

Let's sum up the truth of God's Word concerning who you are in Christ. You are loved by God, created in Christ Jesus, complete in Him. You are not a mistake, for you are His workmanship, created in His image. You are His beloved, saved, and therefore a citizen of the Kingdom of God. For you are His child, chosen by Him. In fact, you are a chosen generation. In view of this truth, you are blessed by Him. You are of worth. You are His bride and forever protected by Him. You are forgiven, set free, victorious and more than a conqueror! You are reconciled to God and are a partaker of His divine nature. You are the temple of the Holy Spirit. Because of this you are able to stand firm, for you are strong in the Lord. In fact, you are strong till the end. You are near to Jesus and you are able to sleep without fear, for you are promised rest. You are at peace with God. You have been justified and you are considered the righteousness of God. You are a new creation in Christ and you are free from condemnation. You are redeemed. In fact, you are redeemed from the curse of the law and redeemed from the hand of the enemy. You are washed clean from your sins. For you are God's. And therefore, know that you are the apple of His eye. You are dead to sin for you have been crucified with Christ and are sealed with the Holy Spirit. You are the salt of the earth and the light of the world. You have been called by God. You are His ambassador. And you must never forget that you are always in His thoughts.

Who You Are in Christ

Because the truth of who you are in Christ is so precious, we are going to take the time to read this truth according to God's Word. Again, we will take turns reading each verse out loud. But this time, place a star or asterisk next to any verse or verses that really touch your heart. Enjoy!

1. I am loved by God:

   > The LORD appeared to him from afar, saying, "I have loved you with an everlasting love; Therefore I have drawn you with lovingkindness."
   >
   > —Jeremiah 31:3, NASB

   > And I am convinced that nothing can ever separate us from God's love. Neither death nor life, neither angels nor demons, neither our fears for today nor our worries about tomorrow—not even the powers of hell can separate us from God's love. No power in the sky above or in the earth below—indeed, nothing in all creation will ever be able to separate us from the love of God that is revealed in Christ Jesus our Lord.
   >
   > —Romans 8:38-39, NLT

   > And I pray that you, being rooted and established in love, may have power, together with all the saints, to grasp how wide and long and high and deep is the love of Christ, and to know this love that surpasses knowledge—that you may be filled to the measure of all the fullness of God.
   >
   > —Ephesians 3:17b-19

   > And so we know and rely on the love God has for us. God is love. Whoever lives in love lives in God, and God in him. In this way, love is made complete among us so that we will have confidence on the day of judgment, because in this world we are like him. There is no fear in love. But perfect love drives out fear, because fear has to do with punishment. The one who fears is not made perfect in love. We love because he first loved us.
   >
   > —1 John 4:16-19

2. I am in Christ Jesus:

   > It is because of him that you are in Christ Jesus, who has become for us wisdom from God—that is, our righteousness, holiness and redemption.
   >
   > —1 Corinthians 1:30

3. I am complete in Him:

> And you are complete in Him, who is the head of all principality and power.
>
> —Colossians 2:10, NKJV

4. I am not a mistake:

> Even if my father and mother abandon me, the LORD will hold me close.
> —Psalm 27:10, NLT

> Your hands made me and formed me; give me understanding to learn your commands.
>
> —Psalm 119:73

> You made all the delicate, inner parts of my body and knit me together in my mother's womb. Thank you for making me so wonderfully complex! Your workmanship is marvelous—and how well I know it. You watched me as I was being formed in utter seclusion, as I was woven together in the dark of the womb. You saw me before I was born. Every day of my life was recorded in your book. Every moment was laid out before a single day had passed.
>
> —Psalm 139:13-16, NLT

5. I am God's workmanship:

> For we are God's workmanship, created in Christ Jesus to do good works, which God prepared in advance for us to do.
>
> —Ephesians 2:10

6. I am created in the image of God:

> Then God said, "Let us make man in our image, after our likeness. And let them have dominion over the fish of the sea and over the birds of the heavens and over the livestock and over all the earth and over every creeping thing that creeps on the earth." So God created man in his own image, in the image of God he created him; male and female he created them.
>
> —Genesis 1:26-27, ESV

7. I am God's beloved:

> Therefore, as the elect of God, holy and beloved, put on tender mercies, kindness, humility, meekness, longsuffering.
>
> —Colossians 3:12, NKJV

But we are bound to give thanks to God always for you, brethren, beloved by the Lord.

—2 Thessalonians 2:13a, NKJV

8. I am saved:

For God did not appoint us to suffer wrath but to receive salvation through our Lord Jesus Christ.

—1 Thessalonians 5:9

He saved us, not because of the righteous things we had done, but because of his mercy. He washed away our sins, giving us a new birth and new life through the Holy Spirit.

—Titus 3:5, NLT

9. I am a citizen of the Kingdom of God:

Consequently, you are no longer foreigners and aliens, but fellow citizens with God's people and members of God's household.

—Ephesians 2:19

10. I am a child of God:

A father to the fatherless, a defender of widows, is God in his holy dwelling.

—Psalm 68:5

Yet to all who received him, to those who believed in his name, he gave the right to become children of God—children born not of natural descent, nor of human decision or a husband's will, but born of God.

—John 1:12-13

Because those who are led by the Spirit of God are sons of God. For you did not receive a spirit that makes you a slave again to fear, but you received the Spirit of sonship. And by him we cry, *"Abba*, Father."

—Romans 8:14-15

Behold what manner of love the Father has bestowed on us, that we should be called children of God!

—1 John 3:1, NKJV

11. I am chosen:

For you are a people holy to the LORD your God. The LORD your God has chosen you out of all the peoples on the face of the earth to be his people,

131

his treasured possession. The LORD did not set his affection on you and choose you because you were more numerous than other peoples, for you were the fewest of all peoples. But it was because the LORD loved you and kept the oath he swore to your forefathers that he brought you out with a mighty hand and redeemed you from the land of slavery, from the power of Pharaoh king of Egypt.

—Deuteronomy 7:6-8

You did not choose me, but I chose you and appointed you to go and bear fruit—fruit that will last. Then the Father will give you whatever you ask in my name.

—John 15:16

For we know, brothers loved by God, that he has chosen you.

—1 Thessalonians 1:4, ESV

For he chose us in him before the creation of the world to be holy and blameless in his sight. In love he predestined us to be adopted as his sons through Jesus Christ, in accordance with his pleasure and will.

—Ephesians 1:4-5

12. I am a chosen generation:

But you are a chosen people, a royal priesthood, a holy nation, a people belonging to God, that you may declare the praises of him who called you out of darkness into his wonderful light.

—1 Peter 2:9

13. I am blessed:

All these blessings will come upon you and accompany you if you obey the LORD your God: You will be blessed in the city and blessed in the country. The fruit of your womb will be blessed, and the crops of your land and the young of your livestock—the calves of your herds and the lambs of your flocks. Your basket and your kneading trough will be blessed. You will be blessed when you come in and blessed when you go out. The LORD will grant that the enemies who rise up against you will be defeated before you. They will come at you from one direction, but flee from you in seven. The LORD will send a blessing on your barns and on everything you put your hand to. The LORD your God will bless you in the land he is giving you. The LORD will establish you as his holy people, as he promised you on oath, if you keep the commands of the LORD your God and walk in his ways. Then all the peoples on earth will see that you are called by the name of the LORD, and they will fear you. The LORD will grant you abundant prosperity—in the fruit of your womb, the young of your livestock and the crops of your ground—in the land he swore to your forefathers to give you. The LORD will open the heavens, the storehouse of his bounty, to send rain on your land in season and to bless all the work of your hands. You will lend to many nations but will borrow from none. The LORD will make you the head, not the tail. If you pay attention to the commands of the LORD your God that I give you this day and carefully follow them, you will always be at the top, never at the bottom. Do not turn aside from any of the commands I give you today, to the right or to the left, following other gods and serving them.

—Deuteronomy 28:2-14

Blessed is the man who does not walk in the counsel of the wicked or stand in the way of sinners or sit in the seat of mockers. But his delight is in the law of the LORD, and on his law he meditates day and night. He is like a tree planted by streams of water, which yields its fruit in season and whose leaf does not wither. Whatever he does prospers.

—Psalm 1:1-3

Blessed is the one you choose and bring near, to dwell in your courts! We shall be satisfied with the goodness of your house, the holiness of your temple!

—Psalm 65:4, ESV

All praise to God, the Father of our Lord Jesus Christ, who has blessed us with every spiritual blessing in the heavenly realms because we are united with Christ.

—Ephesians 1:3, NLT

14. I am of worth:

What is the price of five sparrows—two copper coins? Yet God does not forget a single one of them. And the very hairs on your head are all numbered. So don't be afraid; you are more valuable to God than a whole flock of sparrows.

—Luke 12:6-7, NLT

15. I am the bride of Christ:

And as the bridegroom rejoices over the bride, So your God will rejoice over you.

—Isaiah 62:5b, NASB

Let us rejoice and be glad and give the glory to Him, for the marriage of the Lamb has come and His bride has made herself ready.

—Revelation 19:7, NASB

16. I am protected by God:

No one will be able to stand up against you all the days of your life. As I was with Moses, so I will be with you; I will never leave you nor forsake you. Be strong and courageous, because you will lead these people to inherit the land I swore to their forefathers to give them. Be strong and very courageous. Be careful to obey all the law my servant Moses gave you; do not turn from it to the right or to the left, that you may be successful wherever you go. . . . Be strong and courageous. Do not be terrified; do not be discouraged, for the LORD your God will be with you wherever you go.

—Joshua 1:5-9

When you pass through the waters, I will be with you; And through the rivers, they shall not overflow you. When you walk through the fire, you shall not be burned, Nor shall the flame scorch you.

—Isaiah 43:2, NKJV

17. I am forgiven:

Then David confessed to Nathan, "I have sinned against the LORD." Nathan replied, "Yes, but the LORD has forgiven you, and you won't die for this sin.

—2 Samuel 12:13, NLT

How much more, then, will the blood of Christ, who through the eternal Spirit offered himself unblemished to God, cleanse our consciences from acts that lead to death, so that we may serve the living God!

—Hebrews 9:14

In whom we have redemption through His blood, the forgiveness of sins.

—Colossians 1:14b, NKJV

If we confess our sins, He is faithful and just to forgive us our sins and to cleanse us from all unrighteousness.

—1 John 1:9, NKJV

I write to you, dear children, because your sins have been forgiven on account of his name.

—1 John 2:12

Then Jesus said to her, "Your sins are forgiven. . . . Your faith has saved you; go in peace."

—Luke 7:48,50

18. I am set free:

To the Jews who had believed him, Jesus said, "If you hold to my teaching, you are really my disciples. Then you will know the truth, and the truth will set you free."

—John 8:31-32

I run in the path of your commands, for you have set my heart free.

—Psalm 119:32

You, my brothers, were called to be free. But do not use your freedom to indulge the sinful nature; rather, serve one another in love.

—Galatians 5:13

19. I am victorious:

With God we will gain the victory, and he will trample down our enemies.

—Psalm 60:12

Songs of joy and victory are sung in the camp of the godly. The strong right arm of the LORD has done glorious things!

—Psalm 118:15, NLT

20. I am more than a conqueror:

Yet in all these things we are more than conquerors through Him who loved us.

—Romans 8:37, NKJV

21. I am reconciled to God:

Now all things are of God, who has reconciled us to Himself through Jesus Christ, and has given us the ministry of reconciliation.

—2 Corinthians 5:18, NKJV

22. I am a partaker of His divine nature:

Through these he has given us his very great and precious promises, so that through them you may participate in the divine nature and escape the corruption in the world caused by evil desires.

—2 Peter 1:4

23. I am the temple of the Holy Spirit:

> Do you not know that your body is a temple of the Holy Spirit, who is in you, whom you have received from God? You are not your own; you were bought at a price. Therefore honor God with your body.
>
> —1 Corinthians 6:19-20

24. I am able to stand firm:

> Therefore put on the full armor of God, so that when the day of evil comes, you may be able to stand your ground, and after you have done everything, to stand. Stand firm then, with the belt of truth buckled around your waist. . . .
>
> —Ephesians 6:13-14

25. I am strong in the Lord:

> I love you, O LORD, my strength. The LORD is my rock, my fortress and my deliverer; my God is my rock, in whom I take refuge. He is my shield and the horn of my salvation, my stronghold.
>
> —Psalm 18:1-2

> The LORD is my light and my salvation; Whom shall I fear? The LORD is the strength of my life; Of whom shall I be afraid?
>
> —Psalm 27:1, NKJV

> Finally, my brethren, be strong in the Lord and in the power of His might.
>
> —Ephesians 6:10, NKJV

> He gives power to the weak, And to [those who have] no might He increases strength. Even the youths shall faint and be weary, And the young men shall utterly fall, But those who wait on the LORD shall renew [their] strength; They shall mount up with wings like eagles, They shall run and not be weary, They shall walk and not faint.
>
> —Isaiah 40:29-31, NKJV

26. I am strong till the end:

> He will keep you strong to the end so that you will be free from all blame on the day when our Lord Jesus Christ returns.
>
> —1 Corinthians 1:8, NLT

> Now to him who is able to keep you from stumbling and to present you blameless before the presence of his glory with great joy, to the only God,

our Savior, through Jesus Christ our Lord, be glory, majesty, dominion, and authority, before all time and now and forever. Amen.

—Jude 1:24-25, ESV

27. I am near to Jesus:

Let us draw near to God with a sincere heart in full assurance of faith, having our hearts sprinkled to cleanse us from a guilty conscience and having our bodies washed with pure water.

—Hebrews 10:22

Draw near to God and He will draw near to you.

—James 4:8a, NKJV

But now in Christ Jesus you who once were far off have been brought near by the blood of Christ.

—Ephesians 2:13, NKJV

The Lord is near to all who call on him, to all who call on him in truth.

—Psalm 145:18, ESV

28. I am able to sleep without fear:

I lie down and sleep; I wake again, because the Lord sustains me.

—Psalm 3:5

I will both lie down in peace, and sleep; For You alone, O Lord, make me dwell in safety.

—Psalm 4:8, NKJV

When you lie down, you will not be afraid; Yes, you will lie down and your sleep will be sweet. Do not be afraid of sudden terror, Nor of trouble from the wicked when it comes; For the Lord will be your confidence, And will keep your foot from being caught.

—Proverbs 3:24-26, NKJV

29. I am promised rest:

The Lord replied, "My Presence will go with you, and I will give you rest."

—Exodus 33:14

Come to me, all you who are weary and burdened, and I will give you rest. Take my yoke upon you and learn from me, for I am gentle and humble in heart, and you will find rest for your souls.

—Matthew 11:28-29

There remains therefore a rest for the people of God.

—Hebrews 4:9, NKJV

30. I am at peace with God:

Therefore, since we have been made right in God's sight by faith, we have peace with God because of what Jesus Christ our Lord has done for us.

—Romans 5:1, NLT

The LORD gives strength to his people; the LORD blesses his people with peace.

—Psalm 29:11

I will listen to what God the LORD will say; he promises peace to his people, his saints—but let them not return to folly.

—Psalm 85:8

Great peace have those who love your law; nothing can make them stumble.

—Psalm 119:165, ESV

You will keep in perfect peace him whose mind is steadfast, because he trusts in you.

—Isaiah 26:3

For the mountains may depart and the hills be removed, but my steadfast love shall not depart from you, and my covenant of peace shall not be removed," says the LORD, who has compassion on you.

—Isaiah 54:10, ESV

31. I am justified:

Therefore, having been justified by faith, we have peace with God through our Lord Jesus Christ.

—Romans 5:1, NKJV

And by Him everyone who believes is justified from all things from which you could not be justified by the law of Moses.

—Acts 13:39, NKJV

Being justified freely by His grace through the redemption that is in Christ Jesus.

—Romans 3:24, NKJV

32. I am the righteousness of God:

God made him who had no sin to be sin for us, so that in him we might become the righteousness of God.

—2 Corinthians 5:21

He himself bore our sins in his body on the tree, so that we might die to sin and live for righteousness; by his wounds you have been healed.

—1 Peter 2:24

33. I am a new creation in Christ:

Therefore, if anyone is in Christ, he is a new creation; old things have passed away; behold, all things have become new.

—2 Corinthians 5:17, NKJV

34. I am free from condemnation:

There is therefore now no condemnation to those who are in Christ Jesus, who do not walk according to the flesh, but according to the Spirit.

—Romans 8:1, NKJV

But now he has reconciled you by Christ's physical body through death to present you holy in his sight, without blemish and free from accusation.

—Colossians 1:22

35. I am redeemed:

For you know that it was not with perishable things such as silver or gold that you were redeemed from the empty way of life handed down to you from your forefathers, but with the precious blood of Christ, a lamb without blemish or defect.

—1 Peter 1:18-19

36. I am redeemed from the curse of the law:

Christ has redeemed us from the curse of the law, having become a curse for us (for it is written, "Cursed is everyone who hangs on a tree").

—Galatians 3:13, NKJV

37. I am redeemed from the hand of the enemy:

Let the redeemed of the LORD say so, Whom He has redeemed from the hand of the enemy.

—Psalm 107:2, NKJV

38. I am washed clean from my sins:

"Come now, let us reason together," says the LORD. "Though your sins are like scarlet, they shall be as white as snow; though they are red as crimson, they shall be like wool."

—Isaiah 1:18

I will sprinkle clean water on you, and you will be clean; I will cleanse you from all your impurities and from all your idols.

—Ezekiel 36:25

39. I am God's:

Later I passed by, and when I looked at you and saw that you were old enough for love, I spread the corner of my garment over you and covered your nakedness. I gave you my solemn oath and entered into a covenant with you, declares the Sovereign LORD, and you became mine.

—Ezekiel 16:8

40. I am the apple of God's eye:

Keep me as the apple of your eye; hide me in the shadow of your wings.

—Psalm 17:8, ESV

He found him in a desert land and in the wasteland, a howling wilderness; He encircled him, He instructed him, He kept him as the apple of His eye.

—Deuteronomy 32:10, NKJV

41. I am dead to sin:

What shall we say, then? Shall we go on sinning so that grace may increase? By no means! We died to sin; how can we live in it any longer? Or don't you know that all of us who were baptized into Christ Jesus were baptized into his death? We were therefore buried with him through baptism into death in order that, just as Christ was raised from the dead through the glory of the Father, we too may live a new life. . . . But thanks be to God that, though you used to be slaves to sin, you wholeheartedly obeyed the form of teaching to which you were entrusted. You have been set free from sin and have become slaves to righteousness.

—Romans 6:1-4,17-18

42. I am crucified with Christ:

I have been crucified with Christ and I no longer live, but Christ lives in me. The life I live in the body, I live by faith in the Son of God, who loved me and gave himself for me.

—Galatians 2:20

43. I am sealed with the Holy Spirit:

In him you also, when you heard the word of truth, the gospel of your salvation, and believed in him, were sealed with the promised Holy Spirit.

—Ephesians 1:13, ESV

44. I am the salt of the earth:

> You are the salt of the earth; but if the salt has become tasteless, how can it be made salty again? It is no longer good for anything, except to be thrown out and trampled under foot by men.
>
> —Matthew 5:13, NASB

45. I am the light of the world:

> You are the light of the world—like a city on a hilltop that cannot be hidden. No one lights a lamp and then puts it under a basket. Instead, a lamp is placed on a stand, where it gives light to everyone in the house. In the same way, let your good deeds shine out for all to see, so that everyone will praise your heavenly Father.
>
> —Matthew 5:14-16, NLT

46. I am called by God:

> Who has saved us and called us to a holy life—not because of anything we have done but because of his own purpose and grace. This grace was given us in Christ Jesus before the beginning of time.
>
> —2 Timothy 1:9

47. I am an ambassador for Christ:

> We are therefore Christ's ambassadors, as though God were making his appeal through us. We implore you on Christ's behalf: Be reconciled to God.
>
> —2 Corinthians 5:20

48. I am always in God's thoughts:

> How precious are your thoughts about me, O God. They cannot be numbered! I can't even count them; they outnumber the grains of sand! And when I wake up, you are still with me!
>
> —Psalm 139:17-18, NLT

> Can a mother forget the baby at her breast and have no compassion on the child she has borne? Though she may forget, I will not forget you! See, I have engraved you on the palms of my hands; your walls are ever before me.
>
> —Isaiah 49:15-16

> "For I know the plans I have for you," declares the LORD, "plans to prosper you and not to harm you, plans to give hope and a future."
>
> —Jeremiah 29:11

Assignment

FOR WEEKEND WORKSHOP:

Take a short break and then move onto the next session.

FOR WEEKLY BIBLE STUDY:

Read chapter fifteen titled "Your Worth in Christ" in the book *Go in Peace!* Don't miss reading this chapter. It is totally different from this session. You will be blessed. After reading the chapter spend some time with the Lord and as you do complete the following exercises.

1. As you read the verses in this session, which "I am" statements did you put a star or asterisk next to? List them here.

   _____
   _____
   _____

2. From this list, which "I am" statement spoke the deepest to your heart? And why?

   _____
   _____
   _____

3. Which verse(s) was your favorite? And why?

   _____
   _____
   _____

4. Write out that verse here and take time to memorize it so that it can be life changing.

   _____
   _____
   _____

Session Thirteen

SET APART

> *But know that the LORD has set apart*
> *the godly for himself;*
> *the LORD hears when I call to him.*
>
> PSALM 4:3, ESV

Sanctified

*N*ow that you have learned about who you are in Christ, it is time to learn about the deep, intimate, personal relationship that God desires to have with you. He wants to meet with you in the depths of your innermost being, and it is in this secret place that you will become all that He created you to be.

There is an interesting statement that I think often times we overlook in the first half of Psalm 139:13. It says:

> For you created my inmost being.

What do you think this means? I believe that God created our inmost being as the _____ place that He wants to meet with us in _____, but many times (as you have learned in the previous sessions of this Bible study) our innermost being is so stuffed full of hurt, pain, anger, bitterness and unforgiveness that there is no room to meet with Him. Remember, He is a _____ God, and He does not want to _____ that secret place with _____ or _____.

In view of this, let me share an interesting story I read recently about Queen Victoria's life. She was England's longest-ruling monarch. She became queen when she was only 18 years old and ruled for 64 years. As the account I read stated:

> When she was young, Victoria was shielded from the fact that she would
> be the next ruling monarch of England lest this knowledge spoil her. When
> her teacher finally did let her discover for herself that she would one day be
> Queen of England, Victoria's response was, "Then I will be good!" Her life
> would be controlled by her position. No matter where she was, Victoria was
> governed by the fact that she sat on the throne of England.[1]

From the moment Queen Victoria discovered the truth of who she was, she determined in her heart and mind to be good. She determined to walk worthy of her calling.

Well, much like Queen Victoria's teacher, I would like to help you not only discover who you are in Christ (as we talked about in the last session) but also live who

143

you are in Christ! For you, too, are royalty. You are a child of the King of kings. For this reason, you are sanctified. "Sanctified" means to be "set _____"[2] and "to be _____ from _____."[3] There are two aspects to sanctification—a _____ aspect and a _____ aspect. The *positional aspect* has to do with the moment of your salvation. When you decide to give your heart to God and follow Him, you have immediately been set apart. The *practical aspect* has to do with how you live out your salvation. Each day, you must choose to make wise choices to be set free from sin. Therefore, sanctification is both a _____ event and an _____ process throughout your life.

We see these two aspects in Queen Victoria's life. Because of her royal birth, she knew that she would one day be the future queen of England. This was the _____ aspect of her monarchy—the moment she was born, she was immediately in line to rule the country. However, the _____ aspect of her rule occurred when she learned that she would one day be queen and made the declaration, "Then I will be _____!" From the moment she learned who she was and determined in her heart and in her mind to be good—to be the person that her birth and her position called her to be—she began the _____ process of conducting her life in the way a queen should. In fact, on June 20, 1837, the day that Victoria was told that King William IV had died and she was now Queen of England, she wrote in her journal, "Since it has pleased Providence [God] to place me in this station, I shall do my utmost to fulfill my duty towards my country."[4]

I pray that you will also desire to fulfill your duty to be _____ that God _____ you to be. If you do, you will have a life filled with purpose and meaning and have lasting peace and contentment no matter what is taking place around you. In this session, we will look at who you are in Christ *positionally* and also learn about the special privileges that are yours because of who you are in Christ so that you can *practically* live out your sanctification.

But before we do, let's talk about the Sinful Woman once again. You see, it wasn't only Queen Victoria who experienced both aspects of sanctification in her life. I believe the Sinful Woman experienced both as well. How do I know? Well, the one-time event took place the _____ she accepted Jesus Christ as her Lord and Savior. The moment that Jesus said, "Your faith has saved you" she was set _____. But the on-going process, on the other hand, began the _____ she accepted His challenge to *go in peace*. I believe she not only _____ it, but she _____ it out as well. Why else would her story be preserved throughout the ages if she hadn't accepted Jesus' challenge to *go in peace*? Obviously her life was changed.

Well, your life is changed as well. As you learned in the previous session, you are loved by God, created in Christ Jesus, and complete in Him. You are not a mistake, for you are His workmanship, created in His image. You are His beloved. The moment you become born again and accept Christ as your Lord and Savior, you become a citizen of the kingdom of God. You become His child, chosen by Him, and are forever protected by Him. You are forgiven, redeemed, justified and washed clean from your sins. You are a partaker of His divine nature. You are His and are always in His thoughts.

Now, because of this truth of who you are in Christ, God desires to have a real, personal and _____ relationship with you. The word "intimate" means familiar, _____, dear, personal, confidential, private, _____, secret, deep and _____. These words describe the type of relationship that God truly desires to have with you—yes, you! He wants to be your _____, your confidant, your advocate, your supporter, your _____, your sympathizer and your _____. These are other words that can be used to describe intimate. God desires to be your all-in-all, your best friend—the _____ of your _____.

Now, because of the deep love He has for you, He has given you a choice: You can choose to dwell within the Holy of Holies at the foot of His throne and learn how to be all that He intends you to be, or you can choose to settle for second or even third best. Let me explain about the Holy of Holies in which you are invited to dwell.

It has always been God's desire to dwell among His people. Yet ever since the Garden of Eden when Adam and Eve chose to sin, mankind has wandered from God's presence. Then, at Mount Sinai, God returned His presence and reestablished the long-lost relationship with His people.

It was at this time that God spoke to Moses and said:

> Then have them make a sanctuary for me, and I will dwell among them.
>
> —Exodus 25:8

This was to be a place where God's chosen people could come to _____ from Him. It was a place where they could receive His love, forgiveness and _____. And so they made the Tabernacle. It is important to have a basic understanding of the pattern of this Tabernacle, because found within it was the Holy of Holies, and the _____ to unlocking the _____ of how to have a deep, personal and intimate relationship with God.

God loves you so much that He wants to speak to you. Exodus 33:11a tells us:

> The LORD would speak to Moses face to face, as a man speaks with his friend.

Psalm 84:2 shows how the psalmist yearned to meet with God:

> My soul yearns, even faints, for the courts of the LORD; my heart and my flesh cry out for the living God.

Have you ever spent one day—or even one moment—in the presence of God? If you have, then your soul will _____ to be there again. What is more amazing is that you can spend _____ day in the Holy of Holies with God.

Many times when you are studying God's Word, you will see that God speaks to His people with pictures and parables (which is a biblical name for stories) so that they can picture the spiritual lesson He desires to teach. The Tabernacle is a visual picture of the intimate relationship that God desires to have with you. This visual picture can show you where your heart is spiritually concerning your relationship with God.

THE TABERNACLE
Exodus 25:8

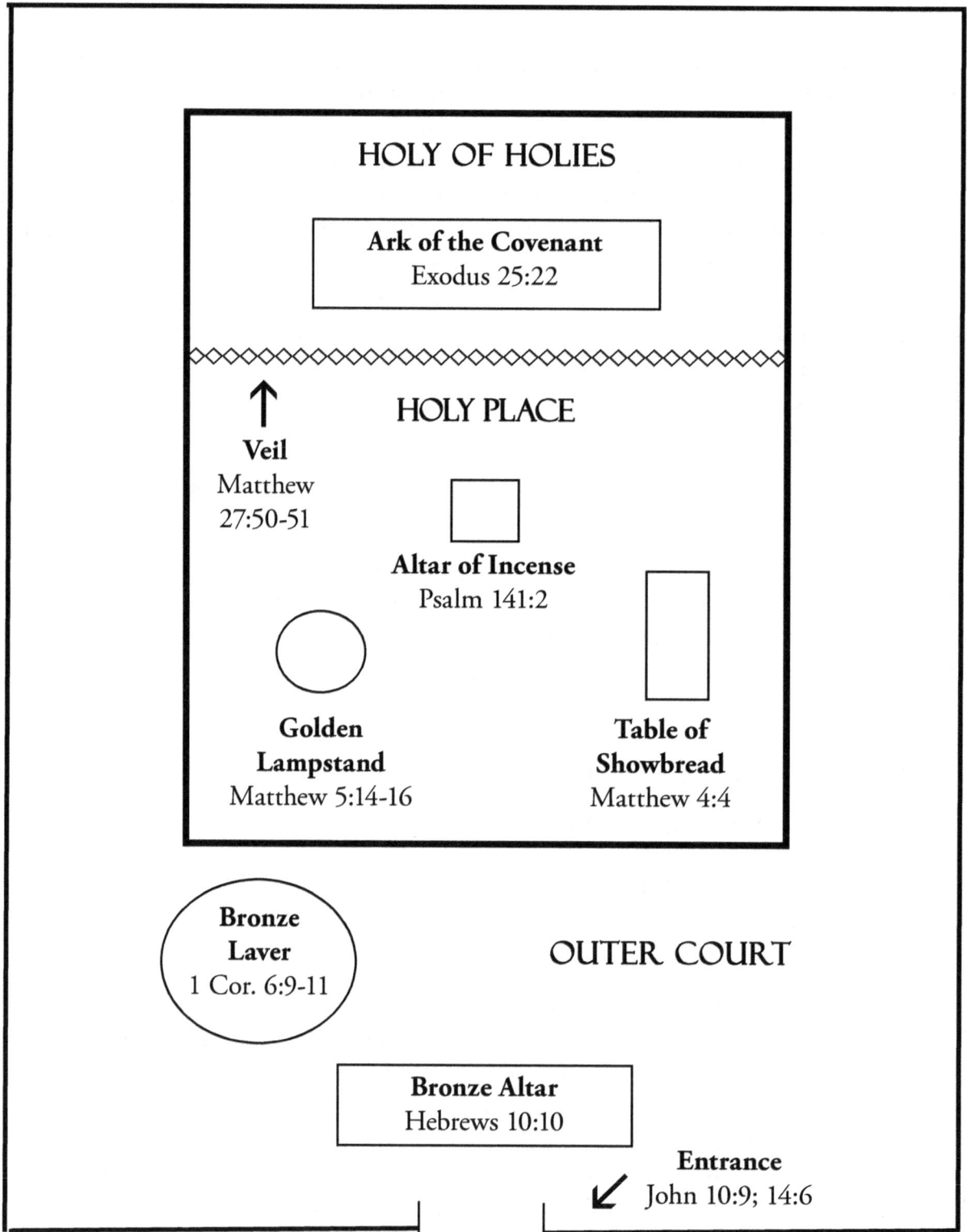

HOLY OF HOLIES

Ark of the Covenant
Exodus 25:22

HOLY PLACE

↑
Veil
Matthew
27:50-51

Altar of Incense
Psalm 141:2

**Golden
Lampstand**
Matthew 5:14-16

**Table of
Showbread**
Matthew 4:4

**Bronze
Laver**
1 Cor. 6:9-11

OUTER COURT

Bronze Altar
Hebrews 10:10

Entrance
↙ John 10:9; 14:6

In her study "Dwelling in the Holy of Holies," Kay Smith states that there are _____ types of believers in regard to where they live _____.[5] We can draw this picture of the three types of believers by relating them to the Tabernacle. Basically, the Tabernacle had three parts: (1) the outer court, (2) the Holy Place and (3) the Holy of Holies. The Holy of Holies was the place where God _____.

1. The _____ Court—There was only one entrance to the Tabernacle, and that was through the door that led into the *outer court*. Now, remember, the Tabernacle can be a visual picture of our relationship with God. In the same way that there was only one way to God in the Tabernacle, there is only one way to God in our lives, and that is by accepting Jesus Christ as our Lord and Savior. In John 14:6, Jesus said:

   > I am the way, and the truth, and the life. No one comes to the Father except through me.
   >
   > —ESV

   He also said:

   > I am the door. If anyone enters by me, he will be saved.
   >
   > —John 10:9a, ESV

   So the moment that you accepted Jesus Christ as your Lord and Savior, you _____ the outer court in your _____ with Him.

   Unfortunately, many believers remain in the outer court and never go any deeper. They never enter into the deep, personal, _____ relationship that God desires to have with them. They have experienced the _____ aspect of salvation, but they are _____ living out their life on a _____ day-by-day basis of following Christ. They are _____ being all that God intends them to be.

   Let's explore this by taking a look at the two items found within the outer court: the Bronze Altar and the Bronze Laver. The *Bronze Altar*, also known as the Altar of Sacrifice, was a large piece of furniture that was used to make sacrifices in Old Testament days before Jesus came.[6] As John Schmitt and Carl Laney explain, "The position of the altar near the entrance of the Tabernacle reminds us of our need for atonement [our need to have our sins paid for by Christ's death] as the basis for approaching a holy God. The altar serves as a _____ lesson, anticipating the _____ sacrifice that Christ offered on the cross."[7]

   Once Christ died on the cross, there was no longer any need to offer sacrifices for man's sin. The sacrifice was made _____, for _____. Hebrews 10:10 teaches about this sacrifice that Jesus made so that we can enter into the outer court:

   > And by that will we have been sanctified through the offering of the body of Jesus Christ once for all.
   >
   > —ESV

The *Bronze Laver* was the second item in the outer court. It was filled with water and was used for ceremonial washings. The Bronze Laver illustrates our _____ for spiritual _____ from sin.[8] Remember, we are all sinners. First Corinthians 6:9-11 explains clearly what would happen to each of us if we were not washed by the blood of Jesus Christ:

> Do you not know that the unrighteous will not inherit the kingdom of God? Do not be deceived: neither the sexually immoral, nor idolaters, nor adulterers, nor men who practice homosexuality, nor thieves, nor the greedy, nor drunkards, nor revilers, nor swindlers will inherit the kingdom of God. And such _____ some of you. But you were washed, you were _____, you were justified in the name of the Lord Jesus Christ and by the Spirit of our God.
>
> —ESV

Keeping these two objects in mind, let's go back to our picture of the Tabernacle and where each type of believer is spiritually in his or her relationship with God. *Outer Court Believers* are those who have received salvation but have gone no further in their relationship with God. They have received the sacrifice that Jesus Christ made on the cross when He died for their sins (as the Bronze Altar represents) and have been washed clean (as the Bronze Laver represents), but that's it. It's as if they entered through the door to the outer court when they accepted Jesus Christ and just _____ there. They have experienced the _____ aspect of salvation, but are _____ practically living out their salvation in the manner God intended.

These believers are _____ becoming all God _____ them to be. They are missing out. They have no witness for God and continue to live their lives by their feelings and their fleshly desires. They will never find purpose for their lives or lasting peace and contentment by remaining in the outer court. They are right where _____ wants them to be.

Remember, there is a battle going on that we cannot see—a battle that includes you and me. Satan does not want us to draw near to God and become all that He desires us to be. Satan wants to keep us ineffective so that we will _____ be a light and impact others for Christ. In view of his schemes, it is important to know that God does _____ want us to live our lives in the outer court. He has so much more for us. He wants a personal and intimate relationship with you and me. Do you desire to be an Outer Court Believer? Or do you want more in your relationship with God?

2. The _____ Place—Now, let's return to our picture of the Tabernacle. Beyond the outer court was the *Holy Place*. There were three items of furniture in the Holy Place that apply to our lives: (1) the Table of Showbread, (2) the Altar of Incense and (3) the Golden Lampstand.

The purpose of the *Table of Showbread* was to display 12 loaves of bread as a continual thank offering to God for His many blessings. Here again is another spiritual lesson.[9] In Matthew 4:4, Jesus said:

> It is written, "Man shall not live by bread alone, but by every word that proceeds from the mouth of God."
>
> —NKJV

This is why the Bible is referred to as "the _____ of Life." It is important to read the Bible _____. We cannot survive on just physical food. We need _____ food as well.

The *Altar of Incense*, as the name implies, was the place in which the priests burned incense as an offering to the Lord. In Scripture, incense often symbolizes _____.[10] Psalm 141:2 teaches:

> Let my prayer be set before You as incense, The lifting up of my hands as the evening sacrifice.
>
> —NKJV

Prayer is the way in which we talk to God.

The oil lamps in the *Golden Lampstand* provided light to the priests who ministered within the darkened interior of the Holy Place. Matthew 5:14-16 explains how this applies to the believer's life.[11] Jesus said:

> You are the light of the world. A city that is set on a hill cannot be hidden. Nor do they light a lamp and put it under a basket, but on a lampstand, and it gives light to all [who are] in the house. Let your light so shine before men, that they may see your good works and glorify your Father in heaven.
>
> —NKJV

As we read God's Word each day and pray, we begin to become a _____ unto the Lord. Others begin to see Christ in us.

Let's go back to our visual of the three types of believers. Unlike the Outer Court Believer, the *Holy Place Believer* enters into the Holy Place by spending time in _____ and _____ God's Word. Thus, his or her life begins to become a _____ unto God. But this believer is still _____ the most important aspect of his or her relationship with God: _____. Because of this, the Holy Place Believer still lives by his or her feelings and desires, which causes no purpose or lasting peace and contentment in his or her life.

"Contentment" means "happiness with one's situation in life."[12] In other words, it means being fulfilled and satisfied regardless of what is happening. Holy Place Believers are _____ truly fulfilled and satisfied. They are _____ content. They spend some time with the Lord, which is a good thing, but then go about their day in their _____ strength. They try to find peace and contentment in _____ and _____, instead of in God. They are still living their lives by feelings and fleshly desires. They are not living by the truth of God's Word or seeking Him for His love, forgiveness and guidance. As Kay Smith notes, "They will give the Lord an hour or two, but that's it. They want the rest of the time for _____."[13] Elisabeth Elliot also explains, "By trying to grab fulfillment everywhere, [they] find it _____."[14]

Like the Outer Court Believer, the Holy Place Believer is also missing out. And you and I will be missing out as well if we remain in the Holy Place. We will not find true purpose in our lives or lasting peace and contentment if we remain in the Holy Place. God desires a deeper intimate relationship with us. In fact, He desires to be involved in every aspect of our lives. He wants to be our all-in-all.

Do you desire to be a Holy Place Believer? Or do you want more in your relationship with God?

3. The _____ of _____—This brings us to the *Holy of Holies*. This was the place where God dwelt. The high priest could only enter the Holy of Holies one day each year. That day was called Yom Kippur, the Day of Atonement. On this day, the high priest would go in and make atonement for the sins of the people.

Because the Holy of Holies was so holy, only the high priest could enter, and he had to go through a whole ritual to cleanse himself beforehand. If the priest wasn't cleansed or his heart wasn't right before God, God could zap him right on the spot. For this reason, the high priest wore bells on his robe so that the others could hear him walking around in the Holy of Holies and know that he was still alive. In addition, because no one else could enter, they tied a rope to his leg in case he got zapped so they could pull him out.

Now, pay attention to this next part—Satan would love for you to miss what you are about to learn. Separating the Holy Place from the Holy of Holies was the _____. This also has significance in our lives. The moment that Jesus Christ died on the cross for you and me, the veil was _____ in _____. Matthew 27:50-51 states it this way:

> And Jesus cried out again with a loud voice, and yielded up His spirit.
> Then, behold, the veil of the temple was torn in two from top to bottom.
>
> —NKJV

This is a visual picture that shows you and me that we are now able to enter into the Holy of Holies and meet with God personally. No matter what we have done or how bad we have been God wants to meet with us! Listen to what Charles Spurgeon said back in the 1800s concerning the veil:

> Yet the rending [tearing] of the veil of the temple is not a miracle to be
> lightly passed over. It was made of "fine twined linen. . . ." This gives the

150

idea of a substantial fabric, a piece of lasting tapestry, which would have endured the severest strain. No human hands could have torn that sacred covering; and it could not have been divided in the midst by any accidental cause; yet, strange to say, on the instant when the holy person of Jesus was rent by death, the great veil which concealed the holiest of all [the Holy of Holies] was "rent in twain [torn in two] from top to the bottom." What did it mean? It meant much more than I can tell you now.[15]

This was a miracle—that's what it means! There was no way that the veil could have been torn by anyone other than God. In fact, some say that the thickness of the fabric was not thin, like the fabric of our day, but it was about a foot thick! Can you imagine? When the veil was torn in two, it _____ that God desires a deep, personal and intimate relationship with _____ and me. We no longer have to go through some cleansing ritual like the high priest had to do to enter the presence of God. No matter where we have been or what we have done, we won't be zapped! God simply wants us to come and spend intimate time with Him in _____. He doesn't want us to be satisfied by _____ reading His Word and praying. He wants _____.

He desires an intimate relationship with you and with me. He loves us. He wants to be our all-in-all, our best friend, the lover of our souls. That is why He made a _____ for us to enter the Holy of Holies—so we can be _____ to Him.

There was one piece of furniture in the Holy of Holies, and that was the *Ark of the Covenant* (also known as the Ark of the Testimony). The Ark was a reminder to the Israelite people of God's personal presence. He desired to meet with them and speak to them.[16] In Exodus 25:22, God declared:

> There, above the cover between the two cherubim that are over the ark of the Testimony, *I will meet with you* (emphasis added).

Let's go back to our visual of the three types of believers. Unlike the Outer Court Believer or even the Holy Place Believer, the *Holy of Holies Believer* desires to become all that God intends him or her to be. Holy of Holies Believers desire for God to be their all-in-all. They _____ by the truth of God's Word, not by their feeling and desires.

The Holy of Holies is not just a place but also an _____ of the heart. This is where our relationship with God moves from our _____ to our _____. It is here in the Holy of Holies that we realize who God is—He is amazing, the almighty God, the King of glory. He is all-powerful, all-knowing and unchanging, yet He loves us and wants to be involved in every aspect of our lives.

It is in the Holy of Holies that we seek God daily, sometimes moment by moment, to receive His love, forgiveness and guidance. It is here that He sees the yuck of our hearts and yet loves us anyway. It is here that we fall to our knees and offer our heart to Him to be changed. When we become Holy of Holies Believers we realize that sin _____

151

a wall between us and God and _____ our fellowship with Him. Therefore, we are continually _____ of the sins in our own hearts and take immediate _____ to admit, confess and repent of it so that our intimate relationship with God is _____. Psalm 139:23-24 becomes a way of life:

> Search me, O God, and know my heart; test me and know my anxious thoughts. See if there is any offensive way in me, and lead me in the way everlasting.

It is in the Holy of Holies that God takes our hearts and molds us into all He desires us to be when we come to Him in truth. It is here that we find our purpose and meaning for life. It is here that we discover lasting peace and contentment for every situation in life.

He wants to be our best friend—the lover of our souls. It is only in the Holy of Holies that we can meet Him and grow to become all that He created for us to be. It is here where we will learn how to _____ live out who we are in Christ.

Which Are You?

Beloved, where have you been dwelling? Put a checkmark next to the one which would best describe your relationship with God?

- ○ *Outer Court Believer*—You are saved, but that's it! You have received the sacrifice that Jesus made on the cross for you. You are washed clean from your sins, but you are missing out on all that God has for you.

- ○ *Holy Place Believer*—You spend time reading God's Word and praying. However, you are still missing the most important aspect of your relationship with God: intimacy. Because of this, there is no lasting contentment in your life. You continue to run after this or that to find satisfaction and pleasure. You don't look to God to be your all and all. And you allow sin (even the sin in the depths of your heart) to break your fellowship with Him.

- ○ *Holy of Holies Believer*—You desire to know God intimately. You realize that sin breaks fellowship with God, and because of this, you search your heart daily to make sure that there is no offensive way in you. You desire to be all that God intends for you to be. You have purpose, meaning, lasting peace and contentment in your life.

Which are you? Is this where you desire to be? If not, what can you do to become a Holy of Holies Believer?

Because of who we are in Christ positionally, you and I have the right to enter into God's presence. We are His children. No one will stop us as we enter into the Holy of Holies, because we have every right to be there. We will not be zapped. God loves us and, according to His Word, we are able to approach Him with confidence. But He gives us a choice: We can choose to sit at His feet in the Holy of Holies and become all He wants us to be, or we can choose to live our lives by our feelings and fleshly desires, running after this or that but never being truly satisfied. The choice is ours.

God truly desires to have a deep, personal, intimate relationship with you. You have the privilege to come into His presence. In fact, because of who you are in Christ positionally, you not only have the privilege but also the right to draw near to Him. You are able to approach Him with confidence.

Satan will do everything in his power to keep you from becoming all that God intends for you to be. Satan is hoping that you will not become a Holy of Holies Believer. In view of this, take some time today to enter the Holy of Holies in your relationship with God. Spend some quiet time reading His Word and in prayer. But don't stop there. Go deeper and enter into the Holy of Holies! Spend time just sitting at God's feet, meeting with Him and listening to His still, small voice. Ask Him to mold you and make you into the person He desires you to be. Ask Him to lead you and guide you. Ask Him to search your heart to see if there is any offensive way in you. Remember, it is _____ which _____ fellowship with Him. It is the sin within your heart that places the _____ between you and Him. Therefore, get your heart right with Him today, so that the veil within your heart may be torn in two, so that you may *go in peace!*

Assignment

FOR WEEKEND WORKSHOP:

Find a quiet place and complete numbers one through five. *Leader's Note:* The students are instructed to put their letters in an envelope and address the envelope to themselves and give it to you. I keep these letters on my desk and occasionally look at them. As I do, I ask the Lord if it is time to mail them. God knows the perfect timing to remind them of what He did in their lives through this workshop.

FOR WEEKLY BIBLE STUDY:

Read chapter sixteen titled "Set Apart" in the book *Go in Peace!* The chapter is basically the same as this session (expect the book does include a story about one of my favorite movies which wasn't included in this Bible study). Although the session is almost the same as the chapter, it is good to review it on your own, and at your own pace, so that the Lord can to speak to you heart as you review the information. After reading the chapter spend some quiet time with the Lord and as you do complete the following exercises.

1. Which type of believer are you—an Outer Court Believer, a Holy Place Believer or a Holy of Holies Believer?

_____

_____

2. Is this where you want to be in your relationship with God?

_____

_____

_____

3. If not, what can you do to become a Holy of Holies Believer?

_____

_____

_____

4. Which verse spoke the deepest to your heart? And why?

_____

_____

_____

5. Now spend some time in the Holy of Holies and listen to His still small voice. He wants to meet with you. He wants to be your all-and-all. As you spend time with the Lord grab some paper and write a letter of how God has ministered to your heart through this Bible study. If you are going through this study with a leader then put the letter in an envelope and address the letter to yourself and seal it. Then give it to the leader who will mail it back to you at a later date to encourage you and remind you of what God did in your life.

_____

_____

_____

IN VIEW OF GOD'S MERCY

Therefore, I urge you, brothers [and sisters],
in view of God's mercy,
to offer your bodies as living sacrifices.
ROMANS 12:1A

Hopes and Goals

*B*efore we begin this session, let's take a look at how God has worked in your life. Turn to page three in session one. Remember the page titled: Hopes and Goals? Let's read the goals out loud and as we do write "yes" next to any of your goals that God has helped you to meet.

In reviewing your hopes and goals, did God work in your life? Were most of your goals answered? Were you surprised? In my many years of discipling, I have seen that God truly does work in a person's life to help him or her meet these goals. Usually, if a person is truly honest with themselves and allows God to do His deep heart surgery, about 90 percent of a person's goals have been met by the time he or she gets to this place in the Bible study. The other 10 percent are typically goals such as, "I want to be used by God to help others," or, "I want my life to have purpose and meaning." Only time will tell if these goals will be met, but this does not mean that God has not answered the person's request. It just means that these are goals for the future. What is really wonderful about these types of hopes and goals is that God desires them as well! Which brings us to the topic of this session.

To set the stage, let's go back to our story of Queen Victoria. Remember that when Victoria discovered for the first time that she would one day be queen of England, she said, "Then I will be good!"[1] The moment she discovered the truth of who she was, she determined to be the person whom her birth and position called her to be. In her heart and her mind, she determined to walk worthy of her calling in a practical manner. Her choice would greatly impact her life and the lives of everyone around her.

Repentant Heart

The same was true for the Sinful Woman as well. The moment that she heard the words "go in peace" she determined in her heart and mind to be the woman that God created her to be. She determined to walk worthy of her calling.

155

How we can learn from this woman! As we blow it in life we need to remember that all we need to do is to come to Jesus in humility, with a broken and repentant heart. Don't be like _____. Don't go back to your old way of thinking. Don't think that the things you are struggling with are all a result of someone else's actions. In fact, what you have learned in this Bible study _____ to become a _____ of life. Keep going through this material about every six months or so as to remind you of the importance of keeping your heart _____.

You see, when Jesus said, "Therefore, I tell you, her many sins have been forgiven—for she loved much [referring to the Sinful Woman]. But he who has been forgiven little loves little [referring to Simon]" (Luke 7:47). Jesus was describing the outcome of a person's life when he or she chooses to be or not to be honest with themselves. Simon was forgiven little, not because he had _____ sin than the Sinful Woman did, but because he *didn't believe* he needed to be forgiven. He *didn't believe* he was a sinful man. He was spiritually righteous within his own sight. And he was _____ himself. Thus he never asked God for forgiveness. But the Sinful Woman _____ her sin and she _____ Jesus' gift and she _____ it to become a way of life as she *practically* lived out who she was in Christ and as a result she _____ much.

Remember, Jesus, being God knew all—including the future—that's why He could say, "Therefore, I tell you, her many sins have been forgiven—for she loved much" (Luke 7:47). Jesus knew what the _____ of her life would be. He knew the love that would be poured forth from her life as a _____ of His wonderful gift to her.

The same is true in my own life. In view of what God has done for me—He forgave me of my sin; He washed me clean; He set me free—can I offer Him anything less than my life?

You also have a choice. You can make the _____ choice to live up to your position in Christ by _____ in your heart and mind to humbly die to self and live for Christ (causing you to dwell in the Holy of Holies), or you can make the _____ choice to live out your life by your feelings and desires (causing you to remain either an Outer Court Believer or a Holy Place Believer). However, it is important to know that your choices _____ greatly impact your life and the lives of those around you.

The Third Element of Repentance

In a previous session, we learned that there are three elements of repentance. The first is a *genuine sorrow* toward God on account of our sin. The second is an *inward repugnance* to sin, which is necessarily followed by the actual *forsaking* of it. Now it is time to look at the third element of repentance, which is: "Humble _____ to the will and service of God."² In other words, the third element of repentance means to walk _____ of our _____ so that we can live out who we are in Christ practically. Listen to what Jeremiah 15:19 says:

Therefore this is what the LORD says: "If you repent, I will restore you that you may serve me; if you utter worthy, not worthless, words, you will be my spokesman. Let this people turn to you, but you must not turn to them.

Because of our _____, you and I have been _____; therefore, it is time for us to _____ the Lord. It's time for us to live out the *practical aspect* of our sanctification. Perhaps the apostle Paul said it best when he wrote:

Therefore, I urge you, brothers, *in view of God's mercy*, to _____ your bodies as living _____, holy and pleasing to God—this is your spiritual act of worship.

—Romans 12:1, emphasis added

In view of God's mercy, we are to offer ourselves as living sacrifices! For this reason, let's take a moment to look at these three aspects of our Christian walk: mercy, offer and living sacrifices.

1. Mercy—Paul urges us that "in view of God's mercy." But what exactly does that mean? What is Paul implying? Mercy is "a form of _____."[3] It is "kindness towards the helpless."[4] It is to have compassion on the suffering.[5] The word itself actually means that the price is _____.[6] Remember, dear beloved, that during the final 18 hours of Christ's life, He paid the ultimate price for our sin with His life. He paid this price so that you and I could be set free. Out of His _____, love, kindness and compassion toward us when we were lost and suffering, He came and saved us, restored us and set us free. In view of this, how can we offer Him anything less than our lives?

2. Offer—To "offer" means "'by a once-for-all presentation to place your bodies [your life] at the disposal of God.' The language here clearly refers to the crisis of _____ consecration."[7] To be "consecrated" means to be _____.[8] It means complete dedication to your Lord and Savior. His sacrifice was complete, and all He wants from you is the same. In view of this, how can you *not* express your faith in Him through love? As Paul wrote in Galatians 5:6b, "The only thing that counts is faith expressing itself through love." God's perfect will for you is to express your faith through love as you _____ yourself to Him and _____ Him. This is exactly what the Sinful Woman did. This is why Jesus said she loved much. She offered herself to serve Him. He wants the same from _____. As Paul states, it is time to be an imitator of God:

Therefore be imitators of God as dear children. And walk in love, as Christ also has loved us and given Himself for us, an offering and a sacrifice to God for a sweet-smelling aroma.

—Ephesians 5:1-2, NKJV

According to Weirsbe in *Be Compassionate*, "What was the proof of [the Sinful Woman's] salvation? Her love for Christ [was] expressed in _____ devotion to Him. For the first time in her life she had *peace with God*."⁹ Dear beloved, do you wish to go forth from this day forward in total peace with God? If so, it is time to _____ yourself to Him. As Paul writes:

> He died for all, that those who live might no longer live for themselves but
> for him who for their sake died and was raised.
>
> —2 Corinthians 5:15, ESV

Since it is time for us to no longer live for ourselves, it brings us to the third point.

3. Living Sacrifices—Perhaps the best way to describe what it means to be a living sacrifice is: It is time to _____ yourself and no longer live according to your own plans. It is death to _____ that is necessary here. That's what it means. It is time to shift your interest from _____ to _____.
    It is time to say no to self-will and self-effort. It is time to take up your cross and live for Christ. Listen to what Jesus said:

> Then he said to the crowd, "If any of you wants to be my follower, you
> must turn from your _____ ways, take up your cross daily,
> and follow me. If you try to hang on to your life, you will lose it. But if
> you give up your life for my sake, you will save it.
>
> —Luke 9:23-24, NLT

Now, to deny yourself daily, moment by moment, you have to make _____ choices over _____ choices. To accomplish this, you must have the attitude of one who believes that it is not about _____ but all about _____. The pity-party attitude of "life is not fair" or "no one loves me" is no longer acceptable. So what if people aren't nice to you? You be the one who is nice no matter what. So what if people don't care about you? You be the one who cares for others no matter what. So what if life isn't fair? You be the one who is fair in every situation. This is what it means to _____ to self and _____ for Christ, and it is when you reach this place that you will bear fruit. Remember that you have been chosen to go and bear such fruit—fruit that will last—because you are Christ's ambassador here on earth. As Jesus said in John 12:24:

> I tell you the truth, unless a kernel of wheat falls to the ground and dies,
> it remains only a single seed. But if it dies, it produces many seeds.

It is time to deny self and die to your wants and desires, for when you deny yourself and live for Him, others will see Christ in you! So let's view our portrait of the Sinful Woman one last time to see how she denied herself and lived for Christ. According to Wiersbe, we learn that "Jesus did not reject either the woman's tears or her gift of ointment, because her works were the evidence of her faith."¹⁰ In fact, some say that the gift she brought was worth a year's wage. As we discussed, it was an alabaster jar that had to be broken in order to be opened. In the book of James, we learn that "faith without works is dead" (James 2:20, NKJV). So, in other words, you are called to do things for God to work out your salvation, just like the Sinful Woman did.

However, it is important to know that works—the things you do for God—cannot save you. These works are merely the _____ of your salvation. In fact, many times it is because of what God has already done in your life that you can begin to do such powerful works. Listen to what Pastor Jon Courson has to say: "[God] takes those of us who have missed the mark or messed up in a certain area, and He delights in using us to bring ministry to others at a later time. He heals the hurts. He restores and rebuilds, renews and revives—and then He releases powerful ministry in the very area where we blew it previously."[11]

Go!

So, are you ready to _____ yourself and _____ for Christ? Are you ready to offer yourself as a living _____? For months now as I have been writing this book, my prayer has been that you would come to know just what Jesus meant when He told the Sinful Woman to "go in peace" and that you would experience that peace in your own life. Well, one morning as I was praying about the title *Go in Peace!* the word "_____" jumped off the page at me. God calls us to go. In fact, one of the last things Jesus said to His disciples before He was taken up into heaven was to go. Listen to what He said:

> All authority has been given to Me in heaven and on earth. Go therefore and make disciples of all the nations, baptizing them in the name of the Father and of the Son and of the Holy Spirit, teaching them to observe all things that I have commanded you; and lo, I am with you always, [even] to the end of the age.
>
> —Matthew 28:18-20, NKJV

Now, some of you may be arguing with me right now and saying, *What could I possibly do for the Lord? I do not know how to share or teach. I have no gifts. I am afraid.* I know the different thoughts that go through a person's mind because, if you remember, I said those same things. But look for a moment at the types of people that God chooses to use. God used Moses mightily, even though he had killed a man.[12] Moses was fearful and said he could not speak, so God gave him Aaron as his spokesman.[13] King David, also a murderer,[14] led the nation of Israel to follow the Lord. God's Word says that he was a man after God's own heart.[15] Look at Saul in the New Testament. He was a man who had persecuted believers and condemned them to death. Yet he became Paul, a man whom God also used mightily.[16] God even used a donkey to speak to Balaam.[17] God truly uses the foolish things of this world to confound the wise.[18] He even used me, a sinful woman.

I know that God also used the Sinful Woman, because Jesus said, "I tell you, her many sins have been forgiven—*for she loved much*" (Luke 7:47a, emphasis added). From the moment Jesus forgave the Sinful Woman of her sins, she was filled with a deep love which reached out and touched other peoples' lives. In fact, to this day, this deep love still touches many lives—mine being one of them. How is it possible that a person could stand in God's presence and be washed clean and forgiven and _____ go out and touch lives?

Dear beloved, we should not question how God could possibly use us when He calls us to serve but instead eagerly respond, "Here I am. Send me!" (Isaiah 6:8b). Jesus Christ said the following before He ascended to heaven:

> But you will receive power when the Holy Spirit has come upon you, and you will be my witnesses in Jerusalem and in all Judea and Samaria, and to the end of the earth.
>
> —Acts 1:8, ESV

God's Word says that you will receive power when the Holy Spirit comes on you. It also says that you will be His _____ in *Jerusalem, Judea, Samaria* and to *the ends of the earth*. So, in view of God's mercy, offer yourself as a living sacrifice and _____ and do whatever He _____ you to do. Go and be His witness.

1. Jerusalem—This call might be in *Jerusalem*, which represents your own _____. If so, *go* and be a living _____ in your home. If you are single, perhaps God is calling you to be a light to your roommates. For some of you women, perhaps your husband is not a believer and God will call you to be the wife described in 1 Peter 3:1-5. Or for you husbands, as Ephesians 5:25-33 teaches, God calls you to love your wife, just as Christ loved the church. If you have a family, raise up your children as unto the Lord. Deny yourself and to live as Christ. Perhaps the Lord will call some of you to homeschool your children. Perhaps He will call some of you to raise foster children, adopt or provide shelter for an unwed mother. Or perhaps He will call you to care for an elderly parent. You are called to be His witness in Jerusalem, in your _____ home.

2. Judea—For others, the call is to *go* into *Judea*, which means to go out into your _____ to be a light for Christ. He wants you to *go* where He sends you and say whatever He commands you to say. If you offer yourself as a living _____, He will be faithful to show you what His good, pleasing and perfect will is. You are now ready to _____! Perhaps He wants you to be a Sunday School teacher or work with the youth group. We definitely need the truth of purity and the sanctity of life taught to our youth, as there are many teens—even teens who follow Christ—who find themselves in crisis pregnancies. Or perhaps He wants you to work at a local crisis pregnancy center which honors life—both born and pre-born. Or perhaps He is calling you to help set the captives free and minister

to those who are hurting. You are ready! You can do it! You can share what you have learned through this Bible study with others. It is as simple as buying this curriculum and taking the time to meet with your friend. (The Leader's Manual and Student Workbook are written in such a way to make it simple to use. Plus in taking another through the study, it helps to reinforce what you learned. Every time I take someone through it, God continues to work in my heart! He wants to do the same in yours! You can do it! You are ready!)

3. Samaria—For some of you, the call is to *go* to *Samaria*, which means to work with the _____. How many end up in juvenile hall or in prison or on the streets because all they were looking for was love and acceptance but found it in all the wrong places? The choices they made to feel loved and accepted led them to make some poor choices. Dear beloved, you know the truth. You may be the only one who will ever share the truth with those who are hurting. Is that scary? Yes! But I've always said, a courageous person is not someone who has no _____; rather, he or she is someone who is _____ to Christ in spite of that fear! So *go* for it! *Go in peace!*

4. The Ends of the Earth—And for some of you, like for me, the call is to *go* to *the ends of the earth*—to another _____. If you feel such a call on your life, remember what Isaiah 26:3 says: "[God] will keep in perfect peace him whose mind is steadfast." He will simply amaze you with the perfect _____ He gives no matter where He sends you.

In 1999 when I went to Macedonia to help the Albanian refugees, because of the war in Kosovo, we were often about 15 miles from the Serbian border, and sometimes less. We could hear the bombs falling and see the smoke from the fires. In fact, the first bomb we heard was so close that we could feel the concussion. But God's tremendous peace was always with us, and never once did I lose that peace. This is because—listen carefully—there is no place safer than in His perfect _____!

Maybe you are unable to go. But you can even be a part of this work by supporting missionaries through your prayers, encouragement and financial support. Check out the missionaries that your church assists and if you can't go to the ends of the earth you can still be a part of this important work. Listen to the words of Jesus in Luke 10:2-3:

> The harvest is great, but the workers are few. So _____ to the Lord who is in charge of the harvest; _____ him to send more workers into his fields. Now _____, and remember that I am sending you out as lambs among wolves.
>
> —NLT

Wherever God sends you—whether it is in your home, your neighborhood, a ghetto, a prison, a different state or even a war-torn country—you are nowhere safer than in God's perfect will!

So, beloved, get ready! Your life will never be the same! He will take you to places and have you do things that you could never even have imagined. Oh, the plans I had for my life years ago, but they did not compare to the plans He had for me. Remember God's wonderful promise in Jeremiah:

> "For I know the plans I have for you," declares the LORD, "plans to prosper you and not to harm you, plans to give you hope and a future."
>
> —Jeremiah 29:11

I wish I had a dollar for every time I heard a person say, "What is God's will for my life?" You have the answer: *In view of God's mercy*, offer yourself as a living sacrifice, for this is your spiritual act of worship, so that you will know what His good, pleasing and perfect will is for your life. Do what He calls you to do, whether it is something little or something big. As you do this, you will continually discover God's will for your life.

Contract

There is one more thing that I would like to ask you to write. This time it is not a letter but a contract. I was at a missionary conference once and Dr. Harold Sala was telling the story of a man. This man decided to enter into a contract with God over all the things he would do for the Lord that year. After he completed his list, he signed it and went into the church sanctuary. He kneeled at the altar and gave the contract to God. But as he was praying, he didn't feel God's presence. So he prayed, "God, here is a list of all the things I can do for You this year. Why do I feel as if You won't accept it?" The Lord began to impress upon his heart, "Those are the things *you* want to do for Me, not the things I want you to do for Me. Are you willing to offer yourself as a living sacrifice? Then sign your name to the bottom of a blank sheet of paper."

Dear beloved, are you willing to offer yourself as a living sacrifice? Are you willing to sign your name at the bottom of a blank sheet of paper? We have done a lot of kneeling throughout this Bible study. Won't you, yet again, come and kneel at the altar and offer yourself as a living sacrifice? As Dr. Sala went onto say, "This is as serious as anything you have ever done. Are you willing to sign your name at the bottom [of a blank sheet of paper] and let God fill it in? The most exciting life in all the world is that of the person who has simply said, 'Lord, I'm Yours! No strings attached, no regrets, no reservations, no bargaining. I'm Yours, period!'"[19]

So I encourage you today to take a piece of paper, date it and write the words of Romans 12:1-2 at the top:

> Therefore, I urge you, brothers, in view of God's mercy, to offer your bodies
> as living sacrifices, holy and pleasing to God—this is your spiritual act of

worship. Do not conform any longer to the pattern of this world, but be transformed by the renewing of your mind. Then you will be able to test and approve what God's will is—his good, pleasing and perfect will.

Leave the rest of the paper blank and sign the bottom. Keep it in your Bible, and throughout the year as God uses *you*, fill in the blanks. You will be amazed at how He uses and blesses yet another sinful person. I challenge you each year on January 1st to sign another contract and watch God work in your life.

May your life never be the same as you live your life worthy of your calling. Serve Him to the best of your ability, and know that "God's gifts and his call are irrevocable" (Romans 11:29). In fact, if you would like to learn more about the gifts God gives, to help fulfill His calling in and through your life, see appendix 3, titled "Spiritual Gifts" which is found in the back. And remember, as you live your life worthy of your calling, you will *go in peace!*

Assignment

FOR WEEKEND WORKSHOP:

The reading of the book *Go in Peace!* is recommended to be read *after* the workshop is completed to reinforce what was learned over the weekend. The weekend workshop is intense and it is best to read the book slowly and contemplate what is written so that God can complete the deep heart work He began during the weekend. But before you do that, take time in the next day or so to complete numbers one through six.

FOR WEEKLY BIBLE STUDY:

Read chapter seventeen titled "In View of God's Mercy" in the book *Go in Peace!* The chapter is basically the same as this session, but it is good to review it on your own, and at your own pace, so that the Lord can to speak to you heart as you read the information. After reading the chapter spend some quiet time with the Lord and as you do complete the following exercises.

1. Which verse spoke the deepest to your heart? And why?

   _____

   _____

   _____

2. Where is God calling you to go—Jerusalem (your home), Judea (your neighborhood), Samaria (the unlovables) or the ends of the earth (another country)?

   _____

   _____

   _____

3. Have you heeded God's calling?

   _____

   _____

   _____

4. If not, what can you do to deny self and offer yourself as a living sacrifice?

   _____

   _____

   _____

5. Are you ready to take a blank piece of paper, date it and write the words of Romans 12:1-2 on top? Are you ready to say, "Here I am Lord, send me!"? If so, do it now and then keep it in your Bible to list how God uses you throughout the year. If not, it's time to start this Bible study over again and this time be honest with yourself! Don't be a Simon. God gave you life for a reason. It's time to go in peace!

   _____

   _____

   _____

6. I do enjoy hearing from my readers through letters, emails or Facebook posts. You can find my contact information in the back.

   _____

   _____

   _____

PROFILE OF AN ABUSER

Then Asa was angry with the seer [the Lord's prophet Hanani]
and put him in the stocks in prison,
for he was in a rage with him because of this.
And Asa inflicted cruelties upon some of the people at the same time
2 CHRONICLES 16:10, ESV

Unfortunately, because of people's sinful behavior, there will be those, both male and female, who will not control their anger and rage and, as a result, will inflict their cruelties on those around them. The issue of abuse is so prevalent in society today that you must know what to look for so you do not end up in an abusive relationship. Abuse is not only physical, such as hitting or slapping, but it can also be verbal, emotional and/or sexual. By knowing what to look for at the beginning of a relationship, you can get out before it is too late. And for those of you who may already be in an abusive relationship, know that there is help.

The profile you are about to read has been compiled from many different sources.[1] Although some of the profiles varied somewhat, I have listed only those traits that were repeated continually. If you would like more information, do an Internet search on the words *profile of an abuser*. You can also visit the website thesheepfold.org, which is a ministry providing help to abuse victims.

If after reading this profile you believe that you are in an abusive relationship, get help! God loves you more than you know, and He does not want you to remain in such a relationship!

Character Traits

Charismatic, Romantic, Devoted and Protective

Is the person charming in public, but degrades you in private? Beware! An abuser is often "charismatic, romantic, devoted and protective. Everyone likes him. On the surface he seems great, so you accept a date with him. He is wonderful. After a few months, you start to notice things but you dismiss them."[2]

Jealous and Possessive

Is the person possessive and jealous? Be careful! Many abusers are often so jealous they could be described as paranoid. They often have trouble trusting people, especially you.

They may continually tell you to "tell the truth" even when you are not lying. Yet, they would describe their possessiveness of you as love.

Controlling

Is the person controlling? Watch out! An abuser likes to be in control at all times. And he likes things his way. He may keep you somewhere against your will or even take away your cell phone. He continually wants to know where you are, who you are with and what you are doing.

Manipulative

Is the person manipulative? Take heed! An abuser will, often times, tell you that he cannot live without you. Or that he would die if you left the relationship. He may talk about hurting or killing himself as a means of keeping you in the relationship. Or he may even threaten to harm or kill you if you leave.

Denies Wrongdoing or Blames Others for Wrongful Behavior

Is the person always blaming someone or something else for their own actions? Or do they act as if nothing happened after a terrible rage? Think twice! An abuser will deny their wrongdoing or blame others and situations for what caused the outburst. Often times, the person will even say that it is your fault.

Other Behavioral Traits

Does the person tease and say things that hurt? Or force you to have sex? Get out! Many times an abuser has an aggressive attitude. Often times, he will try to make others appear less significant than he feels by putting a person down in front of other people. And he may even be so aggressive that he forces you to have sex with him against your will.

Do friends and family members say this person is not good for you? Listen to what friends and family are saying. Sometimes others will see a situation more clearly than you will when you are "in love." The saying "love is blind" is often true. In addition, it is important to remember who you are in Christ. You are the child of the King of kings. God does not want you in an abusive relationship. He has plans to give you a hope and a future.

If you answered yes to many of these questions, please get out of the relationship immediately! If you need to go visit a friend or relative away from home for a while, do it! Get away and get help! There are also shelters and other resources available for abuse victims. Do not allow yourself to be manipulated back into the relationship. Rely on God to be your shield. Ask Him to protect you as you take the steps to protect yourself.

> The Lord is my rock, my fortress, and my savior; my God is my rock, in whom I find protection. He is my shield, the strength of my salvation, and my stronghold, my high tower, my savior, the one who saves me from violence
>
> —2 Samuel 22:2-3, NLT

THE THREE CAUSES OF DEPRESSION

I am utterly bowed down and prostrate;
all the day I go about mourning. . . .
I am feeble and crushed;
I groan because of the tumult of my heart.
PSALM 38:6,8, ESV

Anguish of Heart

Even mighty men and women of God can get to the place in life where they are utterly crushed and groan in anguish of heart. We see this in the life of King David as he described his overwhelming feelings. In fact, take a moment and read the whole chapter of Psalm 38 before we begin this discussion of the three causes of depression. Do you think David was struggling with depression when he wrote this Psalm? It sure sounds like it to me.

In my many years of working with both women and teenagers I have discovered that there are three main causes of depression.

Physical Condition

The first cause of depression that is important to discuss is the possibility of a physical condition which may be causing the despair. A person's thyroid, hormones or even certain diseases are just a few of the causes in which depression can be one of the symptoms. Yet in most cases, these sources can be treated. Therefore, it is important to find a good doctor that will take the time to really get to the bottom of things. If you say to your doctor, "I'm feeling a bit blue lately" and he or she immediately grabs the prescription pad to give you an anti-depressant—run! Don't let the first course of action be, to put you on medication. Instead, find a doctor who will take the time to run blood tests and urinalysis to discover if there truly is a physical condition or a "chemical imbalance" that is causing the depression.

(As a side note, I am not saying anti-depressants are bad or to stop any medication that you may be on. If you are feeling led to stop your medication, only make a decision to stop medication *after* seeking God's will and your doctor's advice. Many anti-depressants must be gradually stopped and therefore you must be under the supervision of a doctor to do this.)

Let me give you an example from my own life concerning a struggle with an unusual case of depression. One day I called my mom crying. She immediately asked me what was wrong. I went on to tell her, my house was a mess, I was tired and I just felt so depressed. She knew this was not the normal me and she urged me to go and see the doctor. Praise the Lord! I had a great doctor and he immediately ran blood tests to see what was the source of the depression. Guess what? I had Mono, also known as Infectious Mononucleosis, the infectious disease that is best known as the "Kissing Disease" since so many teenagers catch it. (I, at the time, was one of the teachers for our youth group and many of the kids would drink out of my cup. Lesson learned—don't share your drink with anyone!)

The cool thing about this was: I learned from the doctor that Mono usually lasts about six months and it causes you to feel extremely tired which can cause the feelings of being overwhelmed and depressed. Therefore, I was to take it easy for the next six months. Great! Permission to do nothing! I went to the bookstore and bought all kinds of books. You see, perspective changes everything! Knowing I had a temporary physical condition in which the treatment was to get lots of rest my depression melted away.

In view of this, we need to educate ourselves. Knowledge is the beginning of freedom and as we educate ourselves we can help to improve our condition—no matter what physical condition we are struggling with. Listen to a recent article I found concerning the Bible and medicine. "In numerous instances the Bible contains medical information that far predates man's actual discoveries of related principles in the field of medicine. The medical instructions given by Moses to the Israelites some 3500 years ago were not only far superior to the practices of contemporary cultures, they also exceeded medical standards practiced as recently as 100 years ago. Where did Moses get this advanced information? . . . . For centuries doctors denied the possibility that disease could be transmitted by invisible agents. However, in the late 19th century Louis Pasteur demonstrated in his *Germ Theory of Disease* that most infectious diseases were caused by microorganisms originating from *outside* the body. This new understanding of germs and their means of transmission led to improved sanitary standards that resulted in an enormous drop in the mortality rate. Yet these core principles of sanitation were being practiced by the Israelites thousands of years earlier.

The Israelites were instructed to wash themselves and their clothes *in running water* if they had a bodily discharge, if they came in contact with another person's discharge, or if they had touched a dead human or animal carcass. They were also instructed to wash any *uncovered* vessels that were in the vicinity of a dead body, and if a dead carcass touched a vessel it was to be destroyed. Items recovered during war were also to be purified through either fire or running water. In addition, the Israelites were instructed to bury their human waste outside of camp, and to burn the waste of their animals (See Numbers 19:3-22, Lev. 11:1-47; 15:1-33, Deut 23:12).

These sanitary practices without question saved countless lives in the Israelite camps by protecting them against infection caused by unseen germs. Meanwhile, their Egyptian peers were dying by the thousands. . . . As mentioned earlier, the sound sanitary practices that we take for granted today only began to flourish about a 100 years ago."[1] Yet what Moses learned from God he taught to his people.

As the Israelites continued to keep themselves educated over the generations to come through the studying of God's Word they were able to improve their physical condition. This is exactly what happened in my own life. I was no longer depressed because I knew what the source of my physical exhaustion was and thus I was able to adapt my daily life to better accommodate my physical condition.

This is still true for me today since I have a condition known as lupus, which can be a very painful, life-threatening, chronic disease. Yet, as I educated myself about this disease and took active measures with both how I care for myself and what I eat, it changed everything. In fact, after many years of research I discovered a dietary supplement, which is one hundred percent natural, which has enabled me to get off of all lupus medication! It's a miracle for me. Plus I have been off all medication since 2003! (If you know someone struggling with lupus and you would like more information about this supplement you can visit the website www.lupusremedy.com or miracinfo.com and read about the supplement called Mirac.)

Just having a chronic condition can be very depressing, but by taking an active role in our own health and educating ourselves it can help to overcome our feelings of despair and may even lead us to a remedy.

Grieving

The second cause of depression can be a grief situation in life. Remember, as you learned in the session titled "Weeping May Last for the Night" we can grieve many different circumstances in life. And as you learned depression is one of the *normal* stages of grief. Although we don't like it; it is normal. Many times we want a quick fix for everything, but that is not the case with the issue of grief. If you are struggling with depression as a result of grief reread session eleven and cling to God as you go through the normal stages of grief. He loves you more than you know and He desires to be a part of your life as you go through the valley (see Psalm 23 for more encouragement).

Out of God's Will

The third cause of depression is being out of God's will. This cause actually has two different sources. But before we discuss these two sources it is important to mention that this cause—being out of God's will—can actually intensify the first two causes—physical condition or grief. Therefore, it is always a good idea for a person who is struggling with depression to be completely honest in the depth of his or her heart so that he or she can be set free and go in peace.

The first source of depression under our third cause—being out of God's will—is what we have discussed much in this Bible study—*an infection in the depths of a person's heart*. As you may recall, hurt not handled in the manner God intended will turn into anger, which in time will turn into bitterness, which will turn into a bitter poison, which will infect every aspect of a person's life. This is what causes the consequences, including the issue of depression. This is why it is important to be honest with ourselves and continue to apply what we learned in this Bible study. Many, as they go through the Bible study again, have discovered that although God may have worked concerning one hurtful issue in the person's life, as he or she goes through it a second, third or even fourth time God was working out other hurtful and infectious issues. We all need to get to the place in our lives that we are cleansed vessels so that we can then be used by God. Which is another great way to make the depression flee! As we take our focus off of self and put it on another it's amazing the satisfaction one can gain by the end of the day.

The second source of depression under our third cause—being out of God's will—is *being disobedient to His will*. Matthew 26:41 is true when it says:

> Watch and pray that you may not enter into temptation. The spirit indeed
> is willing, but the flesh is weak.
>
> —ESV

Our flesh is weak! It's hard to wholeheartedly follow Jesus. And when we choose to live for ourselves we can easily be out of God's will. As we make choices contrary to His will for our lives we lose our way and we lose our joy. Thus depression is soon apart of our lives and we don't even connect it to the wrong turn we made.

In 1996 God called me a third time to go to Bulgaria. Now although it was amazing to go on a short-term missionary trip there were aspects of the trip that I didn't like. I didn't like the oppression I felt in Bulgaria and I especially didn't like the struggles I had to go through to get there. So in February of 1996 although I had God's confirmation to go, I decided in my heart not to. Soon I was in the fog of depression which I *thought* was connected to my physical condition of having Lupus. It wasn't until the week that I needed to make the final decision about the trip to Bulgaria that everything became clear for me. I was confused and depressed, yet I was praying and seeking His will concerning the trip. God amazingly spoke to me through my children's Bible study that morning and I knew that I was to go to Bulgaria. I went to my room and got on my knees. The moment I *repented* of my disobedient heart the fog cleared and I realized that the depression I had been struggling with had been self-inflicted! Self-inflicted for six months! I made a choice from that day forward to be sensitive to the Holy Spirit and to do my upmost to stay within His will!

You can do the same. Take the time to seek God. Ask Him to show you the source of your depression. He wants to set you free so that you can *go in peace!*

Spiritual Gifts

*Now concerning spiritual gifts, brethren,
I do not want you to be ignorant.*
1 Corinthians 12:1, NKJV

The Gifts of the Holy Spirit

God's Word calls us *not* to be ignorant of our spiritual gifts. Yet as Pastor Brian Brodersen writes: "There is probably no greater area of ignorance within the church today than in the area of spiritual gifts."[1] While Warren Wiersbe pens in his book *Be Rich*, "In the Spiritual realm, each believer has at least one spiritual gift no matter what natural abilities he may or may not possess. A spiritual gift is a God-given ability to serve God and other Christians in such a way that Christ is glorified and believers are edified. . . . Gifts are not toys to play with, they are tools to build with."[2] Pastor Gary Nelson substantiates this teaching when he says concerning the gifts, "They are not something that we bring and put on display—like a big show. . . . They are for the benefit and a blessing for the body of Christ."[3]

God has a *call* on each one of our lives and He equips us for that call with the gifts that He gives. Each day is a precious gift from Him in which He desires us to be busy about His work. In view of the calling on our lives, let's learn more about our gifts so that we will not be ignorant. And better yet, so our days will not be wasted away, instead, we will be busy about our call glorifying God and building up others through the gifts He has given us.

Spiritual gifts are taught about in Romans 12:3-8, 1 Corinthians chapters 12 through 14, Ephesians 4:11-16 and 1 Peter 4:8-11. There are three categories that the gifts fall under: speaking gifts, serving gifts and sign gifts.

Speaking Gifts Include:

1. The Gift of Prophecy—A person with this gift has the ability to boldly declare the truth of God, regardless of the consequences. In other words, as the *NIV Study Bible* points out, it is "a communication of the mind of God imparted to a believer by the Holy Spirit. It may be a prediction or an indication of the will of God in a given situation."[4] Sometimes it is specific words. The person with the gift of prophecy causes the Word of God to shine. They encourage people to turn back to God and obey His

Word. Perhaps 1 Corinthians 14:1 says it best. "But one who prophesies strengthens others, encourages them, and comforts them" (NLT). If you would like more information concerning this gift turn to 1 Corinthians 12:10,28; Romans 12:6; Ephesians 4:11-12 and don't miss Deuteronomy 18:22.

2. The Gift of Teaching—The person who has the gift of teaching has the ability to make the Word of God clear and understandable. The person with this gift deeply enjoys studying the Bible. "And God has appointed these in the church. . . . teachers" (1 Corinthians 12:28, NKJV). For more information concerning this gift also see Romans 12:7 and Ephesians 4:11-12.

3. The Gift of Evangelist—As Ephesians 4:11 says, "And He gave some as. . . evangelists (NASB). Some, such as, Billy Graham and Greg Laurie are names which come to mind when we think of those with the gift of evangelist. The person with this gift has the ability to share the gospel in a way that many come to accept Jesus Christ as their Savior. But be aware, if you have this gift, don't expect that all other believers have this gift also! God only called *some* to be evangelists. To read more about this gift see 2 Timothy 4:5.

4. The Gift of Exhortation or Encouraging—The person with the gift of exhortation, or also known as encouraging, comes alongside and uplifts. The person with this gift has the ability to speak words of encouragement, challenge or rebuke in a way that others are unable. In the counseling situation the person with this gift takes the Word and applies it to the situation at hand. Listen to what Romans 12:6-8 says, "In his grace, God has given us different gifts for doing certain things well. . . . If your gift is to encourage others, be encouraging (NLT).

Serving Gifts Include:

5. The Gift of Pastor/Shepherd—The gift of pastor is the image of shepherding. The person with this gift has the ability to assume responsibility for the spiritual growth of a group of believers. Many who have the gift of pastor also has the gift of teaching because it is natural for this person to want to provide "food" from God's Word to feed his sheep. "And He gave. . . .some as pastors and teachers, for the equipping of the saints for the work of service, to the building up of the body of Christ (Ephesians 4:11-12, NASB).

6. The Gift of Apostle—According to *Strong's* "apostle" means "a delegate, messenger, [or] one sent forth with orders."[5] I personally believe that this gift is a gifting missionaries have because each one is sent out to do God's work. If you would like to learn more concerning this particular gift read 1 Corinthians 12:27-28 and Ephesians 4:11-12.

7. The Gift of Wisdom—According to God's Word, "To one there is given through the Spirit the message of wisdom, to another the message of knowledge by means of the same Spirit" (1 Corinthians 12:8). The gift of wisdom and the gift of knowledge are very closely related. The difference is very slight, but it is important. The gift of wisdom is having specific insight into something. It is knowing what to do—it is having wisdom and guidance for a specific situation. Example: perhaps you have a very specific situation and you are not sure what to do. You seek counsel from another believer and the Holy Spirit, through the gift of that believer, will minister something to you. He or she gives you counsel in what to do and you instantaneously know in your heart that what is being shared is right, that the advice given is from God. When this takes place this is the gift of wisdom.

8. The Gift of Knowledge—On the other hand, the gift of knowledge is the ability to know what the *root* of a problem is. It is not so much what to do, as we saw with the gift of wisdom, but it is knowing what the real problem is—the root issue. As Brodersen writes, "The gift is not divine assistance in the accumulation of knowledge, but rather knowledge previously unknown which is supernaturally and instantly imparted to the believer by the Holy Spirit."[6] Both the gift of wisdom and the gift of knowledge are important gifts for one who desires to biblically counsel. See 1 Corinthians 12:8 if you would like to learn more.

9. The Gift of Discernment—This gift, which is also known as the gift of distinguishing between spirits, is the ability to recognize counterfeits. In other words, the person with this gift will recognize false teaching and false teachers. (This is true even if the person is ignorant of his or her gift or perhaps young in the Lord. Because of this, the person may not be able to pinpoint exactly what is off. Yet he or she realizes that something is not quite right.) This gift is necessary in the Church to distinguish the true from the false. The person with this gift also has the ability to recognize when something spiritual is happening, and to especially discern spiritual warfare. "But the manifestation of the Spirit is given to each one for the profit [of all]: for to one is given. . . . discerning of spirits" (1 Corinthians 12:7-8,10, NKJV).

10. The Gift of Faith—As the *NIV Study Bible* points out, "Not saving faith, which all Christians have, but faith to meet a specific need within the body of Christ."[7] The gift of faith is the ability to trust God in a greater way—to a greater and higher degree. You can find this gift mentioned in 1 Corinthians 12:9.

11. The Gift of Serving or Ministry—The gift of serving is practical hands on kinds of ministry. The person with this gift has the ability to identify and meet the practical needs of others and of the Church. It is dedicated hands such as cleaning ministry or sound ministry. Usually this gift is displayed behind the scenes and unto the Lord. Check out Romans 12:7 and 1 Peter 4:10-11 for more insight into this most needed gift.

12. The Gift of Contributing or Giving—The person with this gift loves to give above and beyond regular tithes. This gift is a huge blessing to the work of God around the world! In fact, we couldn't do our work in Bulgaria with out so many of you who have this wonderful gift, who have blessed our ministry tremendously. There are rewards awaiting you in heaven! See Romans 12:8 and 2 Corinthians 9:7 if you want to learn more.

13. The Gift of Leadership—The person with the gift of leadership has the ability to influence others according to a specific purpose, mission or plan. This person naturally takes charge if no one else is doing anything. They lead with diligence, zeal, and eagerness. You can learn more in Romans 12:8.

14. The Gift of Administration—The person with the gift of administration has the ability to coordinate and organize people, projects and things. They have talents of organization, talents to oversee and talents to attend to details. In fact, I call this gift, "the gift of things and stuff." First Corinthians 12:28 speaks of this gift.

15. The Gift of Mercy—The person with this gift usually will have a kind word to say. They naturally show mercy with kindness and compassion. They see the need to help. But be careful, do not be ignorant of your gifts; I have seen that people with this gift sometimes pick boyfriends or girlfriends who need fixing! You can learn more about this gift inRomans 12:8 and Proverbs 17:22.

16. The Gift of Hospitality—A person with this gift has the ability to make others feel welcome, cared for and/or a part of the group. In other words, the person with this gift makes people feel at home. Now don't be ignorant of your gift, you do not have to be a good cook to have this gift. I can't tell you how many times I have met someone with this gift, but they don't think they have it because they can't cook! It's not that at all! It's just a love for making people feel welcomed. Read Romans 12:13 and 1 Peter 4:9 to learn more.

Sign Gifts Include:

17. The Gift of Tongues—Pastor Brodersen writes, "Tongues is a language given by the Holy Spirit, unknown to the speaker, by which the believers prays to God."[8] According to God's Word we learn, "For anyone who speaks in a tongue does not speak to men but to God" (1 Corinthians 14:2). The gift of tongues can be an actual existing language on earth or a language that is from heaven. Although there is much controversy among the Church today about the gift of tongues, which we don't have time to address in this short study, perhaps the apostle Paul said it best, "If I speak in the tongues of men and of angels, but have not love, I am only a resounding gong or a clanging cymbal (1 Corinthians 13:1). You can also read 1 Corinthians chapter 14 to learn more about this interesting gift.

18. **The Gift of Interpretation of Tongues**—This gift works along with the gift of tongues. As Brodersen goes onto say, "Paul states that tongues are not to be exercised in the public assembly unless there is someone present with the *gift of interpretation* (See 1 Corinthians 14:19). Every time there is a public utterance in tongues, an interpretation should follow it. According to the Scriptures, the one who is speaking in tongues is speaking to God and not to men, so the interpretation should be giving praise and glory to God (See 1 Corinthians 14:2)."[9] Perhaps 1 Corinthians 14:40 says it best concerning the gifts: "Let all things be done decently and in order" (NKJV).

19. **The Gift of Healing**—This gift is the ability to be used supernaturally by God to heal someone. Perhaps this is the most sought after gift. In view of this, it's important to learn what Pastor Brodersen has to say, "Although some might have a more frequent manifestation of some of the spiritual gifts, there is nothing in Scripture that indicates someone could have a permanent gift of healing, which they could exercise at anytime they choose. Therefore, you do not need to make special plans to go and see that self-acclaimed 'healing evangelist.' Instead, you can 'call the elders of the church, and let them pray over [you], anointing [you] with oil in the name of the Lord. . . that you may be healed' (James 5:14,16, NKJV)." You can read more about this gift in 1 Corinthians 12:9,28.

20. **The Gift of Miracles or Miraculous Powers**—This gift is the ability to be used supernaturally by God in a miraculous way. Here is an example of this gift: An accident happens and a car rolls on top of someone. The person manifesting the gift of miracles is given the supernatural power to lift the car off of the person. See 1 Corinthians 12:10,28 to learn more.

God has a calling on your life and He has gifted you to fulfill that calling. But perhaps the most important thing to remember concerning the gifts is what Paul wrote in 1 Corinthians 13:1-3:

> If I speak with the tongues of men and of angels, but do not have *love*, I have become a noisy gong or a clanging cymbal. If I have the gift of prophecy, and know all mysteries and all knowledge; and if I have all faith, so as to remove mountains, but do not have *love*, I am nothing. And if I give all my possessions to feed the poor; and if I surrender my body to be burned, but do not have *love*, it profits me nothing.
>
> —NASB, emphasis added

God has done a mighty work and has prepared you to become all that He created you to be. In view of His mercy, go out and serve Him with a grateful heart. As you go, no matter where He sends you, remember that God's supernatural love is the key, which will unlock doors of opportunity for you. You are ready! *Go in peace!*

THE JUDGMENT SEAT OF CHRIST

For we must all appear before the judgment seat of Christ,
that each one may receive what is due him
for the things done while in the body, whether good or bad.
2 CORINTHIANS 5:10

Rewarded for the Things Done

As the name implies, the Judgment Seat of Christ, can conjure up thoughts of fear and trembling. But if we truly understand what it represents it can beacon us to live the life that God created us to live, to become all that He intends us to be. For the Judgment Seat of Christ has nothing to do with justification; the moment you accepted Jesus Christ as your Lord and Savior all your sins were covered by His blood, instead this accounting has to do with the rewards or lack of rewards you will receive in heaven for the things God called you to do while in the body.

In view of this, it is important to note that there are two judgment seats talked about in the Bible—the Great White Throne Judgment and the Judgment Seat of Christ. In Revelation 20:11-15 we learn about the first one spoken of here.

> Then I saw a great white throne and Him who sat on it, from whose face the earth and the heaven fled away. And there was found no place for them. And I saw the dead, small and great, standing before God, and books were opened. And another book was opened, which is [the Book] of Life. And the dead were judged according to their works, by the things which were written in the books. The sea gave up the dead who were in it, and Death and Hades delivered up the dead who were in them. And they were judged, each one according to his works. Then Death and Hades were cast into the lake of fire. This is the second death. And anyone not found written in the Book of Life was cast into the lake of fire.
>
> —NKJV

This judgment is the one which should cause thoughts of fear and trembling. But again, if you have truly accepted Jesus Christ as your Lord and Savior you need not worry about this judgment. I like what Pastor David Guzik has to say. "Bible scholars believe that Christians will never appear before the Great White Throne. It isn't because we can hide from it—no one can. The idea is that we are spared from this awesome throne of judgment because our sins are already judged in Jesus at the Cross. We don't escape God's judgment; we satisfy it in Jesus."[1]

Therefore, the moment you accepted Jesus Christ as your Lord and Savior all your sins—past, present and future—were atoned for by the blood of Jesus Christ. You see, God the Father cannot look upon sin, therefore, at the moment of your salvation you are covered by Christ's righteousness which restores you to the place that God the Father can look upon you in love because your sins have been paid for.

However, there is a second judgment seat and that is called the Judgment Seat of Christ. There are many verses and passages within the Bible that speak of this judgment but the one that truly beacons me to become all that God created me to be is found in 2 Corinthians 5:10. In fact, I encourage you to memorize it. Listen to what is written there.

> For we must all appear before the judgment seat of Christ, that each one may receive what is due him for the things done while in the body, *whether good or bad.*
>
> —emphasis added

This judgment has nothing to do with our sins which as we talked about earlier were covered by the blood of Jesus Christ, but it has everything to do with how we live our lives! According to God's Word we will be rewarded for the things done while in this body of ours—whether good or bad. This judgment doesn't have to do with punishment like the Great White Throne Judgment does for unbelievers, but it has everything to do with receiving or even *not* receiving rewards in heaven.

I believe that we will somehow be aware of both the rewards we receive *and* the rewards we missed out on because *we did not do* that which God was calling us to do.

If God calls you to minister to someone and you minister to them with the right heart attitude you will receive a reward in heaven. However, if God calls you, for example, to walk in purity so that you can be a light to those around you who are watching and you *don't* walk in purity you will lose your reward. You won't be *punished* and suffer eternal separation from the Lord like the unbelievers because you have been saved by Jesus Christ and your sin has been covered by His blood, *but you will lose your reward* and you will be aware that you lost your reward.

Now, there is no sadness in heaven. According to Revelation 7:17 God is going to wipe away every tear. But we will somehow be aware of the rewards we missed out on because of our disobedience to God.

In view of this truth, I want to live my life in such a way that I will hear, "Well done good and faithful servant." My life is not my own! Nor, if you are really truthful with yourself, is yours.

Many believe that verses such as 2 Corinthians 5:10 apply to just our ministry, or in other words, the work we do for the Lord. But I have a question for you to consider: *Is our ministry that the Lord will judge and reward, work such as serving in the Sunday school or feeding the poor or some other type of ministry such as this? Or is our whole life to be our ministry?*

If our whole life is to be our ministry work unto the Lord, which this is what I believe to be the correct answer, then it is time for us to live our lives differently! Each day is a gift from God and I believe we need to live our lives, daily, in such a way that it counts! Therefore, consider this for a moment.

> But do not forget this one thing, dear friends: With the Lord a day is like a thousand years, and a thousand years are like a day.
>
> —2 Peter 3:8

So many times we look at this verse and use it to explain why the Lord is tarrying. Since it has been a little over two thousand years since Christ was here, in God's economy it's only been a couple of days. Yet we miss the part of the verse which says: *With the Lord a day is like a thousand years.* What do you think this means?

A Day is Like a Thousand Years

I had the privilege once of hearing Joni Eareckson Tada teach at a conference I attended. She shared an interesting concept that not only caught my attention but changed my thinking and my life. She was teaching on 2 Peter 3:8 and she challenged everyone present with this question: *What if we had the ability within each day to build up a thousand years of rewards in heaven would we live our lives differently?*

Think about this for a moment. What if, as we were living our lives for the Lord, we truly did have the ability to build up a thousand years of rewards within each day? What if, as you gave a cup of cold water to a little child (see Matthew 10:42) you had the ability to store up in heaven 112 years worth of rewards would you look for ways to serve the Lord even in the little things? What if, as you visited someone who was sick or in prison (see Matthew 25:35-36) you had the ability to build up in heaven 362 years of rewards would you find more time in your busy schedule to visit more often? Or what if, as you went to work you worked as if you were working for the Lord and not for man (see Colossians 3:23) you had the ability to store up in heaven 587 years of rewards would you work differently? What if each day that God has given you, you had the ability to store up in heaven one thousand years of precious treasures—would you live your life differently?

As the Unger's Bible Dictionary says, "Rewards are offered by God to a believer on the basis of faithful service rendered after salvation."[2]

In view of this, I want to list some of the other verses that have to do with this biblical concept below. Look them up in your Bible, read them for yourself and allow God to speak to your heart. It is my prayer that at the end of your life you will receive many rewards because you lived your life with purpose. Enjoy!

Bible Study

- We are to store up treasures in heaven: Matthew 6:19-21
- We will be rewarded for what we have done: Matthew 16:24-27
- We will be rewarded according to our conduct: Matthew 25:31-46
- We should offer ourselves as living sacrifices: Romans 12:1-2
- We must all give an account: Romans 14:10-12
- Our work will be tested by fire: 1 Corinthians 3:8-15
- We are to run in such as way as to receive the prize: 1 Corinthians 9:24
- We must all appear before the Judgment Seat: 2 Corinthians 5:9-10
- We will be rewarded for service: Ephesians 6:7-8
- Look here to discover more about rewards: Colossians 3:23-25
- Here is another interesting reward: 2 Timothy 4:7-8
- We need to persevere to receive the reward: Hebrews 10:35-39

ENDNOTES

Session 1: Introduction

1. Warren W. Wiersbe, *Be Compassionate* (Colorado Springs, CO: Chariot Victor Publishing, 1988), p. 80.
2. "History of Psychology" Wikipedia, December 28, 2010. http://en.wikipedia.org/wiki/History_of_psychology#The_word_itself. (accessed 1/27/2011).
3. "History of Psychology" Wikipedia, December 28, 2010. http://en.wikipedia.org/wiki/History_of_psychology#The_word_itself. (accessed 1/27/2011).
4. See 1 Corinthians 3:11.

Session 2: Do Not Be Deceived

1. Warren W. Wiersbe, *Be Compassionate* (Colorado Springs, CO: Chariot Victor Publishing, 1988), p. 80.

Session 3: Take Every Thought Captive

1. *The Merriam-Webster Dictionary* (Springfield, MA; Merriam-Webster, 2004), s.v. "pretense," p. 570.
2. "Conscious," c. 1600, from Latin conscious, knowing, aware," from conscire; probably a loan-translation of Greek syneidos. A word adopted from the Latin poets and much mocked at first. The sense of "active and awake" is from 1837.
3. Douglas Harper, historian, *Dictionary.com. Online Etymology Dictionary*, s.v. "subconscious." http://dictionary.reference.com/browse/subconscious (accessed: February 21, 2011).
4. *The NIV Study Bible* (Grand Rapids, MI: Zondervan Bible Publishers, 1985), study notes for Psalm 4:7; 7:9 and 139:13.
5. *Dictionary.com. The American Heritage® Stedman's Medical Dictionary.* Houghton Mifflin Company, s.v. "suppression." http://dictionary.reference.com/browse/suppression. (accessed: February 1, 2011).
6. Dan B. Allender, *The Wounded Heart* (Colorado Springs, CO: Navpress, 1990), p. 36.
7. *Webster's Ninth New Collegiate Dictionary* (Springfield, MA: A Merriam-Webster, 1988), s.v. "cover."

8. *Webster's Ninth New Collegiate Dictionary* (Springfield, MA: A Merriam-Webster, 1988), s.v. "rationalization."

9. Michael T. Mannion, *Abortion and Healing*: A Cry to Be Whole (Kansas City, MO: Sheed & Ward, 1992), p. 44.

10. *Webster's 21st Century Dictionary* (Nashville, TN; Thomas Nelson, Inc., Publishers, 1993), s.v. "blame," p. 29.

11. *Dictionary.com. Collins English Dictionary—Complete & Unabridged 10th Edition*. HarperCollins Publishers, s.v. "denial." https://dictionary.reference.com/browse/denial. (accessed: February 1, 2011).

12. *Webster's Ninth New Collegiate Dictionary* (Springfield, MA: A Merriam-Webster, 1988), s.v. "denial."

13. *Webster's Ninth New Collegiate Dictionary* (Springfield, MA: A Merriam-Webster, 1988), s.v. "hide."

14. Fillmore H. Sanford and Lawrence S. Wrightsman, "Reaction Formation," *Psychology: A Scientific Study of Man, 3rd edition* (Belmont, CA: Brooks/Cole Pub. Co., 1970).

15. See 1 John 1:9.

16. *Webster's Ninth New Collegiate Dictionary* (Springfield, MA: A Merriam-Webster, 1988), s.v. "justify."

17. *Dictionary.cambridge.org. Cambridge Dictionaries Online*. Cambridge University Press, "afraid." http://dictionary.cambridge.org/dictionary/british/afraid_1?q=afraid. (accessed: August 18, 2011).

Session 4: Deprived of Peace

1. Jon Courson, "Ten Commandments: Do Not Murder—Part Two," lecture on cassette tape (Jacksonville, OR: Applegate Christian Fellowship, 1999).

2. Charles H. Spurgeon, *Jesus the Substitute for His People—Booklet Vol. 21, Number 1223* (Pensacola, FL: Chapel Library), p. 3.

3. *Webster's 21st Century Dictionary* (Nashville, TN: Thomas Nelson Publisher, 1993), s.v. "tangible."

4. *Blue Letter Bible*, s.v. "offensive" (Strong's Hebrew # 06090, dictionary and word search for otseb). http://cf.blueletterbible.org/lang/lexicon/lexicon.cfm?strongs=H06090&Version=kjv.

5. Ralph Earle, *Word Meaning in the New Testament* (Peabody, MA: Hendrickson Publishers, 1998), p. 61.

Session 5: Forgiveness Is Not an Option

1. *Blue Letter Bible*, s.v. "bitterness," dictionary and word search for *la`anah* (Strong's Hebrew #3939). http:// cf.blueletterbible.org/lang/lexicon/lexicon.cfm?Strongs=H03939&Version=kjv.

2. *Blue Letter Bible*, s.v. "bitterness," dictionary and word search for *pikria* (Strong's Greek #4088).

http:// cf.blueletterbible.org/lang/lexicon/lexicon.cfm?Strongs=G4088&Version=kjv.

3. See Deuteronomy 29:18.

4. *Blue Letter Bible*, s.v. "forgive," dictionary and word search for *aphiēmi* (Strong's Greek #863).
http:// cf.blueletterbible.org/lang/lexicon/lexicon.cfm?Strongs=G863&Version=kjv.

5. Warren W. Wiersbe, *The Cross of Jesus* (Grand Rapids, MI: Baker Books, 1997), p. 54.

6. The idea for the phrases "forgiveness is and forgiveness in not" was adapted from Sharon Pearce, *Silent Voices Post Abortion Syndrome Healing and Recovery Leader's Manual* (Chula Vista, CA: Silent Voices, 1993), pp. 53-55.

7. *The Wesley Bible New King James Version* (Nashville, TN: Thomas Nelson, Inc., 1990), p. 1447.

8. Jay Adams, *From Forgiven to Forgiving* (Amityville, NY: Calvary Press, 1994), p. 12.

9. Ibid., p.11.

10. Kathleen White, *Corrie ten Boom* (Minneapolis, MN: Bethany House Publishers, 1983), pp. 106-107.

11. *Merriam-Webster Dictionary* (Springfield, MA: Merriam-Webster, Inc., 2004), s.v. "grudge."

12. *Blue Letter Bible*, s.v. "grudge," dictionary and word search for natar (Strong's Hebrew #05201). http:// cf.blueletterbible.org/lang/lexicon/lexicon. cfm?Strongs=H05201&Version=kjv.

13. Lewis B. Smedes, *Forgive and Forget* (New York, NY: Pocket Books, 1984), p. 57.

14. *WordNet® 3.0* (Princeton, NJ: Princeton University, 2007), s.v. "tolerate." http:// dictionary.reference.com/browse/tolerate.

15. Adams, *From Forgiven to Forgiving*, p. 57.

16. See Isaiah 43:25; Jeremiah 31:34.

17. Adams, *From Forgiven to Forgiving*, p. 12.

18. Wiersbe, *The Cross of Jesus*, p. 53.

Session 6: The Weapons of Victory

1. *The NIV Study Bible*, study notes on Revelation 12:10 (Grand Rapids, MI: Zondervan Bible Publishers, 1985).

2. *The NIV Study Bible*, study notes on Revelation 2:10.

3. See Job 1:6-11; Revelation 12:7-11.

4. *Holman Bible Dictionary* on CD-ROM, Quick Verse 6.0 (Hiawatha, Iowa: Parsons Technology, 1999), s.v. "satan."

5. See Genesis 3:1; Revelation 12:9.

6. See 1 Peter 5:8.

7. See 2 Corinthians 4:4.

8. See 2 Corinthians 11:13-15.

9. See John 12:31; 14:30-31.

10. See Revelation 12:4,7-9.

11. See Daniel 10:12-20.

12. *Dictionary.com Unabridged*, v 1.1 (New York: Random House, Inc., 2007), s.v. "faith." http://dictionary.reference.com/browse/faith.

13. Lance Wubbels, ed., *Charles Spurgeon on Prayer: A 30-day Devotional Treasury* (Lynnwood, WA: Emerald Books, 1998), Day 6.

Session 7: A Broken and Contrite Heart

1. *Dictionary.com, Collins English Dictionary—Complete & Unabridged 10th Edition* (HarperCollins Publishers.), s.v. "contrite." http://dictionary.reference.com/browse/contrite.

2. Ralph Earle, *Word Meanings in the New Testament.* (Peabody, MA: Hendrickson Publisher, 1998), p. 30.

3. See Romans 2:4

4. Merrill F. Unger, *The New Unger's Bible Dictionary* (Chicago, IL: Moody Press, 1988), p. 1073.

5. Unger, *The New Unger's Bible Dictionary*, p. 1073.

6. *The Merriam-Webster Dictionary* (Springfield, MA: Merriam-Webster, Inc., 2004), s.v. "repugnance."

7. *Roget's 21st Century Thesaurus* (Nashville, TN: Thomas Nelson Publishers, 1992), "repugnant."

8. Unger, *The New Unger's Bible Dictionary*, p. 1073.

9. *NIV Study Bible*, Study Notes on Isaiah 64:6.

Session 8: The Price is Paid

1. Warren W. Wiersbe, *The Cross of Jesus* (Grand Rapids, MI: Baker Books, 1997), p. 8.

2. David Hocking, "The Execution of the Messiah," (Tustin, CA: Hope for Today, 1999), lecture on tape.

3. Jon Courson, *The Gospel According to John, Volume III* (Jacksonville, OR: Olive Press, 1997). pp. 109-110.

4. Wiersbe, *The Cross of Jesus*, p. 32.

5. See Revelation 13:8.

6. Wiersbe, *The Cross of Jesus*, p. 12.

7. Ibid., p. 16.

8. Henry H. Halley, *Halley's Bible Handbook* (Grand Rapids, MI: Zondervan Publishing House, 1980), p. 303.

9. Jon Courson, *Jon Courson's Application Commentary New Testament* (Nashville, TN: Thomas Nelson, Inc., 2003), p. 193.

10. Jon Courson, *The Gospel According to Matthew, Volume II* (Jacksonville, OR: Olive Press, 1997), p. 241.

11. Dr. Frederick Zugibe (Chief Medical Examiner, Rockland County, New York) *How Jesus Died: The Final Eighteen Hours*. Trinity Pictures, 1994.

12. Robert Beck, M.D., "A Physician's Look at the Death of Jesus" (Temecula, CA: Calvary Chapel Temecula Valley, 1991), lecture on tape.

13. Hocking, "The Execution of the Messiah."

14. See Isaiah 50:7.

15. See Psalm 41:9.

16. See Matthew 26:48-49; Luke 22:48; John 18:3-4.

17. Jon Courson, *The Gospel According to John, Volume III*, p. 93.

18. Jon Courson, *Jon Courson's Application Commentary New Testament*, p. 582.

19. *The NIV Study Bible* (Grand Rapids, MI: Zondervan Bible Publishers, 1985), p. 1631.

20. See Matthew 26:50b

21. See Matthew 26:51; Mark 14:47: Luke 22:50; John 18:10.

22. Jon Courson, *The Gospel According to Matthew, Volume II*, p. 246.

23. Jon Courson, *The Gospel According to John, Volume III*, p. 96.

24. See John 18:13,24.

25. Jon Courson, *The Gospel According to Matthew, Volume II*, p. 248.

26. Ibid., p. 261.

27. See Mark 15:3-5.

28. Jon Courson, *The Gospel According to John, Volume III*, p. 110.

29. See Matthew 27:3-5.

30. See Luke 23:7.

31. Courson, *The Gospel According to Matthew, Volume II*, p. 268.

32. Beck, "A Physician's Look at the Death of Jesus."

33. Dr. James Strange, (Professor of Religious Science University of Southern Florida), *How Jesus Died: The Final Eighteen Hours*. Trinity Pictures, 1994.

34. Beck, "A Physician's Look at the Death of Jesus."

35. Courson, *The Gospel According to Matthew, Volume II*, p. 268.

36. See Isaiah 53:5.

37. See Isaiah 52:14.

38. Courson, *The Gospel According to Matthew, Volume II*, p. 250.

39. Strange, *How Jesus Died: The Final Eighteen Hours*, Trinity Pictures, 1994.

40. Beck, "A Physician's Look at the Death of Jesus."

41. Hocking, "The Execution of the Messiah."

42. Wiersbe, *The Cross of Jesus*, p. 56.

43. Dr. John Bonica (pain specialist), *How Jesus Died: The Final Eighteen Hours*. Trinity Pictures, 1994.

44. Strange, *How Jesus Died: The Final Eighteen Hours*.

45. Courson, p. 125.

46. Beck, "A Physician's Look at the Death of Jesus."

47. Ibid.
48. Zugibe, *How Jesus Died: The Final Eighteen Hours.*
49. Courson, *The Gospel According to Matthew, Volume II*, p. 115.
50. Wiersbe, *The Cross of Jesus*, p. 53.
51. Beck, "A Physician's Look at the Death of Jesus."
52. Wiersbe, *The Cross of Jesus*, p. 42.
53. See Habakkuk 1:13.
54. See 2 Corinthians 5:21.
55. Wiersbe, *The Cross of Jesus*, p. 105.
56. Ibid., p. 109.
57. Ibid., p. 42.
58. Courson, *The Gospel According to Matthew, Volume II*, p. 120.
59. Ibid., p. 121.
60. Halley, *Halley's Bible Handbook*, p. 549.
61. Courson, *The Gospel According to Matthew, Volume II*, p. 142.

Session 9: The Temple of the Holy Spirit

1. *The NIV Study Bible* (Grand Rapids, MI: Zondervan Bible Publishers, 1985), study notes for Psalm 4:7; 7:9 and 139:13.
2. *The NIV Study Bible* Study note on Matthew 5:8.
3. *Vine's Complete Expository Dictionary* (Nashville, TN: Thomas Nelson, Inc., 1996), s.v. "flesh," p. 242.
4. *The Merriam Webster Dictionary* (Springfield, MA: Merriam-Webster, Inc., 2004), s.v. "thought," p. 744.
5. *The Webster's Ninth New Collegiate Dictionary* (Springfield, MA: Merriam-Webster, 1988), s.v. "desire."
6. *The Webster's Ninth New Collegiate Dictionary* (Springfield, MA: Merriam-Webster, 1988), s.v. "action."
7. *Dictionary.com Unabridged* (Random House, Inc.), s.v. "recompensed," http://dictionary.reference.com/browsed/recompensed.
8. *The NIV Study Bible*, study note on Jeremiah 17:9.
9. Franklin Graham with Donna Lee Toney *Billy Graham in Quotes* (Nashville, TN: Thomas Nelson, 2011), p. 342.
10. *Blue Letter Bible*, s.v. "saw" (Strong's Hebrew #07200, dictionary and word search for ra'ah.)
    http://cf.blueletterbible.orglang/lexicon/lexicon.cfm?Strongs=H07200&Version=kjv.
11. Ibid.
    http://cf.blueletterbible.orglang/lexicon/lexicon.cfm?Strongs=H07200&Version=kjv [Mood-Imperfect See 08811].
12. See Hebrews 11:25.

13. *Webster's Ninth New Collegiate Dictionary* (Springfield, MA: Merriam-Webster, 1988), s.v. "romance," emphasis added.

14. Ibid., s.v. "romantic," emphasis added.

15. *Roget's 21st Century Thesaurus* (Nashville, TN: Thomas Nelson Publishers, 1992), s.v. "romantic."

16. *The NIV Study Bible*, study note on Exodus 20:17.

Session 10: Brephos

1. Sharon Pearce, *Silent Voices: Post Abortion Syndrome Healing and Recovery Leader's Manual* (Chula Vista, CA: Silent Voices, 1993), p. 70.

2. *The First Nine Months*, Booklet LF177/3608 (Colorado Springs, CO: Focus on the Family, Rev. 12/93), Day 1.

3. Bart T. Hefferman, M.D., "The Early Biography of Everyman," a chapter within F.J. Beckwith, *Politically Correct Death* (Grand Rapids, CO: Baker Books House Co., 1993), pp. 43-44.

4. Keith Moore, *Before We Are Born: Basic Embryology and Birth Defects, 5th ed.* (Philadelphia, PA: W.B. Saunders Company, 1989), p. 52.

5. *The First Nine Months*, Day 20.

6. *The First Nine Months*, Day 40 and Week 6.

7. J.I.P. de Vries, G.H.A. Visser and H.F.R. Prechtl, "The Emergence of Fetal Behavior I. Qualitative Aspects," *Early Human Development 7* (1982), p. 311.

8. William A. Liley, M.D., "The Fetus as a Personality," *Fetal Therapy 1*, (1986), pp. 8-17.

9. *The First Nine Months*, Week 8.

10. de Vries, Visser, and Prechtl, The Emergence of Fetal Behavior I. Qualitative Aspects," pp. 301-322.

11. *What They Never Told You About the Facts of Life* (Norcross, GA: Human Development Resource Council, Inc., 1992), brochure.

12. *The First Nine Months*, Week 9

13. K.L. Moore, Ph.D. and T.V.N. Persaud, M.D., *The Developing Human: Clinically Oriented Embryology*, 5th ed. (Philadelphia, PA: W.B. Saunders Company, 1993), p. 95.

14. *The First Nine Months*, Week 12.

15. *The First Nine Months*, Month 4.

16. *What They Never Told You About the Facts of Life*.

Session 11: Weeping May Last for the Night

1. Lance Wubbels, ed., *Charles Spurgeon The Power of Christ's Tears* (Lynnwood, WA: Emerald Books, 1996), p. 16.

2. Warren W. Wiersbe and David W. Wiersbe, *Comforting the Bereaved* (Chicago, IL: Moody Press, 1985), p. 21.

3. *The NIV Study Bible* (Grand Rapids, MI: Zondervan Bible Publishers, 1985), study notes p. 1215.

4. J.I. Packer, Merrill C. Tenney and William White, Jr., *Illustrated Encyclopedia of Bible Facts* (Nashville, TN: Thomas Nelson Publishers, 1995), p. 580.

5. James Strong, *Strong's Exhaustive Concordance of the Bible* (Peabody, MA: Hendrickson Publishers), Hebrew #349, p. 11 in the *Hebrew and Chaldee Dictionary* portion.

6. *Webster's Ninth New Collegiate Dictionary* (Springfield, MA: A Merrian-Webster, 1988), s.v. "lament."

7. Wiersbe and Wiersbe, *Comforting the Bereaved*, p. 131.

8. *The NIV Study Bible*, p. 1217.

9. Wiersbe and Wiersbe, *Comforting the Bereaved*, p. 22.

10. Wiersbe, p. 22.

11. Wiersbe, p. 22.

12. See Proverbs 18:24.

13. Wiersbe and Wiersbe, *Comforting the Bereaved*, p. 22.

14. Wiersbe, pp. 22-23.

15. Wiersbe, p. 23.

16. Delores Kuenning, *Helping People Through Grief* (Minneapolis, MI: Bethany House Publishers, 1987), p. 25.

17. Warren W. Wiersbe, *Why Us? When Bad Things Happen to God's People* (Old Tappan, NJ: Fleming H. Revell Company, 1984), p. 96.

18. *Webster's Ninth New Collegiate Dictionary* (Springfield, MA: A Merrian-Webster, 1988), s.v. "apathy."

19. Wiersbe and Wiersbe, *Comforting the Bereaved*, p. 23.

20. Wiersbe, p. 23.

21. See 2 Peter 3:9.

22. See Luke 16:19-31.

23. *National Memorial for the Unborn* (Chattanooga, TN: National Memorial for the Unborn), brochure.

Session 13: Set Apart

1. Warren W. Wiersbe, *Be Rich* (Colorado Springs, CO: Chariot Victor Publishing, 1998), pp. 13-14.

2. Ibid., p. 10.

3. *Webster's Ninth New Collegiate Dictionary* (Springfield, MA: Merriam-Webster, 1988), s.v. "sanctified."

4. "Historic Royal Speeches and Writings Victoria (r. 1837-1901)," The British Monarchy website, November 11 2007. http://royal.gov.uk/files/pdf/victoria.pdf.

5. Kay Smith, "Dwelling in the Holy of Holies" (Santa Ana, CA: The Word of Today, 2003), lecture on CD.

6. Stephen F. Olford, *The Tabernacle Camping with God* (Grand Rapids, MI: Kregel Publications, 2004), p. 76.

7. John W. Schmitt and J. Carl Laney, *Messiah's Coming Temple: Ezekiel's Prophetic Vision of the Future Temple* (Grand Rapids, MI: Kregel Publications, 1997), p. 28.

8. Ibid., p. 28.

9. Ibid., p. 29.

10. Ibid., p. 30.

11. Ibid.

12. *WordNet® 3.0* (Princeton, NJ: Princeton University, 2007), s.v. "contentment." http://dictionary.reference.com/browse/contentment.

13. Smith, "Dwelling in the Holy of Holies."

14. Elisabeth Elliot, *Passion and Purity* (Grand Rapids, MI: Fleming H. Revell, 1984), p. 21.

15. Charles Spurgeon, "The Rent Veil," sermon delivered at the Metropolitan Tabernacle Pulpit, March 25, 1888. http://www.blueletterbible.org/Comm/charles_spurgeon/sermons/2015.html.

16. Schmitt and Laney, *Messiah's Coming Temple: Ezekiel's Prophetic Vision of the Future Temple* p. 31.

Session 14: In View of God's Mercy

1. Warren W. Wiersbe, *Be Rich* (Colorado Springs, CO: Chariot Victor Publishing, 1998), pp. 13-14.

2. Merrill F. Unger, *The New Unger's Bible Dictionary* (Chicago, IL: Moody Press, 1988), p. 1073.

3. Unger, *The New Unger's Bible Dictionary* p. 835.

4. *Webster's 21st Century Dictionary* (Nashville, TN: Thomas Nelson Publishers, 1993), s.v. "mercy."

5. Ralph Earle, *Word Meaning in the New Testament* (Peabody, MA: Hendrickson Publishers, 1998), p. 191.

6. *Webster's Ninth New Collegiate Dictionary* (Springfield, MA: Merriam-Webster, 1988), s.v. "mercy."

7. Earle, quoting Kenneth S. Wuest, *The New Testament: An Expanded Translation*, p. 198.

8. *Webster's 21st Century Dictionary* Nashville, TN: Thomas Nelson Publisher, 1993), s.v. "consecrated."

9. Warren W. Wiersbe, *Be Compassionate* (Colorado Springs, CO: Chariot Victor Publishing, 1988), p. 81. emphasis added.

10. Wiersbe, *Be Compassionate* p. 81.

11. Jon Courson, *The Gospel According to Matthew, Volume II* Jacksonville, OR: Olive Press, 1997), p. 312.

12. See Exodus 2:11-12.

13. See Exodus 4:1-17.

14. See 2 Samuel 11:14-17.

15. See Acts 13:22.

16. See Acts 13:9; 22:1-10

17. See Numbers 22:28-30.
18. See 1 Corinthians 1:27.
19. Dr. Harold Sala, "Why Unlikely Candidates" (Murrieta, CA: Missions Conference 1999), lecture on tape.

Appendix 1: Profile of an Abuser

1. Adapted from www.tearmann.net/defndv.htm; www.brokenspirits.com/information/the_abuser.asp; www.paralumun.com/issuesabuser.htm> researched on 3/12/2008. Additional resources Gaddis, Patricia Riddle Dangerous Dating. Colorado Springs, Colorado: Waterbrook Press, 2000:p. 117-119.
2. The Sheepfold, *"Profile of a Batterer"*, June 24, 2008. http://www.thesheepfold.org/victim/victim-batterer.htm.

Appendix 2: The Three Causes of Depression

1. "Advance Medical Knowledge," Bibleevidences.com website, October 28 2011. http://www.bibleevidences.com/medical.htm.

Appendix 3: Spiritual Gifts

1. Brian Brodersen, *The Gifts of the Holy Spirit* (Costa Mesa, CA: Back to Basics, 2000), p. 3.
2. Warren W. Wiersbe, *Be Rich* (Colorado Springs, CO: Chariot Victor Publishing, 1998) pp. 99-100.
3. Gary Nelson, Gary. "He Has a Gift for You" (Temecula, CA: Grace for Living), lecture on cassette tape.
4. *The NIV Study Bible* (Grand Rapids, MI: Zondervan Bible Publishers, 1985), study notes p. 1750.
5. Blue Letter Bible. s.v. "apostle" (Strong's Greek #652, dictionary and word Search for apostolos) http:// cf.blueletterbible.org/lang/lexicon/lexicon.cfm?strongs=652&version=kjv&page=4.
6. Brodersen, *The Gifts of the Holy Spirit* p.10.
7. *The NIV Study Bible*, p. 1750
8. Brodersen, *The Gifts of the Holy Spirit* p. 29.
9. Brodersen, *The Gifts of the Holy Spirit* p. 33.

Appendix 4: The Judgment Seat of Christ

1. David Guzik, "Study Guide for Revelation 20." Enduring Word. *Blue Letter Bible*, 7 Jul 2006. 2012. 13 Apr 2012. <http://www.blueletterbible.org/commentaries/comm_view.cfm? AuthorID=2&contentID=8122&commInfo=31&topic=Revelation& ar=Rev_20_11 >
2. *The New Unger's Bible Dictionary* (Chicago, IL; The Moody Bible Institute of Chicago, 1988), s.v. "rewards," p. 1080

ABOUT THE AUTHOR

In 1988, Cherie rededicated her life to the Lord, and soon after, God began performing His gentle surgery deep within her heart to heal her of her deep heart hurts. After leading her through a process of recovery, God began impressing on her that she needed to help others with similar hurts and show them how to apply His Word to their lives. In 1993, she co-founded Strong-ARM (Abortion Recovery Ministry) to help women deal with issues of abortion and teaching purity seminars to help teens make wiser choices. When many women began to attend her workshops for issues other than abortion, she changed the name to the Truth and Hope Ministry to better encompass the scope of the work.

In 1999, Cherie wrote her first book titled *Go in Peace!* to help women deal with post-abortion issues. When she was unable to find a curriculum for her workshop that was 100 percent biblically-based, she began writing the *Go in Peace! Leader's Manual* and *Go in Peace! Student Workbook*. This curriculum was written for individuals attending her seminars who were suffering from any deep heart hurt issues—such as rejection, rape, abortion and abuse, to name just a few.

In 2001, Cherie and her husband, Keith, opened the non-profit Truth and Hope Foundation in Sofia, Bulgaria, to help women and teens heal from their deep heart hurts. In 2006, she joined the staff of Calvary Chapel Murrieta, where she is the overseer and trainer of the women's biblical counseling ministry. In 2011 she also became the overseer of the women's discipleship ministry at Calvary Chapel of the Harbour. Today, in addition to writing, Cherie loves to travel and teach God's Word and can often be found teaching various topics at women's retreats and teen's seminars. Cherie has two daughters, who are both married to godly young men, and one grandson.

The sale of this book helps to further Cherie and her husband's ministry work in the United States, Eastern Europe and wherever God sends them.

If you enjoyed this study and you know a teenager who would benefit in learning the same biblical concepts checkout Cherie's book *Go in Peace for Teens*.
For more information about Cherie's books, products or teaching schedule, visit

www.cheriefresonke.com
www.sunflowerpress.net

Don't forget to visit her blog while on the webpage. Simply click on "Blog" and it will take you to the page. She usually posts a new blog weekly to encourage her readers. You can also subscribe to this by clicking on the "Subscribe to Feed" button.

For more information about the Truth and Hope Foundation in Sofia, Bulgaria, visit
www.truthandhope.net

If you want to know what Cherie is up to follow her on Facebook or Twitter at
www.facebook.com/cherie.fresonke
www.twitter.com/CherieFresonke

To order additional copies of this title please visit our website at (quantity discounts are available)
www.sunflowerpress.net

Or write to

Sunflower Press
P.O. Box 813
Seal Beach, CA 90740